1870
Prelude 1900

TIME LIFE BOOKS ®

THE ART OF SEWING
THE OLD WEST
THE EMERGENCE OF MAN
THE AMERICAN WILDERNESS
THE TIME-LIFE ENCYCLOPEDIA OF GARDENING
LIFE LIBRARY OF PHOTOGRAPHY
THIS FABULOUS CENTURY
FOODS OF THE WORLD
TIME-LIFE LIBRARY OF AMERICA
TIME-LIFE LIBRARY OF ART
GREAT AGES OF MAN
LIFE SCIENCE LIBRARY
THE LIFE HISTORY OF THE UNITED STATES
TIME READING PROGRAM
LIFE NATURE LIBRARY
LIFE WORLD LIBRARY
FAMILY LIBRARY:
THE TIME-LIFE BOOK OF THE FAMILY CAR
THE TIME-LIFE FAMILY LEGAL GUIDE
THE TIME-LIFE BOOK OF FAMILY FINANCE

This Fabulous Century

1870 Prelude 1900

By the Editors of TIME-LIFE BOOKS

Time-Life Books, New York

The following individuals and departments of Time Inc. were helpful in preparing this book: Editorial Production, Norman Airey; Library, Benjamin Lightman; Picture Collection, Doris O'Neil; Photographic Laboratory, George Karas; TIME-LIFE News Service, Murray J. Gart; Correspondents J. Patrick Barker (Oklahoma City), Jane Beatty (Philadelphia), Robert Buyer (Buffalo), Patricia Chandler (New Orleans), Jane Estes (Seattle), Juliane Greenwalt (Detroit), Blanche Hardin (Denver), Sandra Hinson (Orlando), Holland McCombs (Dallas), Jerry Madden (Helena), Jeff Nesmith (Atlanta), Jane Rieker (Miami), Gayle Rosenberg (Los Angeles), Margot Sider (Chicago), Patrick Strickler (St. Louis), Judith Topaz (Madison), Nelson Wadsworth (Salt Lake City), Phyllis Wise (Washington, D.C.), Richard Wootten (Cleveland), Sue Wymelenberg (Boston), Earl Zarbin (Phoenix).

Published simultaneously in Canada. Reprinted 1974.
Library of Congress catalogue card number 69–16698.
School and library distribution by Silver Burdett Company, Morristown, New Jersey.

Contents

America 1870-1900

Paddle-boating party on California's Feather River, circa 1870.

Posturing in the park, Tallahassee, Florida, 1880s.

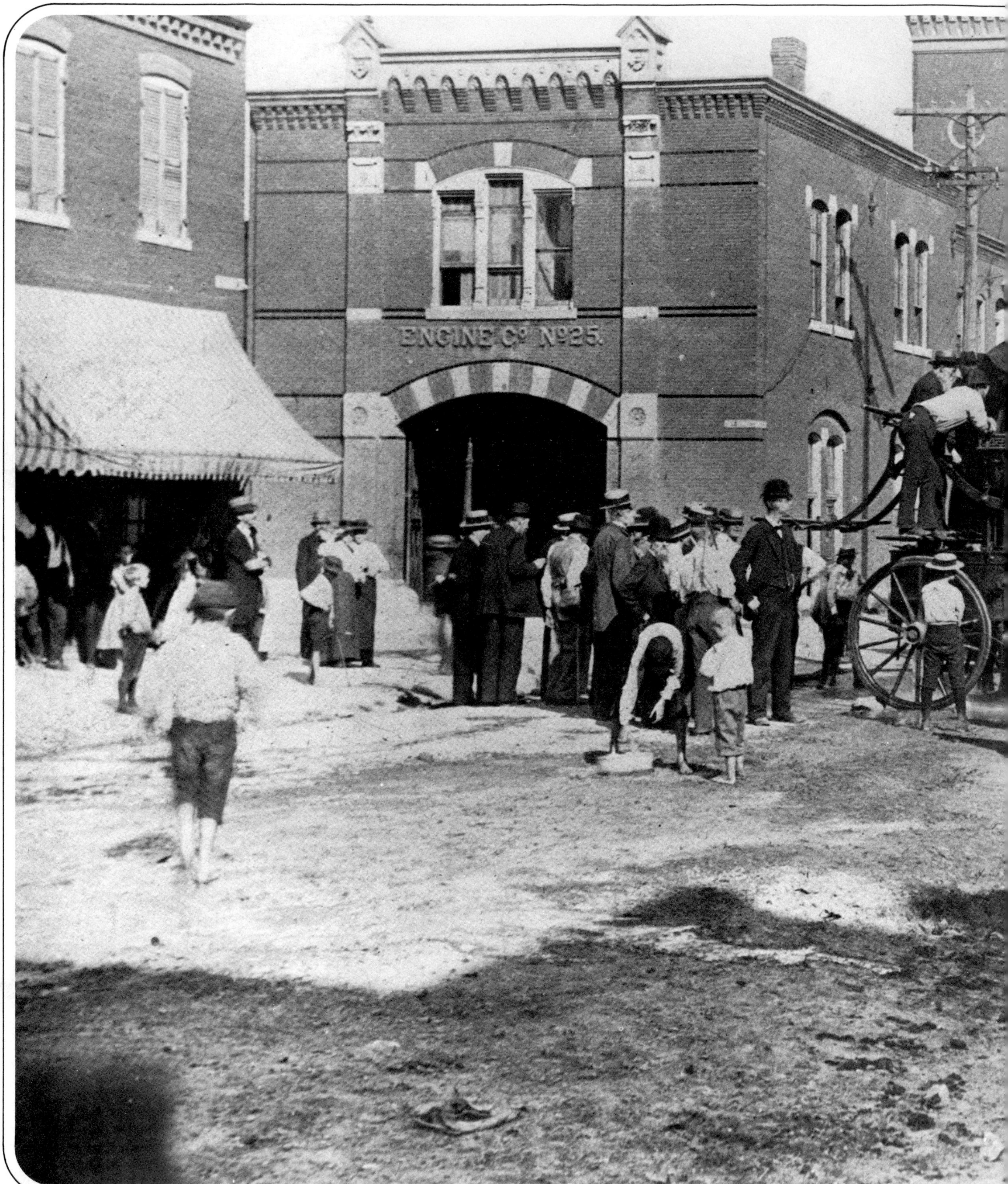
ENGINE Co No25.

Testing the fire engine, St. Louis, Missouri, 1894.

CURES
CELERY
CONSTIPATION
DAMSCHINSKY'S
LIQUID
Hair Dye
GUARANTEED HARMLESS
HENDERSON'S
DIGESTIVE
TOOTHACHE GUM
LICORICE PASTILLES MINT AND ASSORTED JUJUBES 5¢ BOXES

Soda fountain, western Massachusetts, 1890s.

A tot of rum on the afterdeck, San Francisco Bay, 1880s.

Under the elms along State Street, Jacksonville, Illinois, 1889.

Parlor duet, Chicago, 1890.

NELLIE PECK
WESTERN
WESTERN

Steamboats at the levee, Bismarck, Dakota Territory, 1877.

UNCLE TOM'S CABIN
UNCLE TOM'S CABIN
UNCLE TOM'S CABIN

Lumber-camp string trio, in the chow hall, Minnesota, 1890s.

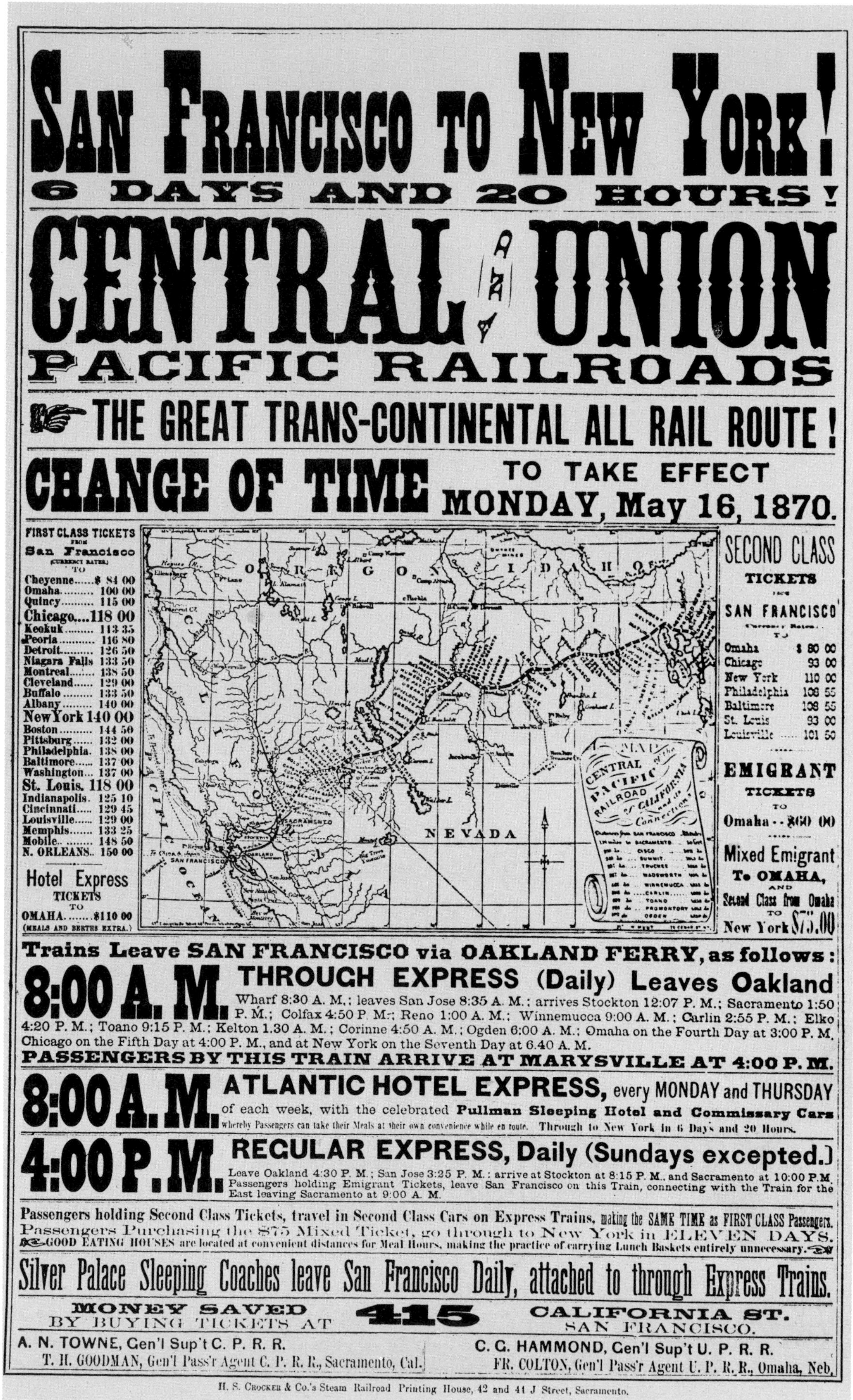

SAN FRANCISCO TO NEW YORK!

6 DAYS AND 20 HOURS!

CENTRAL AND UNION PACIFIC RAILROADS

THE GREAT TRANS-CONTINENTAL ALL RAIL ROUTE!

CHANGE OF TIME TO TAKE EFFECT MONDAY, May 16, 1870.

FIRST CLASS TICKETS FROM San Francisco (CURRENCY RATES.) TO

Cheyenne	$ 84 00
Omaha	100 00
Quincy	115 00
Chicago	118 00
Keokuk	113 35
Peoria	116 80
Detroit	126 50
Niagara Falls	133 50
Montreal	138 50
Cleveland	129 00
Buffalo	133 50
Albany	140 00
New York	140 00
Boston	144 50
Pittsburg	132 00
Philadelphia	138 00
Baltimore	137 00
Washington	137 00
St. Louis	118 00
Indianapolis	125 10
Cincinnati	129 45
Louisville	129 00
Memphis	133 25
Mobile	148 50
N. ORLEANS	150 00

Hotel Express TICKETS TO OMAHA .... $110 00 (MEALS AND BERTHS EXTRA.)

SECOND CLASS TICKETS FROM SAN FRANCISCO (Currency Rates.) TO

Omaha	$ 80 00
Chicago	93 00
New York	110 00
Philadelphia	108 55
Baltimore	108 55
St. Louis	93 00
Louisville	101 50

EMIGRANT TICKETS TO Omaha -- $60 00

Mixed Emigrant To OMAHA, AND Second Class from Omaha TO New York $75.00

Trains Leave SAN FRANCISCO via OAKLAND FERRY, as follows:

8:00 A. M. THROUGH EXPRESS (Daily) Leaves Oakland Wharf 8:30 A. M.; leaves San Jose 8:35 A. M.; arrives Stockton 12:07 P. M.; Sacramento 1:50 P. M.; Colfax 4:50 P. M.; Reno 1:00 A. M.; Winnemucca 9:00 A. M.; Carlin 2:55 P. M.; Elko 4:20 P. M.; Toano 9:15 P. M.; Kelton 1.30 A. M.; Corinne 4:50 A. M.; Ogden 6:00 A. M.; Omaha on the Fourth Day at 3:00 P. M. Chicago on the Fifth Day at 4:00 P. M., and at New York on the Seventh Day at 6.40 A. M.

PASSENGERS BY THIS TRAIN ARRIVE AT MARYSVILLE AT 4:00 P. M.

8:00 A. M. ATLANTIC HOTEL EXPRESS, every MONDAY and THURSDAY of each week, with the celebrated **Pullman Sleeping Hotel and Commissary Cars** whereby Passengers can take their Meals at their own convenience while en route. Through to New York in 6 Days and 20 Hours.

4:00 P. M. REGULAR EXPRESS, Daily (Sundays excepted.) Leave Oakland 4:30 P. M.; San Jose 3:25 P. M.: arrive at Stockton at 8:15 P. M., and Sacramento at 10:00 P.M. Passengers holding Emigrant Tickets, leave San Francisco on this Train, connecting with the Train for the East leaving Sacramento at 9:00 A. M.

Passengers holding Second Class Tickets, travel in Second Class Cars on Express Trains, making the SAME TIME as FIRST CLASS Passengers.
Passengers Purchasing the $75 Mixed Ticket, go through to New York in ELEVEN DAYS.
GOOD EATING HOUSES are located at convenient distances for Meal Hours, making the practice of carrying Lunch Baskets entirely unnecessary.

Silver Palace Sleeping Coaches leave San Francisco Daily, attached to through Express Trains.

MONEY SAVED BY BUYING TICKETS AT **415** CALIFORNIA ST. SAN FRANCISCO.

A. N. TOWNE, Gen'l Sup't C. P. R. R.
T. H. GOODMAN, Gen'l Pass'r Agent C. P. R. R., Sacramento, Cal.

C. G. HAMMOND, Gen'l Sup't U. P. R. R.
FR. COLTON, Gen'l Pass'r Agent U. P. R. R., Omaha, Neb.

H. S. Crocker & Co.'s Steam Railroad Printing House, 42 and 44 J Street, Sacramento.

When direct cross-country service opened in 1870, Americans could take the longest rail trip in the world.

Nation on the Move

The last hundred years have been the most fruitful and the most glorious period of equal length in the history of the human race. . . . We are entering a year which will be ever memorable in our annals.

NEW YORK *HERALD*, JANUARY 1, 1876

Two events, both occurring in the decade just after the Civil War, summed up the exhilarating conditions of life in America during the last third of the 19th Century. One was the climax of a superb feat of technology, the opening of direct coast-to-coast service on the first transcontinental railway *(left)*. The other had its roots in pure sentiment, the celebration in 1876 of the hundredth anniversary of the nation's founding.

The completion of the railroad had for most Americans a more tangible and immediate significance. For when the tracks of the Central and Union Pacific lines were joined at Promontory Point, Utah, in 1869, the opposite shores of a half-wild continent 3,000 miles wide suddenly were only seven days apart. Until then the United States had remained a house truly divided, not only by the lingering bitterness of the war, but also by distance and the attendant hazards of travel by shipboard or wagon. San Francisco had been a full month from New York by uncertain rail and stagecoach connections, up to five months by wagon train from Missouri and six months by windjammer around the Horn from East Coast ports. Under these circumstances, people, goods and ideas traveled slowly and not very far. Over half the population still made its living on farms, and many Americans never left the towns where they had been born. They were simple people, straightforward with neighbors but sometimes suspicious of strangers; and a harsh streak of backwoods violence still showed across the land. Statistics indicated that the state of Alabama, and doubtless several others like it, contained more guns and dirks than farm implements. Fewer than two U.S. citizens in every hundred between the ages of 18 and 21 went to college. And there was not a town between St. Louis and San Francisco whose population numbered more than 35,000 souls.

Thus the new transcontinental railroad and the other lines that soon paralleled it over the plains meant much more than a simple saving of time or improvement in comfort and safety for travelers; they meant a spreading and melding of the American people and an acceleration of their commerce. In the late spring of 1884, with four railroads crisscrossing the prairie, more than 800,000 head of cattle were shipped out of Dodge City and Abilene, bound for the big markets of the East. San Francisco importers could send silks to Chicago in two days. Omaha could dine on fresh-caught Pacific salmon, which was brought to it in refrigerator cars. Pittsburgh steel reached out across the

Electricity was a fascination in the late 19th Century, when Thomas Edison was a leading American hero. For example, when Anaheim, California, inaugurated its lighting system in 1895, the town celebrated with a variety show of music and recitations (upper right). Below the program from that event are a flier and a poster advertising two other marvels for which Edison was responsible, the kinetoscope and the motion picture.

nation to create soaring bridges and great buildings in the booming cities. And if business temporarily slowed (as it did in the depressions of 1873, 1884 and 1893), the trains carried the seeds of recovery into the country as salesmen brought big-city ideas into small towns—and took back signed order blanks to the home factory.

The railroad was a new market entirely on its own. Between 1870 and 1900, for example, about 60 per cent of all steel manufactured in the U.S. went into rails. And all the Western roads did a rousing business speculating in land—and in people. The first trains to leave Oakland and Sacramento in 1870 offered special rates for emigrants, many of whom succumbed to the beguilements of railroad agents *(page 91)* who were peddling land-grant property at up to $14 per acre.

By 1898 the U.S. boasted nearly half the railway mileage in the world, and U.S. trains carried 800 million tons of goods, or half the world's rail freight. To most people, though not all *(below)*, that growth spelled progress and wealth, two concepts dear to the hearts of 19th Century Americans. And it was directly in line with the perceptions of the late President James A. Garfield. "The changes now taking place have been wrought and are being wrought, mainly, almost wholly, by a single mechanical contrivance, the steam locomotive," he told an audience at Hudson College, New York, in 1873. "The railway is the greatest centralizing force of modern times."

> *Progress cannot be reckoned in railroads and steamboats, or counted in money, or decided in any way by the census tables. Are we producing better children and better men and women? This is the question which decides everything.*
>
> JOURNALIST JOSIAH GILBERT HOLLAND

While the railroads were building up their head of steam, the nation was preoccupied with the excitement of its hundredth anniversary. Few Americans questioned the premise that the Centennial Year was worthy of observance, but how to do the occasion justice was an absorbing matter. "Is self-jollification . . . getting up a grand magnificent exposition, a function of government?" asked New York Representative Benjamin Willis when the question of an appropriation came before Congress. "Rather than expend money for a jubilee in 1876," he answered himself, "we should bequeath to our posterity the privilege of celebrating the continued existence of the Republic in 1976."

Patriotism and dreams of profit, however, won over puritan thrift. When the Centennial time came round, the whole year, from the ringing in of January 1, 1876, to the close of the following December, was filled with celebrations all across the country. The dazzler of them all was a fair, officially called the Centennial Exhibition and appropriately staged in Philadelphia, scene of the signing of the Declaration of Independence 100 years before. To underwrite the Exhibition, Congress came up with $1.5 million to match the $1.5 million that Philadelphia and the state of Pennsylvania had already raised.

When the Centennial, as it was called for short, got ready to open on May 10, 1876, there was no doubt in the minds of most observers that the money had been well spent. "In all its features," predicted the Philadelphia *Inquirer* in a sanguine front-page story that appeared on the morning of the fair's debut, "the occasion will be grand and imposing, as the magnificence of the event itself demands it shall be." And as if closing the door forever on the civil strife of the previous decade, the newspaper went on: "The dazzling pageantry is not to be of war."

In the first reports on the fair, other members of the national press agreed that the show was everything that any good American could have hoped for. The highly respected novelist, critic and editor of the *Atlantic Monthly*, William Dean Howells, had this to say: "The undertaking merits all possible prosperity, and whatever were the various minds in regard to celebrating the Centennial by an international fair, no one can now see the fair without a thrill of patriotic pride."

The New York Times concurred, giving almost as much attention to the spectators as to the displays to be seen at the Centennial. "The crowd was nothing if not American,"

Souvenir Programme

. . OF THE . .

CELEBRATION OF THE COMPLETION

OF THE

Electric Light System

. . IN . .

ANAHEIM

THURSDAY, APRIL 11, 1895

Programme.

Music by the Band

Opening remarks by Chairman Mr. W. J. Fay.

General Illumination

The "Button" will be pressed by the oldest living resident of Anaheim, Charles Lorenz.

1. Song....................German Singing Society
2. Address..........................Mr. R. Melrose
3. Whistling Solo....Miss Harriette True Regan
4. Athletic Exhibition....Anaheim Turn Verein
5. Solo.................................Rev. F. Reiser
6. Recitation (Darkness)...........Mrs. Cushing
7. Recitation (Light, Original Poem)..Mrs. Rugg
8. Guitar Solo..........................Mr. Grannis
9. Recitation.....................Mr. P. A. Brown
10. Whistling Solo.......................Miss Regan

Order of March.

The procession will form in front of the City Hall at 7:30 p. m. sharp, in the following order:

Orange Brass Band.

City Officials in Carriages.

Company F, N. G., Ninth Inf. Regiment.

Company G, N. G., Seventh Inf. Regiment.

Chairman, Speaker, Orange County Chamber of Commerce, Anaheim Chamber of Commerce and Invited Guests in Carriages.

School Children.

Bicycle Corps.

Anaheim Turn Verein.

Candle Brigade.

Citizens in Carriages.

N. F. STEADMAN,
GRAND MARSHAL

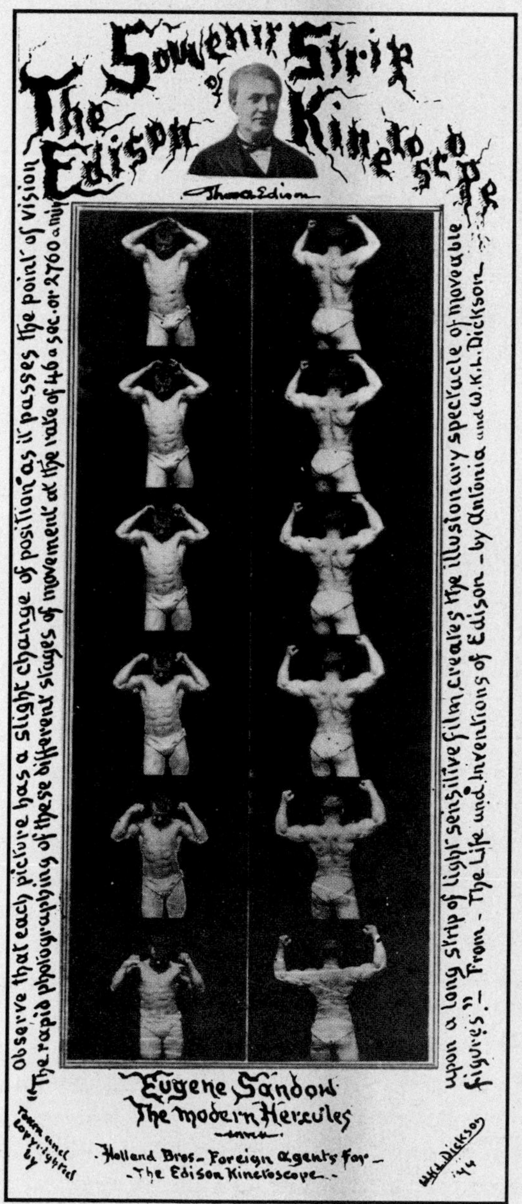

GRAND POPULAR

ENTERTAINMENT

DON'T FAIL...

TO TAKE ADVANTAGE OF THIS OPPORTUNITY.

BRING CHILDREN AND FRIENDS . . .

CONSISTING OF

LIFE-SIZE MOTION PICTURES

PROJECTED UPON A LARGE SCREEN BY MEANS OF THAT MOST WONDERFUL OF ALL MODERN INVENTIONS.

The Edison Moving Picture Machine

This part of the entertainment will consist of:

Views of Railroad Trains going at full speed, Street and Domestic Scenes of interest, Comic Actions, etc., with figures composing the pictures in natural motion.

So Life-like, so true to nature, so perfect in detail are this pictures, that the audience can scarcely realize that what they see is only a picture and not reality.

GRAND TALKING MACHINE

ENTERTAINMENT

During which will be rendered the LATEST MUSICAL SELECTIONS as played by the best Bands and Orchestras of this country; VOCAL SELECTIONS, as sung by the most noted Comic and Sentimental Singers; SPEECHES of our most noted Men;

AND A SPLENDID

PANORAMIC EXHIBITION

of high-grade Magic Lantern Views thrown upon a screen in largely magnified form by means of a

FIRST CLASS **STEREOPTICON**

The Views will consist of a fine selection of Subjects of Popular Interest and will be fully explained in an interesting Lecture.

The entertainment will be given at June

Admission Adults______Cents. Children 10 Cents. Entertainment begins at______P. M.

rhapsodized the *Times*. "In it were fair ladies gorgeously attired, plain workwomen from workshops and factories, cooks and servant-maids, dandies in broadcloth, Western farmers in homespun, workmen fresh from their benches —rich men and poor men were all mingled together. There never was a more good-natured crowd. It was an honor to the country that produced it."

So, of course, was the fair itself, which spread through some 180 buildings laid out on 450 acres of exhibition grounds, all accessible for the modest admission fee of 50 cents. There were displays from 25 foreign countries: jewelry from India, a new contraption called a bicycle *(page 110)* from England, porcelain from Germany, textiles from France and 6,000 live Chinese silkworms obligingly spinning silk. Most conspicuous were the marvels of American technology. In Machinery Hall there was the Corliss 1500-horsepower steam engine, the biggest and most powerful in all the world. Near it was a machine called a typewriter, on which an attendant would write a letter home for any visitor willing to fork up 50 cents. In Agricultural Hall, farmers were impressed by a steam-powered thresher-separator that could thresh and clean from 800 to 1,000 bushels of wheat per day. At the Main Building, housewives marveled at a new floor covering, a waterproof, washable surface that could last a dozen years or more; it was called linoleum.

This government is not a Republic, but a hateful oligarchy of sex. ANONYMOUS SUFFRAGIST, 1876

Many of the scientific exhibits at the Centennial were futuristic curios whose impact on the daily lives of Americans was yet to be imagined. The telephone on display, for example, was one of 3,000 in the entire country. So new was the concept of this voice-carrying machine that the suave Emperor Dom Pedro of Brazil, invited to test the device, exclaimed, "My God, it talks!" and dropped the receiver. But within 25 years there would be 1.356 million telephones spread across the U.S. The Otis elevator, a wonderful machine that could effortlessly whisk a dozen passengers to the top of a tall building, was still more of a fright than a convenience in the minds of most Americans.

In the French exhibit there were a few glaring electric arc lights, like those already in use in Paris. The incandescent lamp to be devised by Thomas Edison was still three years in the future; but only 20 years after that there would be more than 20 million of them lighting the homes and streets of the nation, and one billion dollars of capital invested in the venture.

Here and there a few naysayers grumbled that the Centennial Year fell short of expectations. Among the shrillest of the critics were the suffragists, champions of the feminist cause in the 19th Century. Simultaneous with the fair's opening, the National Woman Suffrage Association met in New York and let it be known that any celebration of the country's achievements was premature and unjustified; one speaker was reported to have said that "there must be a Mrs. President before this Republic could become full and grand and rounded." But such voices were in the minority; Americans were more inclined to think like the flamboyant circus promoter Phineas Taylor Barnum, who papered the barns of the Eastern Seaboard with copies of a poster that measured 7 by 47 feet. It was the largest show bill ever printed in the world and advertised the Barnum circus of 1876 as "surpassing anything before attempted in this country."

Barnum's grandiloquent boast summed up the way Americans felt generally about their country and its place in the world: that it surpassed anything before attempted. It also reflected what every man alive, in this time of bursting progress, felt the future would bring to him in the way of fame and fortune. Historian Henry Adams, great-grandson of President John Adams, found that the average New Yorker or Chicagoan was "a pushing, energetic, ingenious person, always awake and trying to get ahead of his neighbors." Newspaper pundit Finley Peter Dunne, whose pen spouted the wisdom of Mr. Dooley, was more specific. The "crownin' wurruk iv our civilization," he asserted, "is th' cash raygister."

Mark Twain, writing in a solemn mood, agreed with

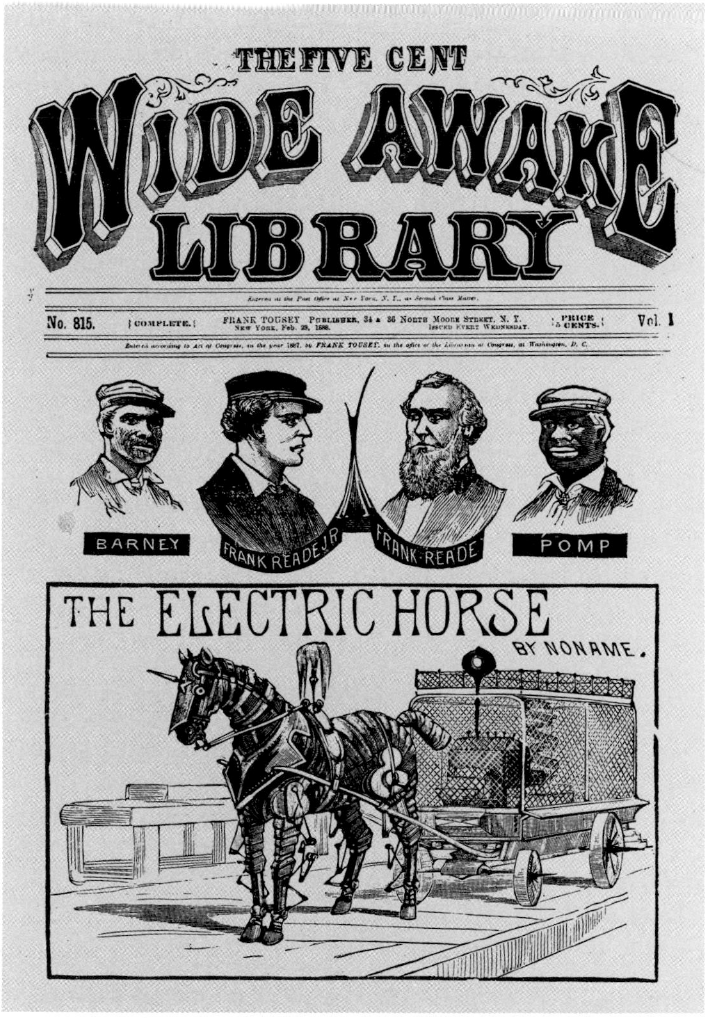

Pulp novels leaned heavily for plots on the wonders of electricity.

Adams and Dunne and offered this insight into the competitive drives of the average American. "Nearly every man," he wrote, "has his dream, his pet scheme, whereby he is to advance himself socially or pecuniarily. It is a characteristic which is both bad and good, for both the individual and the nation. Good, because it allows neither to stand still, but drives both for ever on, toward some point or other which is ahead, not behind nor at one side. Bad, because the chosen point is often badly chosen, and then the individual is wrecked; the aggregation of such cases affects the nation, and so is bad for the nation."

Most people ignored such complex philosophies. Moneymaking was good for everybody, good for the individual man and good for the country. Money was, in fact, the consuming passion of virtually all Americans, rich and poor, old families and new immigrants alike, through the remainder of the century. Those who already had it strove mightily to accumulate more; those who did not yet have money set their sights on getting some as quickly as possible. And the current of optimism ran so strong through most veins that it rarely occurred to those who had not yet succeeded that the goal was out of reach.

And why should it be? The marketplace and the drawing room alike abounded with living examples of rags-to-riches achievements. In this era, for instance, a one-time soap salesman from Philadelphia named William Wrigley Jr. promoted a candy-flavored novelty called chewing gum. "Tell 'em quick and tell 'em often," Wrigley said in explaining his technique of salesmanship, and he obviously had something. So swiftly did his product catch on that in just a few years teenagers were using the slang phrase "Wipe the gum off your lip" to mean "Behave yourself," and a traveler in the West, commenting on gum-chewing, described a railway car as "filled with young women, nearly every one of whose jaws and pretty mouths was engaged in this pleasing occupation; and so much power was generated that it would, if applied, have kept the car in motion if the steam had been shut off." With similar, though less spectacular, ambition and shrewd business sense, August Brentano won success in another field. He began as an immigrant peddler of newspapers and magazines on New York's lower Broadway back in 1853, and by the Centennial Year he was the owner of the most elegant bookstore on the East Coast, a half-million-dollar establishment on fashionable Union Square.

Perhaps the most dazzling success story of all was that of James Buchanan Duke, heir to a small cigarette factory near Durham, North Carolina, where smoking tobacco was rolled by hand. When young Buck, as he was called, took over his father's shop in 1881, he hired a French actress to endorse his cigarettes and sent a troop of minions to hand out free sample packages to new arrivals at the New York Immigration Station. Then he retained a young inventor named James Bonsack to perfect a machine that could roll cigarettes by the hundred thousand without the touch of a human hand. By 1889 Americans were smoking 2.1 billion cigarettes a year, almost a tenfold increase in only eight years, and Duke had 50 per cent of the market. Next he absorbed four of his major competitors into the American Tobacco Company, a coup that gave him a full 90 per cent of the thriving U.S. cigarette business. A few years later, when the rest of the country was sunk in the trough of a depression, Duke's American Tobacco Company brought in an enviable net profit of five million dollars.

All this seemed a just reward for good, hard work. "No man now standing on an eminence of influence and power," said the editor of the dignified *Scribner's Monthly*, "has arrived at his position by going up in an elevator. He took the stairway, step by step. He climbed the rocks, of-

First, you hit your enemies in the pocketbook, hit 'em hard. Then you either buy 'em out or take 'em in with you.
JAMES BUCHANAN DUKE

ten with bleeding hands." To some, the reward was not only just but divinely ordained as well. William S. Speer, a Methodist teacher, wrote in an inspirational book of "the commercial value of the Ten Commandments and a righteous life." James Fullarton Muirhead, a British writer who spent three years exploring the U.S. while preparing a Baedeker's guide to the young nation, noted that a baritone entertaining in a California hotel followed a rendition of "The Man Who Broke the Bank at Monte Carlo" with "Nearer, My God, to Thee"—and "no one in the room except myself," wrote Muirhead, "seemed to find it in the least incongruous or funny."

As their country aimed toward ever greater prosperity, even the periodic depressions that hit the economy did not shake the nation's faith in its inevitable progress. For business climbed out of each slump in better health than before. Wages *(page 248)* kept going higher all the time—which meant that laborers could buy the chewing gum and cigarettes that the entrepreneurs were turning out; that many a housewife could afford one of the newfangled carpet sweepers or sewing machines that were making housekeeping so much easier; that even a modest farmer could aspire to harvest his wheat with an automatic thresher like the one on display at the Centennial Exhibition in Philadelphia.

Before the end of the century, the U.S. had established itself as the industrial giant of the world. It was the biggest maker of most heavy goods and the biggest consumer as well. The production of steel had leaped from 569,000 long tons just after the Centennial to nearly five million in 1892. During the same time the mining of bituminous coal had risen from 35 million tons to 127 million. Copper, oil, textiles and electrical goods all went up commensurately; and even agriculture, since prehistoric times a slow, manual occupation, shared in the sense of progress. Before the Civil War 61 hours of labor had been necessary to produce an acre of hand-grown wheat; by the 1890s machinery yielded the same amount in 3 hours and 19 minutes. And by 1900 the nation had also grown physically to include 45 states plus the offshore territories of Hawaii, American Samoa, Guam, the Philippine Islands and Puerto Rico, a fact that moved the economic frontier outward.

Occasionally, thoughtful critics would ask whether all this progress was in the right direction. "Who will teach us incessant workers how to achieve leisure and enjoy it?" editor Horace Greeley wanted to know in 1876; and reformer Henry George intoned that "Amid the greatest accumulations of wealth, men die of starvation, and puny infants suckle dry breasts; while everywhere the greed of gain, the worship of wealth, shows the force of the fear of want." But such observations were generally lost in the din as Americans pursued their ambitions with single-minded zeal. And as they surveyed the scene when the century drew to a close, there seemed to be no end in sight to the good things their bounteous land still had to offer.

SCHMIDT LABEL & LITH. CO. S. F.

A DEATH TRAP.

The hazards of elevator travel in the 1880s were spoofed in cartoons like this one from The Wasp, a Western magazine.

Law and Order

A New York City copper bringing in his man, circa 1897.

An Eye for an Eye

There must be some way to stay this mad rush of crime; some remedy for this bacteria which is poisoning the fountains of moral and physical health.

THE MEDICAL TIMES, APRIL 1893

I never killed nary a feller what didn't need it. NEW MEXICO MARSHAL CLAY ALLISON

Not far beneath the prim lace-curtain surface of Victorian America lay a deep and abiding potential for violence. In 1870, only five years after the Civil War and the assassination of President Lincoln, the odor of blood still lingered across the land. Bands of outlaws terrorized the border states of the Midwest, in defiance of police and militia; many of the badmen, like two brothers named Frank and Jesse James, were discharged Confederate soldiers who continued to live by the gun long after their side had surrendered at Appomattox. In the raw-boned mining camps and cattle towns of the Western frontier, the deeds of gunslingers, claim jumpers and cattle rustlers were accepted conditions of life. And while many Western sheriffs worked hard and honestly to keep the peace, many other purported representatives of law and order were simply quick-triggered hoodlums. Sheriff Wyatt Earp, himself a saloon bouncer, deputized a card sharp called Bat Masterson to help him clean up Dodge City, Kansas, and later drafted an alcoholic murderer named Doc Holliday to pacify Tombstone, Arizona. Wild Bill Hickok, the high-rolling marshal of Abilene, Kansas, calmly boasted that he was responsible for "considerably over a hundred" deaths, several of them rumored to be outside the line of duty; and no one believed frontier marshal Clay Allison when he denied that he killed for pleasure.

In the big cities of the East, another type of social upheaval bred its own form of violence and crime. As thousands of penniless European immigrants poured into the urban ghettos, the efforts of local police forces to keep order collapsed under the impact of sheer numbers. By 1870 gangs of young toughs were ravaging the poorer areas of most big cities almost at will. On one single street in New York City's Lower East Side, murders averaged one a night. And in the last decade of the century, an ominous and totally new criminal phenomenon appeared on the American scene: an internationally controlled underground of organized racketeering. In 1890 the nation was appalled to learn that New Orleans' upstanding, two-fisted police chief, David Hennessy, had been assassinated by a secret criminal group from Sicily called the Mafia. Fifteen Mafia leaders were captured and tried, but the jury, harassed both by underworld threats and attempted bribes, did not manage to convict even a single one. Incensed at this obvious dereliction of duty, a group of New Orleans' most zealous citizens formed a posse, stormed the jailhouse, and shot, clubbed or hanged 11 of the Sicilians.

Lynched by the angry burghers of Minneapolis in 1882, rapist Frank McManus swings from a tree limb after being dragged from jail.

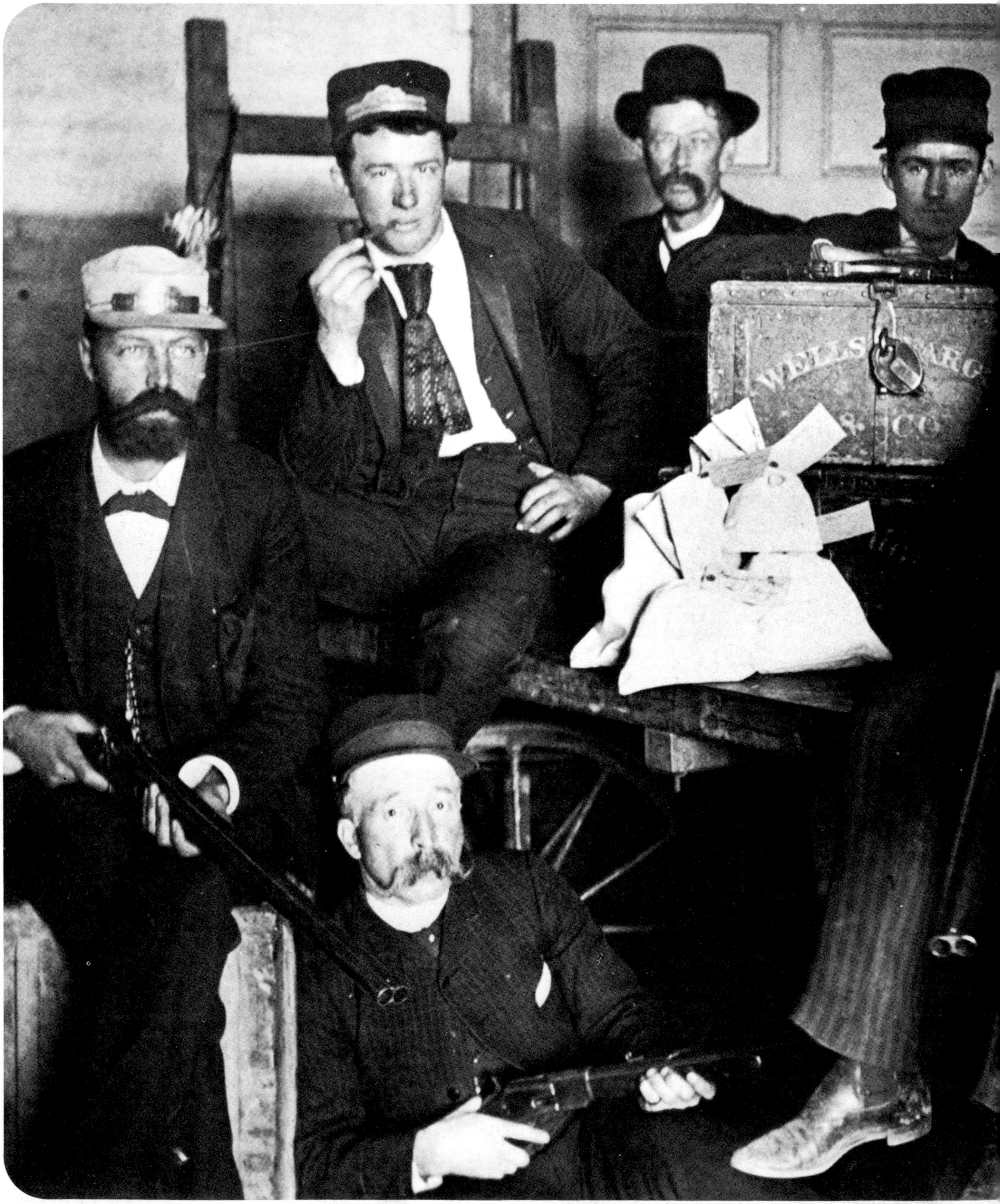

An intrepid squad of agents keeps watch over bags and strongboxes full of Nevada silver at the Wells Fargo branch office in Reno.

"Alert and Faithful"

Guards ride shotgun on a Wells Fargo shipment worth $350,000.

One of the staunchest defenders of law and order on the Western frontier was an express agency called Wells Fargo, the trans-Mississippi arm of the American Express Company. Set up in 1852 initially to speed gold shipments from the California minefields to the banks and minting offices back East, Wells Fargo by 1870 had expanded into a network of 396 branch offices, stage coach routes and railway express franchises that reached into virtually every cowtown and mining camp in the West.

For a fee, the company would carry just about anything: mail, bank notes, brides en route from the East to booming California, and on at least one occasion a battalion of soldiers to fight an Indian war. However, the backbone of the firm's trade was the gold and silver that it transported in the padlocked green strongboxes that became a Wells Fargo trademark.

Tempted by such rich prizes, bands of outlaws hovered around the Wells Fargo routes like flies around honey. But true to its motto—Alert and Faithful—the company hired gun-toting guards to fend off these marauders. And to track down any outlaws who might grab the gold and get away, in 1873 Wells Fargo hired a California sheriff named James B. Hume, who steadfastly pursued Wells Fargo robbers for the next 31 years. A burly six-footer, Hume was a maverick among the West's gun-slinging lawmen. His favorite diversions were tending his rose garden and savoring fine claret and imported French cheese. To the tough business of frontier crime detection, he added such refinements of science as ballistics and his own annotated photographic rogue's gallery *(below)*. So successful were his methods that he was able to report after a 14-year period that only $415,312.55 out of the hundreds of millions of dollars' worth of treasure shipped by Wells Fargo had been lost to outlaws. And of this, Wells Fargo customers lost not a penny. For it was a bedrock company policy to guarantee that every cent lost would instantly be refunded.

MR. JNO. J. VALENTINE
Wells, Fargo & Company,
San Francisco,

Dear Sir:—

We have compiled from the records in our Department the following data, extending over a period of fourteen years —from November 5th, 1870, to November 5th, 1884.

Total amount taken from W. F. & Co.'s Express by stage robbers, train robbers and burglars during the fourteen years beginning November 5, 1870. *$415,312.55*

Rewards paid for arrest and conviction of said robbers, etc., and percentage paid on treasure recovered *$73,451.00*

Frank Miller

Robbed Stage Six miles above Ukiah. Jany 15th 1896 Sent to State Prison for a term of 15 years.

Jesus Marea

Robbed three Stages in 1875 Butte Co. with Pardilla, Red Antone" and others

Hugh McGregor

A Crank

Wm Corbet - Stage Robber.

John D. Ruggles.

In an attempt to rob the Weaver-ville Stage. murdered W. F. & Cos Mess. Buck Montgomery. May 14-92 Taken from prison and hunged by the mob July 24. 1892.

Eugene Tyler

(Negro) Robbed Los Baños Stage May 7-1877 with Dan McCarty

Number of Stage Robberies and Attempted Stage Robberies	*347*
" *Burglaries*	*23*
" *Train Robberies and Attempted Train Robberies*	*8*
" *Convictions for Robbery and Attempt at Stage Robbery*	*206*
" *Convictions for Train Robbery and attempt at same*	*20*
" *Convictions for Burglary*	*14*
" *W. F. & Co.'s Guards killed while in discharge of duty, by stage robbers*	*2*
" *Stage Drivers killed by robbers*	*4*
Number of Passengers killed by stage robbers	*4*
" *Stage Robbers killed while in the act of robbing or attempting to rob the express on stages, by W. F. & Co's guard*	*5*
" *Robbers killed while resisting arrest*	*11*
" *Robbers hanged by citizens*	*7*

You will notice by the foregoing that the number of lives lost, as the result of the above enumerated robberies and attempted robberies, amounts to THIRTY-THREE.

There have also been seven horses killed, and thirteen stolen from the various stage teams.

Respectfully submitted,

J. B. HUME, J. N. THACKER, *Special Officers*

J. R. Todd
Robbed stage near Glendale Or
alone July 25/83

Geo Harris
Attempted to rob Stage
from Yreka to Redding
alone June 26" 1882

Geo N. Rugg
Robbed Marysville Stage
July 31-1877 with
Eph White

John Mc Cabe
Burglarized R.R. & Ex.
Safe Madison. Yolo Co.
June 14-84

Tom Horn
Letter Thief

John A. Toney
Robbed Shasta Stage three
times in one week in 1876
with Frank Chapman

A sheriff's posse rings wounded Wells Fargo bandit John Sontag, captured after an eight-hour gunfight at Sampson's Flats, California.

Six-Gun Justice

In many parts of the wide-open West, the law was nothing more than an angry citizen with a gun or a rope. Sometimes these citizens banded together into vigilante committees, such as the ones that first warned *(below)* and then shot or hanged misbehavers in the Montana Territory. In other cases, outraged individuals just grabbed their six-shooters and started firing.

One memorable instance occurred during 1876 in Northfield, Minnesota, when the swift trigger fingers of local citizens broke up the most notorious outlaw gang in all the West. It began quietly enough. At midmorning on September 7, 1876, five tall, handsome strangers trotted into Northfield, mounted on fine horses with fancy saddles. "Nobler looking fellows I never saw," exclaimed one witness later. The strangers idled about town until two in the afternoon, when they rode up to the bank. At that moment, two additional strangers came galloping onto the main street, yelling and firing off their revolvers in an attempt to frighten people into taking cover. "Them men are going for the town, they mean to rob the bank!" a bystander shouted.

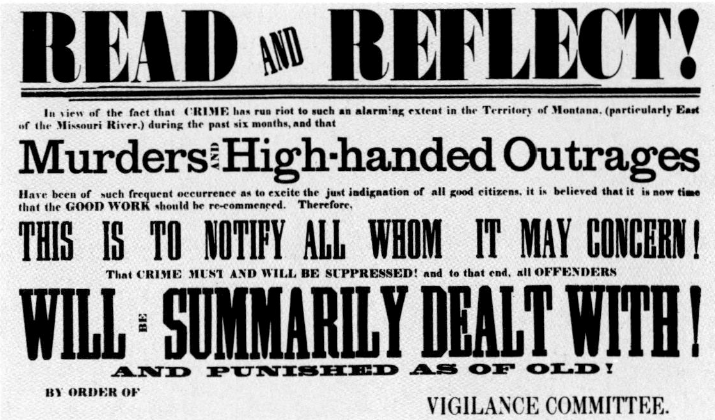
READ AND REFLECT!

In view of the fact that CRIME has run riot to such an alarming extent in the Territory of Montana, (particularly East of the Missouri River,) during the past six months, and that

Murders AND High-handed Outrages

Have been of such frequent occurrence as to excite the just indignation of all good citizens, it is believed that it is now time that the GOOD WORK should be re-commenced. Therefore,

THIS IS TO NOTIFY ALL WHOM IT MAY CONCERN!

That CRIME MUST AND WILL BE SUPPRESSED! and to that end, all OFFENDERS

WILL BE SUMMARILY DEALT WITH!

AND PUNISHED AS OF OLD!

BY ORDER OF

VIGILANCE COMMITTEE.

And indeed they did. The invaders grabbed all the cash they could find, which turned out to be only $12 in loose scrip, fatally shot cashier Joseph Heywood and ran outside —to find not a deserted street but a crowd of gunslinging citizens. Henry M. Wheeler, a medical student home in Northfield for the summer, picked off one horseman, a man named Clell Miller. Another robber, Bill Chadwell, was cut down by hardware merchant A. R. Manning. The other desperadoes rapidly fled town.

During the next two weeks, while posses hunted the robbers, state police authorities speculated that the gang leaders were none other than Jesse James and the Younger brothers. The outlaw band they headed had already knocked over 10 other banks, pillaged four trains and two stage coaches, snatched the gate receipts of the Kansas City Fair and gunned down 15 people.

Acting on a tip from a youth named August Suborn, a posse under Sheriff James Glispin ran the fugitives to earth on September 21, some 80 miles southwest of Northfield. A second gun battle erupted, and when the smoke had cleared, the posse had killed one more desperado, Charlie Pitts, and captured three more—who turned out to be the nefarious Younger brothers. Jesse James had split off from the gang earlier and remained at large.

Hurting from many bullet wounds and in mortal fear of being lynched, the three Youngers were carted back to jail. To their surprise, they were treated like celebrities. The good Minnesota farmers felt a begrudging admiration for the bandits, and they flocked to the jailhouse by the thousands to see what the men looked like. Photographers took pictures of the gang members, both living and dead, and sold over 50,000 souvenir prints—some with misspelled names *(right)*—in a single month. Awaiting trial, the brothers shrewdly played up to their public by sweet-talking visitors, displaying just the right note of contrition ("We were drove to it, sir," Cole Younger declared; "circumstances sometimes makes men what they are") and graciously accepting the gifts of food, cigars and flowers brought by admiring ladies. ("I love flowers, because those I love loves flowers," Cole was overheard to murmur.) In this aura of good will the Youngers managed to beat the hangman and got off with life sentences. As for Jesse James, he went on robbing and killing for another six years, until he was shot in the head by a member of his own gang, Bob Ford, in 1882, for $10,000 in reward money.

A Northfield souvenir card showed the good guys (top) and the bad guys. The photographs of Chadwell, Miller and Pitts are posthumous.

The Pioneering Private Eye

In the free enterprise spirit of the 19th Century, the most powerful U.S. organization for catching crooks was neither the federal government nor the local police, but a private detective company run by a Scottish immigrant named Allan Pinkerton. In the best Horatio Alger style, Pinkerton had come off the boat from Glasgow a penniless young man, and before 1900 his National Detective Agency had become a million-dollar empire whose activities were worldwide. When, for example, in 1876, master thief Adam Worth made the biggest haul in his 35-year career by making off with a Gainsborough painting, Pinkerton's men hounded him for more than 20 years until they recovered the painting. In October 1873, when trouble was brewing in the Pennsylvania coalfields between mine owners and labor agitators called the Molly Maguires, it was a Pinkerton man who gathered enough evidence to hang 19 men and break up the movement. And it was the Pinkertons who, in 1895, helped unearth the evidence to convict the most dastardly criminal of the age, Herman Webster Mudgett, a murderous Lothario whose Chicago mansion contained a lime kiln, an acid barrel and the charred remains of some of his 27 victims.

For the self-assured Pinkerton such prodigies of sleuthing were the merest routine. In one of the books he wrote dramatizing his own exploits, he recorded this monologue with an awed bank president: "On reading a telegraphic newspaper report of a large or small robbery, with the aid of my vast records and great personal experience, I can tell at once the character of the work, and then, knowing the names, history, habits, and quite frequently the rendezvous of the men doing that class of work, am able to determine, with almost unerring certainty, not only the very parties who committed the robberies, but also what disposition they are likely to make of the plunder."

So much for the art of crime detection. There were times, however, in his earlier years, when life cannot have seemed all that simple for Allan Pinkerton. The son of a Glasgow police sergeant, he had been forced to flee Scotland in 1842 at age 23 to avoid arrest for taking part in political riots. En route to America, his sailing packet was wrecked on an island off Nova Scotia. Making shore in a lifeboat, Pinkerton was set upon by Indians. He escaped, later hitched a ride on a riverboat up the St. Lawrence to Detroit and finally trekked across country into the Chicago area, where he arrived with total assets of one silver dollar tied up in a handkerchief.

To earn a few more silver dollars, Pinkerton started making barrels for local farmers. One day, while cutting barrel staves on a small island, the sharp-eyed Scot came upon a campsite that struck him as suspicious, for the island was uninhabited and a poor place for casual camping. Pinkerton knew that the local sheriff was gunning for a gang of counterfeiters said to be somewhere in the area. Could this be their hideout? Indeed it was. Pinkerton legged it to the sheriff. Together they returned, staked out the island and nabbed the crooks.

From then on, Pinkerton was in the crime-busting business. Appointed a deputy sheriff, he acquired such a reputation at running in malefactors that Chicago's chief law officer hired him as an investigator. Two years later he struck out on his own as a private detective. Lining up clients among the city's railroads, he put together a 10-man organization he called Pinkerton's National Detective Agency. To dramatize its promised vigilance in pursuit of criminals, he later took for his trademark an unsleeping, all-seeing eye *(above, right)*.

And indeed, the canny Pinkerton did seem blessed with an extraordinary ability to pinpoint just the right clue—a telltale laundry mark, a whiff of some special perfume or tobacco—that would lead him straight to the culprit. Like other top lawmen of the day, he leaned heavily on his extraordinary memory, which allowed him to recall most of the material in the agency's enormous rogues' gallery after only one reading. And once he had nailed his man, Pinkerton had a unique talent for encouraging the unhappy felon to confess. "A guilty conscience is a detective's best friend," Pinkerton would remind his agents solemnly.

His men learned well, for the National Detective Agency quickly built a solid record of solving major thefts. Soon Chicago's harried thieves began referring to the company

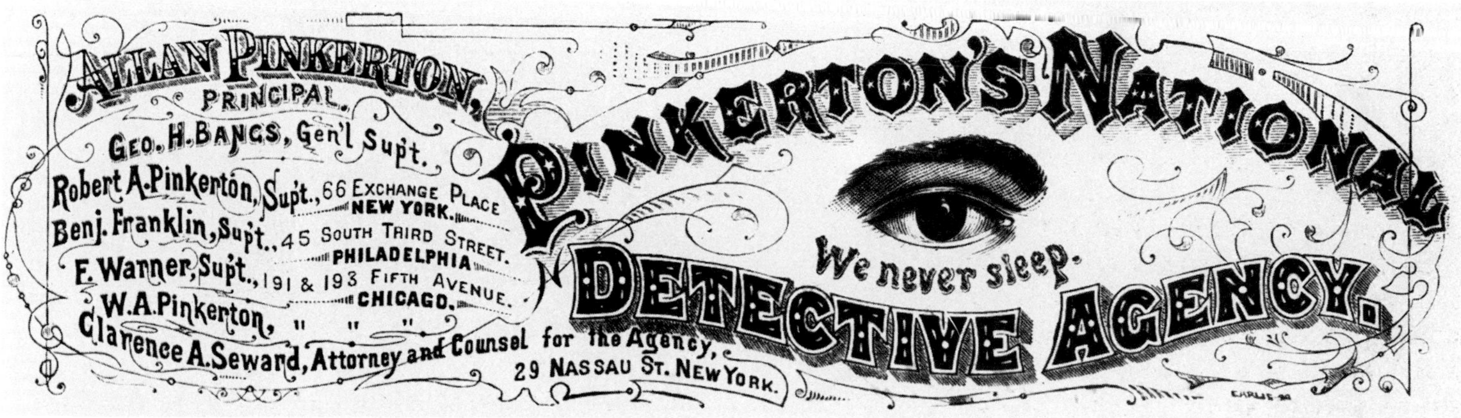

as "The Eye." And eventually the phrase "private eye" became a universal nickname for all private detectives.

Pinkerton himself became a national hero in 1861, when he foiled an early assassination plot against Abraham Lincoln. The President-elect was about to entrain from Springfield, Illinois, for his inauguration when a rumor broke that secessionists were planning to shoot him as he changed trains in Maryland. Pinkerton sent an agent to infiltrate the radicals. Then he personally persuaded Lincoln to change his travel schedule for Washington and to disguise himself by wrapping up in a woolen shawl. The President never forgot Pinkerton's imaginative, decisive way of foiling the plotters. During the Civil War Pinkerton was asked to set up America's first official secret service, whose principal wartime catch was one Mrs. Rose Greenhow, a Washington hostess with a popular salon that turned out to be headquarters for one of the Confederacy's most active spy rings.

At war's end Pinkerton went back to his detective agency, which by 1870 had become the world's largest. In all, thousands of highly trained men operated out of offices in key cities across the U.S. Through them, the eye that never slept was keeping watch over banks, department stores, factories and railway express agencies, to name just a few. In addition, hard-riding Pinkerton agents were chasing badmen on the Western frontier *(overleaf)*. They dogged the heels of Jesse James so closely that the master outlaw went gunning—unsuccessfully—for Allan Pinkerton and his son William, who by 1875 was one of the agency's top detectives. James vowed a slow death for father Allan, saying: "I want him to feel it. I want to watch him." But Jesse never got his man.

By the early 1880s, however, the elder Pinkerton, ailing and bored with the increasing administrative burden of running his empire of paid snoopers, turned over much of the day-to-day operation to his deputies. From then on, Pinkerton spent most of his time either writing some 18 volumes of blood-and-thunder detective stories based on his own files, or disguising himself with eyeglasses and false whiskers to hunt down crooks for the sheer fun of it. He never lost this joy in the hunt, and he continued personally to chase criminals in the field until his ignominious death in 1884, from gangrene that developed after he had tripped and bitten his tongue during his customary morning constitutional.

The will of the once penniless immigrant left an estate of half a million dollars; William and another son, Robert, inherited control of the agency. And they continued to run it in steadfast adherence to their father's deep faith in law and order, as expressed in the preface to one of his books: "Vice may triumph for a time, crime may flaunt its victories in the face of honest toilers, but in the end the law will follow the wrong-doer to a bitter fate, and dishonor and punishment will be the portion of those who sin."

The Wild Bunch: Sundance Kid sits at left, Cassidy at right.

In 1897 William Pinkerton was handed a report on a band of swaggering outlaws that was pillaging Union Pacific trains. The gang was composed, the report said, "of outlaws and former cowboys, headed by George LeRoy Parker, alias Butch Cassidy, a cowboy, rustler, and gambler. We must use every facility to break up this gang." Cassidy, a likable bandit with an infectious smile and twinkling eyes, had left his father's Utah ranch in the late 1880s to follow the outlaw trail simply for the glamor of it. And a glamorous time he had, pulling together a swashbuckling crew known as the Wild Bunch.

To stop them William Pinkerton sent out the renowned cowboy detective Charlie Siringo. Posing as a Texas gunslinger, Siringo joined the Bunch and tipped off the railroad whenever a heist was planned. As Siringo's cover wore thin, forcing him to quit the gang, the railroad adopted other tactics—a pioneer type of mobile striking force *(right)*. So successful were these tactics in frustrating the train robbers that Cassidy and company were forced to lay off the U. P. for easier game—like other railroads.

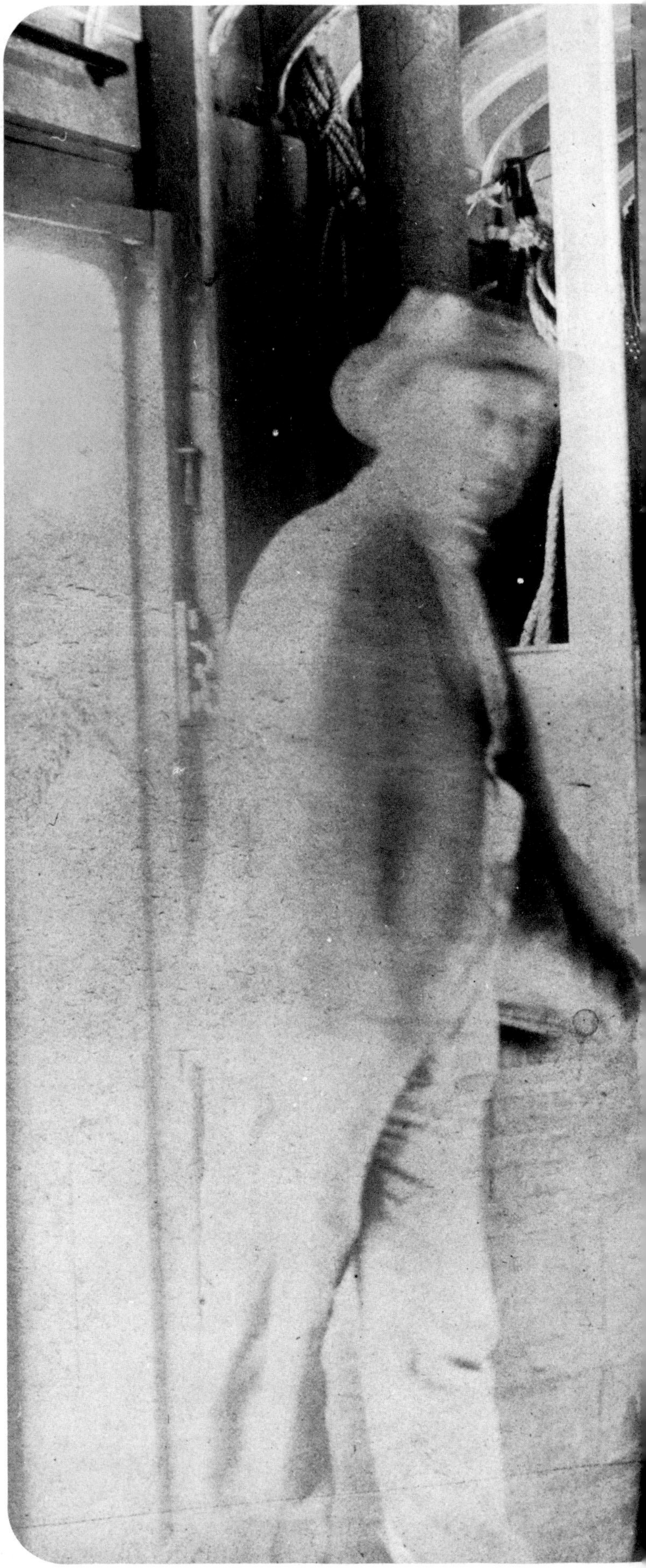

To foil the Wild Bunch, the Union Pacific outfitted a high-speed train with horse stalls and this posse of determined manhunters.

Victorian police, like this proud Richmond, Virginia, officer, posed as models of virtue, but police corruption was the scandal of the day.

Tarnish on the Copper's Badge

To all appearances, the smartly uniformed police who stood guard against crime in the nation's big cities were the pride of their communities. In tribute to the men of his force, New York City police chief George Walling dubbed them "the City's Finest." But in New York, as elsewhere, it turned out that the Victorian copper, for all his spit and polish, could be a darker villain than the crooks he was supposed to catch.

The most appalling police scandal of the era was uncovered by a crusading New York cleric, Dr. Charles H. Parkhurst, who was a leading member of a citizen's group called the Society for the Prevention of Crime. Infuriated by well-substantiated tales of corruption, Dr. Parkhurst mounted his pulpit at the Madison Square Presbyterian Church one Sunday in 1892 to blast the city's Tammany Hall politicians and by implication the police department that they controlled, for being a "lying, perjured, rum-soaked, and libidinous lot." Then he sallied forth in person to gather enough proof to punish the malefactors. Posing as a tramp and guided by a private detective in similar disguise, he spent four hard nights touring the city's most disreputable fleshpots. "'Show me something worse,' was his constant cry," said the detective later. The good reverend saw enough to prove that most of the city's gambling parlors, policy shops and after-hours saloons were handing over a good piece of their take to the police for protection. Newspapers and magazines *(below)* broke the story, and a State Senate hearing was called. As a result, every single top police official in the city was forced to resign, including Superintendent Thomas Byrnes *(overleaf)*, who had been thoroughly respected up to that moment as the fine, crusading leader of the city's finest.

The Committee investigating New York's police-department has been literally turning the city inside out, as one turns an old stocking to examine its seamy side, and see what has lodged in its dark recesses. New York has had investigations in plenty—but never, at least, not for many years—such an one as this, and every day furnishes fresh revelations and sensations. Bawdy-house keepers have taken the stand, and have told the secrets of the "trade," and especially those that pertain to hush money for the police. Gamblers, saloonkeepers, and "green goods" men (swindlers dealing in counterfeit money), have followed in succession, with equal candor and detail.

As a result of it all, it is hardly too much to say that every bluecoat and brass button in the city rests under suspicion of complicity with crime. So sweeping has the implication of the police been that Delancey Nicoll, their "counsel" before the Committee, savagely intimates that if the things go much farther the militia will have to be called on to guard the city, for there will be nobody else left to do it.

Additional testimony has been offered to prove that gamblers, liquor dealers, and keepers of bawdy-houses paid fees for immunity from prosecution. The evidence indicates that the usual price of admission to the police-force has for years been $200, and as each Commissioner has his proportion of vacancies to fill, he draws an income of about $3,000 a year from this source alone. The civil service examinations are evaded by substituting other men than the applicants for admission to the force. It was shown that police justices were "counsel" for disorderly houses, and that ex-Assemblyman Wissig had leased property for disorderly purposes.

But perhaps the most startling testimony of all was that of an ex-convict named Appo, who had long been engaged in the "green goods" business. He swore that men engaged in this business are under police protection, and that the police were paid for the license to rob country people by pretending to sell them counterfeit money.

THE LITERARY DIGEST, JUNE 23, 1894

IKE VAIL *alias*
OLD IKE

CONFIDENCE MAN: *Their form of roguery has been said to be the safest and most amusing way for a shrewd thief to make his living. There certainly must be a strange fascination about these methods of swindling, for in the ranks of the sharpers has been discovered an ex-Governor and many others, who have at one time figured in good society.*

The operators are very careful in their personal appearance, and endeavor to attain an easy respectability. Confidence men have more than once declared a tinge of grey in their side whiskers to be a great advantage and a bald head a fortune.

JOHN CANNON *alias*
OLD JACK

CHRISTINE MAYER *alias*
KID GLOVE ROSEY

SHOPLIFTER: *There are few ladies to whom the visitation of the shops and the handling of the wares are not joys which transcend all others on earth. And the female shoplifter has that touch of nature left in her which makes a clothing store, variety bazaar or jewelry establishment the most delightful spot to exercise her cunning. In the last few years professionals of this order have wonderfully multiplied in this city, but their increase has been no more than commensurate with that of the metropolitan bazaars. It is these very places which are most preyed upon and in which the temptation to larceny is most freely offered.*

STEPHEN RAYMOND *alias*
MARSHAL

JOHN CLARE *alias*
GILMORE

BANK BURGLAR: *It requires rare qualities in a criminal to become an expert bank-safe robber. Thieves of this high grade stand unrivaled among their kind. The professional bank burglar must have patience, intelligence, mechanical knowledge, industry, determination, fertility of resources and courage—all in high degree. But, even if he possess all these, they cannot be utilized unless he can find suitable associates or gain admission to one of the already organized gangs. Sometimes the arrest of a single man out of a gang will put a stop to the operations of the remainder for a long time.*

JOSEPH LEWIS *alias*
HUNGRY JOE

Before his retirement in the corruption scandal of 1894, Superintendent Byrnes had prepared for publication a gallery of well-known crooks.

HOTEL THIEF: *When the unsuspecting prey, fatigued by travel, gives proof of his unconsciousness by deep, stertorous breathing, the hotel thief steals silently from his hiding-place. A slight push may let him enter the apartment, or it may be necessary to use a gimlet and a small piece of crooked wire to slide back the bolt, or a pair of nippers to turn the key left in the lock. Sometimes as many as a dozen rooms in the same hotel have been plundered in one night and none of the watchmen saw or heard the thief. The old style of climbing through transoms or unkeyed windows is at present not much in vogue.*

MARGRET BROWN *alias*
OLD MOTHER HUBBARD

PICKPOCKET: *Women make the most patient and dangerous pickpockets. Humble in their attire, and seemingly unassuming in their demeanor, without attracting any notice or particular attention, they slip into an excited crowd in a store or in front of a shop window. A quick eye or a delicate touch will locate for them without difficulty the resting-place of a well filled purse. That discovered, they follow the victim about until the proper opportunity presents itself and they capture the prize. Sometimes they go off on thieving excursions in pairs, but an expert female pickpocket invariably prefers to work alone.*

FORGER: *All told there are not more than two dozen expert penmen and engravers who prostitute their talents by imitating the handwriting and workmanship of others. Occasionally they suddenly launch forth some gigantic scheme, flooding the principal cities with their spurious and worthless paper. Some of the most prominent forgers are chemists, and by the aid of a secret mixture of acids, they are able to erase figures in ink from the face of notes without destroying or damaging the paper. Thus genuine orders upon banks or brokers for a few dollars are easily raised up into the thousands.*

HENRY HOFFMAN *alias*
MEYERS

RECEIVER OF STOLEN GOODS: *Receivers, while they rarely pay more than one-quarter of the value of the stolen article, run no risks. They never make a settlement with the thieves until the proceeds of the robbery have been removed to a place the location of which the gang they are dealing with knows nothing about. The reason why the rogues are kept in ignorance is to prevent them, should there be any bickering as to the price, from betraying the buyer. The simple testimony of the self-confessed thief that he sold the stolen goods would be of no value in a legal sense without the proof of the seizure of the plunder.*

BANCO MAN: *"Banco" is the old English game of "eight dice cloth." It was introduced into this country some thirty years ago by a noted sharper who operated throughout the West. The dupe is lured into the banco men's shop by the usual story about a book or a painting drawn in a lottery, then the cash prize and the rest of it. The stranger usually bites; he is anxious to get $500 for $100; puts down his wad of bills, and the operators capture it, and he walks out in a brown study, not knowing exactly how he was done up, but quite sure he has been swindled. The victim does not complain because he is ashamed to tell how green he was.*

CHARLES WOODWARD *alias*
THE DIAMOND SWALLOWER

SNEAK THIEF: *Some housebreakers are daring and desperate rascals. These are the ones that enter dwellings in the night-time in search of plunder and with masks on their faces and murder in their heart. Other thieves, who also pillage houses during the supper hour, pick the lock of the front door and steal in without making any noise. They wear rubbers or woolen shoes, and succeed at intervals in making large hauls. Some sneaks go about as peddlers, piano tuners, health and building inspectors, book canvassers, life and fire insurance agents, and in various other roles. Cash, jewelry, and valuables is the plunder.*

With the pictures were Byrnes's own oddly respectful descriptions (excerpted above) of the various criminal types represented by each rogue.

The Wages of Crime

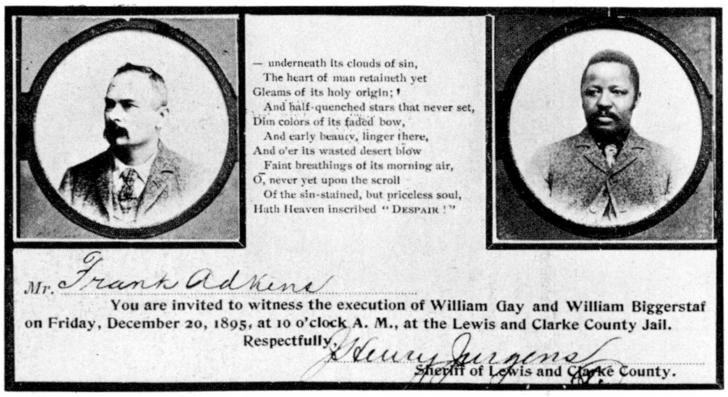

— underneath its clouds of sin,
The heart of man retaineth yet
Gleams of its holy origin;
And half-quenched stars that never set,
Dim colors of its faded bow,
And early beaucy, linger there,
And o'er its wasted desert blow
Faint breathings of its morning air,
O, never yet upon the scroll
Of the sin-stained, but priceless soul,
Hath Heaven inscribed "DESPAIR!"

Mr. Frank Adkins

You are invited to witness the execution of William Gay and William Biggerstaf on Friday, December 20, 1895, at 10 o'clock A. M., at the Lewis and Clarke County Jail.

Respectfully,
Henry Jurgens
Sheriff of Lewis and Clarke County.

Special invitations were sent out to guests for a Montana hanging.

Once caught, 19th Century crooks met with harsh justice. On the frontier, murderers, cattle rustlers and horse thieves were often sent straight to the gallows—with or without due ceremony. In the cities, offenders were tossed into foul, disease-ridden prisons. Toward the end of the century, reformers managed to see to the building of more antiseptic prisons *(right)* and tried to abolish capital punishment. But on the latter point they were shouted down by hard-liners such as Theodore Roosevelt, who served as Police Commissioner of New York City from 1895 to 1897.

The gallows produced no deterrent effect on the violent. The electrical chair seems to have no terrors to those of ungovernable passion. Yet the State—the great, calm, judicial, unimpressionable State—which should be superior to ordinary humanity's weaknesses takes life, nevertheless, as the maddened, frenzied, or ignorant, irresponsible individual might do.

THE EXPRESS, ALBANY, NEW YORK, 1893

You don't want any mushy sentimentality when you are dealing with criminals. One of the things that many of our good reformers should learn is that fellow-feeling for the criminal is out of place.

THEODORE ROOSEVELT, 1895

Sitting bolt upright in tightly disciplined rows, convicts wait to rise after dinner at the model State Prison in St. Cloud, Minnesota.

Holidays

High-schoolers preparing to decorate veterans' graves.

The Luxury of Guilt

I have been out paying New Year's calls since twelve o'clock. A tiresome, hollow sham it is, but I must keep it up until near midnight.

GODEY'S LADY'S BOOK, JANUARY 1870

In an era of hard work, rural isolation and monumental inhibition, holidays were liberating occasions. Easter parades offered a socially acceptable chance to show off; Valentine's Day afforded an opportunity for shy maidens to send ornate tokens of affection to their beaux. On the warm-weather holidays, frontier farmers who had endured the frozen isolation of the winter prairie came to town to crack open a convivial keg or two, and to find out —often for the first time in months—what had been happening to their neighbors and to their nation. So strongly felt was the need for this kind of lusty communalizing that many U.S. holidays got their start as national institutions in the decade just after the Civil War.

One such was Arbor Day, launched April 22, 1875, by J. Sterling Morton of Nebraska as part of a campaign to get people to plant trees on the bare prairie. Within a dozen years, 40 states had named April 22 an official holiday, and schoolchildren, church and temperance groups had adorned the plains with the awesome total of 600 million newly planted trees. Another of the new observances was Memorial Day, whose date was designated as May 30 by John A. Logan of the Grand Army of the Republic (but as April 26 by an unreconstructed band of Mississippi ladies) to honor the Civil War dead. The scene on Memorial Day was much the same in thousands of small towns across the U.S. The day opened typically with a parade led by a brass band and the volunteer firemen hand-pulling their pumping engine. Following them were the Mexican War veterans and, for a few years anyhow, an occasional, shuffling old-timer from the War of 1812 and finally, splendid in their visored caps and coats, the Civil War veterans. At midday came the patriotic speeches. And afterward, while children raced underfoot, the elders gossiped over fried chicken, home-made pickles and angel-food cake eaten on broad-planked tables set up on the town common.

Throughout these extravagant celebrations there was always the nagging counterpoint of moralistic preaching. Before each holiday feast, Americans were sternly reminded by their clergy that they should be sharing with less fortunate neighbors. Newspapers and magazines were full of editorial scoldings: Christmas gifts had become too lavish, Easter parades too gaudy. Americans suffered suitable guilt and struggled to reconcile the doctrine of deprivation with their own need to bust loose once in a while. But it was a case of protesting too much. The fact was that in this era, holidays were a particular lot of fun.

Go help the lonely Child to play,
Beside the weary sick one stay,
Go make some little sad heart gay,
On Christmas Day in the morning.
MAY YOUR Christmas BE AS HAPPY AS OURS

Christmas cards like this one, with its cherubic children and moralistic messages, were often framed and hung in Victorian living rooms.

The New Year

GENTLEMAN'S CALLING CARD

PROPER CALLING

Ladies expecting calls on New Year's should be in readiness to receive from 10 a.m. to 9 p.m. Upon calling, the gentlemen are invited to remove overcoat and hat, which invitation is accepted unless it is the design to make the call very brief. Gloves are sometimes retained upon the hand during the call, but this is optional. The call should not exceed ten or fifteen minutes, unless it is mutually agreeable to prolong the stay. The ladies should have a bright, cheerful fire and a table, conveniently located in the room, with refreshments, consisting of fruits, cakes, bread and other food, such as may be deemed desirable. No intoxicating drinks should be allowed.

MANUAL OF SOCIAL AND BUSINESS FORMS, 1873

HAND-TINTED CALLING CARD

HOLIDAY POSTCARD

ILLUSTRATED CALENDAR

In the late 1800s the great New Year's rite was not a big party the night before, but quieter customs on the day itself. During the '70s single gentlemen armed with fancy calling cards went on a round of visits to ladies of their acquaintance, aided by local newspapers, which printed long lists of damsels who would be "at home" to such callers. But by 1880, bachelors had so abused the custom ("This is my 47th call!" shouted one swain on the run) that it died of social disapproval. Married men, however, continued to observe the day, either by taking their families to fancy restaurants or by going calling *en famille*—a practice that, like bachelor calling, did not always fall within the bounds of etiquette *(below)*.

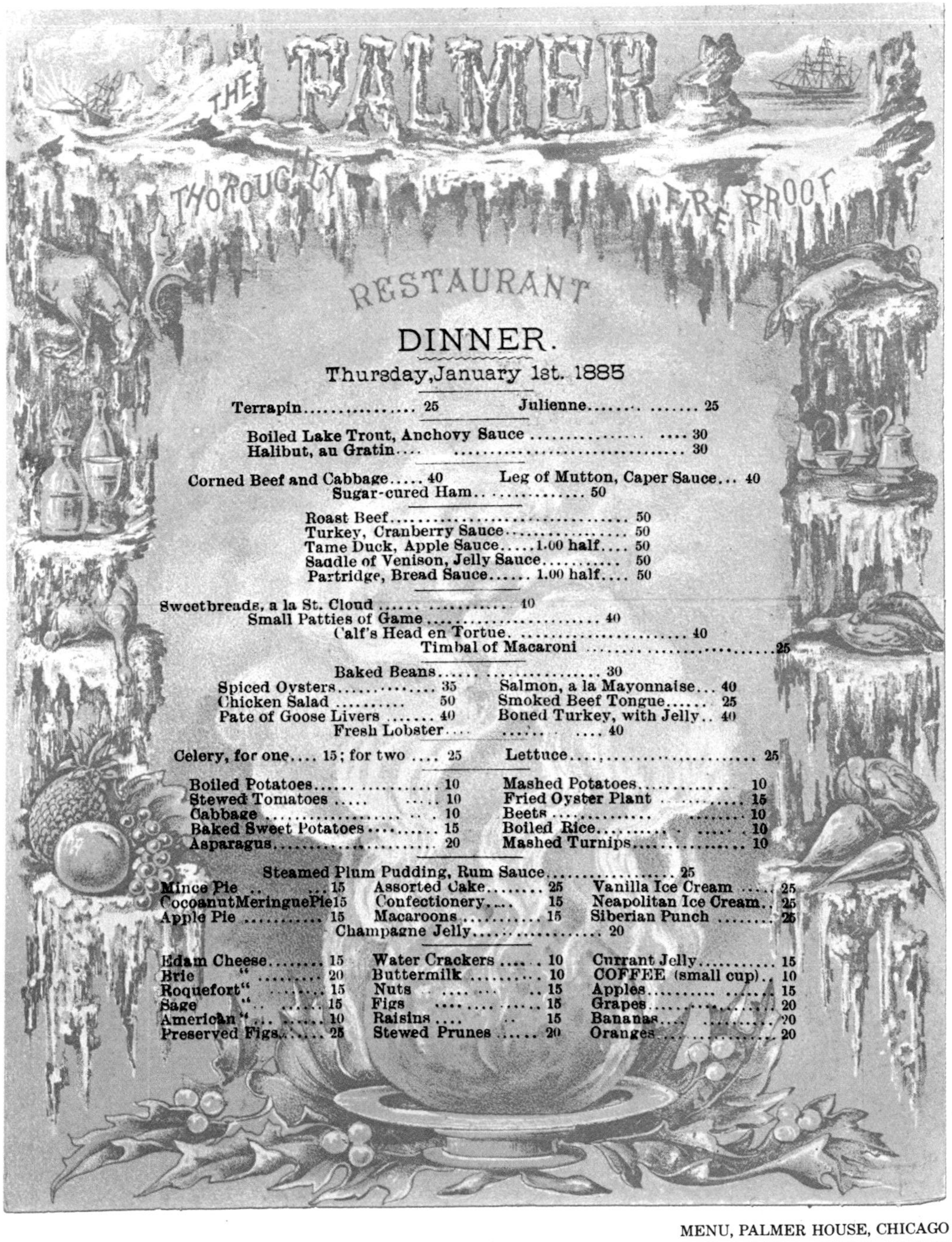

THE PALMER

THOROUGHLY FIRE PROOF

RESTAURANT

DINNER.

Thursday, January 1st. 1885

Terrapin................ 25 Julienne....... 25

Boiled Lake Trout, Anchovy Sauce 30
Halibut, au Gratin.... 30

Corned Beef and Cabbage..... 40 Leg of Mutton, Caper Sauce... 40
Sugar-cured Ham.. 50

Roast Beef.................................. 50
Turkey, Cranberry Sauce................. 50
Tame Duck, Apple Sauce.....1.00 half.... 50
Saddle of Venison, Jelly Sauce........... 50
Partridge, Bread Sauce...... 1.00 half.... 50

Sweetbreads, a la St. Cloud 40
Small Patties of Game........................ 40
Calf's Head en Tortue. 40
Timbal of Macaroni 25

Baked Beans...... 30
Spiced Oysters.............. 35 Salmon, a la Mayonnaise... 40
Chicken Salad .... 50 Smoked Beef Tongue...... 25
Pate of Goose Livers .... 40 Boned Turkey, with Jelly.. 40
Fresh Lobster.... 40

Celery, for one.... 15; for two .... 25 Lettuce........................ 25

Boiled Potatoes..... .... 10 Mashed Potatoes............ 10
Stewed Tomatoes .... 10 Fried Oyster Plant 15
Cabbage .... 10 Beets 10
Baked Sweet Potatoes.......... 15 Boiled Rice.......... 10
Asparagus..................... 20 Mashed Turnips............... 10

Steamed Plum Pudding, Rum Sauce................. 25
Mince Pie .. ... 15 Assorted Cake........ 25 Vanilla Ice Cream 25
CocoanutMeringuePie15 Confectionery..... 15 Neapolitan Ice Cream.. 25
Apple Pie .... 15 Macaroons .... 15 Siberian Punch 25
Champagne Jelly.................. 20

Edam Cheese........ 15 Water Crackers ..... 10 Currant Jelly.......... 15
Brie " .... 20 Buttermilk .... 10 COFFEE (small cup).. 10
Roquefort" .... 15 Nuts .... 15 Apples........ 15
Sage " ...... 15 Figs .... 15 Grapes.............. 20
American " .... 10 Raisins .... .. 15 Bananas.... 20
Preserved Figs...... 25 Stewed Prunes ...... 20 Oranges 20

MENU, PALMER HOUSE, CHICAGO

THE NEW YORK HERALD, 1896

IMPROPER CALLING

Disagreeable callers are the husband and wife who come with a child and a small dog; the husband making himself familiar with the hostess, the dog barking at the cat, the child taking free run of the house, while the wife, passes around the room, handling and examining the ornaments.

Some evening callers make themselves odious by continuing their visit too long, and even when they have risen to depart they lack decision to go but will stand several minutes before taking final leave, and then when wraps are on, will tell one more story while the hostess protects herself as best she can from the incoming gusts of wind and storm, sometimes thus taking a cold that ends in death. When the guest is ready to go—go.

MANUAL OF SOCIAL AND BUSINESS FORMS, 1873

A sentimental holiday like Valentine's Day called forth, naturally, the most dewy effusions, as saccharine cards designed in the most elaborate shapes, and adorned with ribbons, blossoms, fringes and bows, transmitted the seasonal message of love in glorious papier-mâché. In an effort to stem the flow of treacle, magazines like *Harper's (below)* might sniff at the vulgarization of the valentine custom, but in vain. The high priestess of the cult of complex valentines was a genteel Mount Holyoke graduate, Esther Howland of Worcester, Massachusetts, whose lacy handmade creations sold for as much as $50. Alas, though her valentine messages helped the romantic lives of many others, they did not benefit Esther herself; she died a spinster.

FOLD-OUT SEAL

NOTEPAPER

TRINKET BOX

CANDY-BOX CARD

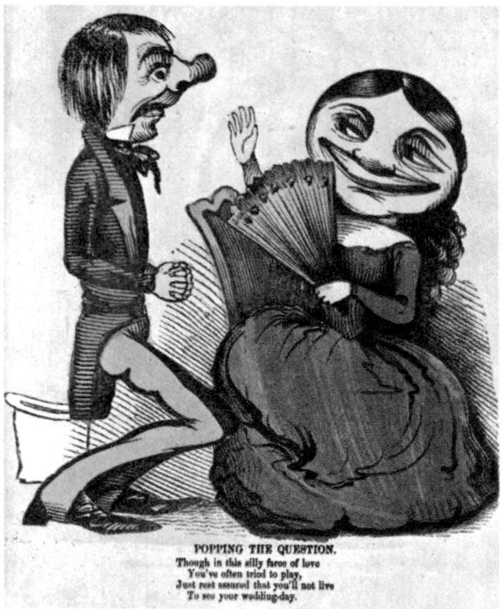

COMIC VALENTINE

CANDY HEART, 1890

Valentine's Day

FOLD-OUT VALENTINE

REQUIEM FOR ST. VALENTINE

The spirit and sentiment of St. Valentine's Day are fading. The world is growing too prosaic. Lovemaking and matrimony are no longer conducted on the principle of a bashful lover worshipping from afar off, and under the disguise of some incognito, some shrinking maiden who revels in the mystery of an unknown adorer. Marriage is walked up to by both parties in a business-like fashion. Neither is in the least timid, and the matter is put through according to rule, and as if it wore only the features of an ordinary contract. This has nearly done away with the occupation of good St. Valentine, and the missives he

CALLING CARD

now presides over are too often only annoying communications, and sent by persons who have no regard for the feelings of others. His fairy gifts, his turtle doves and tender verses have been nearly hustled off our soil by a struggle to adapt him to the customs of our commercial country and make him pay.

Clearly it is impossible to expect that delicate or sensitive people can hereafter make use of the valentine. There seems nothing to do but resign it with a sigh as one more of the pleasant customs of our forefathers, which for some reason we have concluded to abandon.

HARPER'S WEEKLY, FEBRUARY 21, 1880

FLOWER-BASKET VALENTINE

To my Sweetheart
TAKE my heart sweet Valentine
And promise to be true
Then come what may I'll be for aye over fond to you.

VALENTINE FAN

In the first 60 years of the century, Easter was little celebrated in the U.S. The country's Protestant majority scorned the day as Papist, though during the Civil War some communities had set it aside as a day of mourning for fallen soldiers. In the postwar years, however, Easter suddenly emerged as a favored holiday. Youngsters took up those ancient Easter symbols, the egg and the rabbit, and in 1878 President Hayes inaugurated the annual Easter egg roll on the White House lawn. Gentlemen sent cards to ladies. And both sexes turned the holiday into a fashion show, as people of all shapes and tastes paraded their brightest spring outfits up and down the main streets of their towns.

THREE-DIMENSIONAL CARD

GIFT EASTER EGGS

Easter

AN APPEAL FOR ELEGANCE

Everybody is young on Easter Sunday. Matrons throw off their staid airs, and old men rustle bravely. But may Life be permitted one suggestion. Year after year, the homeliest people have inevitably appeared Easter Sunday in the most conspicuous of garments, thus attracting special attention to their lack of natural attractions. If the homely people would either stay home tomorrow or, if they venture out, array themselves in proper garments, the symphonic essence of the street parade would better be preserved.

BROOKLYN LIFE, APRIL 5, 1890

EASTER GREETING CARDS

MOLDED-PLASTER CANDY BOX

MILLINERY TRADE CARD

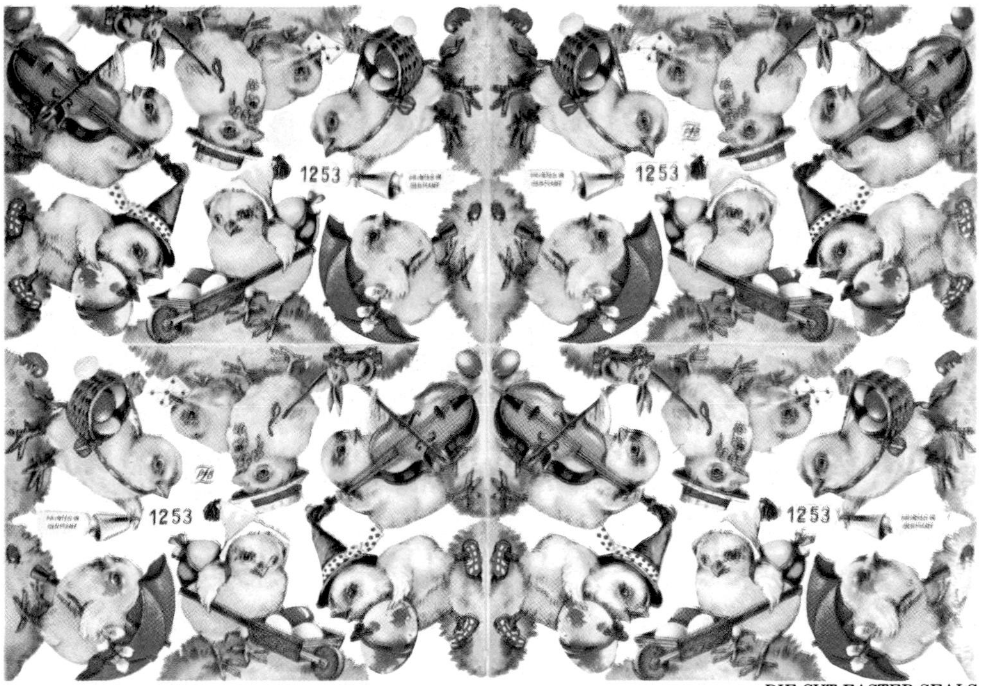

DIE-CUT EASTER SEALS

The loudest, most bumptious holiday of all was the Fourth of July. Every town throughout America had its patriotic parade, accompanied by a cacophony of brass bands, booming fireworks, sham battles and flag-draped oratory—often heavily political in content. Yet while most of the nation was hailing Old Glory, the flag was also being desecrated and bitterly fought over. Advertisers and politicians overprinted slogans and pictures upon it. In the heat of partisan battles, the flag was torn, and shots were even fired in real anger *(overleaf)*, giving an unwelcome tinge of realism to the raucous cannonading on the glorious Fourth of July.

POSTCARD EMBLEM

JULY FOURTH PARADE IN EVANSTON, ILLINOIS

Independence Day

PROGRAM POSTER, 1879

POSTCARD

IN DEFENSE OF OLD GLORY

Southport, Conn., July 2—I write, as chairman of the flag committee of the Connecticut Daughters of the Revolution, to tell you of the work we are doing to foster a feeling of loyalty to the flag that has been honored and guarded in weary marches and perilous voyages. We need such an education of public sentiment as will loyally support righteous legislation for the purpose of enforcing respect for Old Glory.

It should hardly be a question of argument whether a man may wantonly and maliciously tear our country's flag into shreds or trample it; hardly less a question whether it ought to be used as a vehicle of advertisement for nostrums or liquors; yet instances of such misuse are too well known.

A stranger in Council Bluffs, Ia., rode up to a large American flag bearing a partisan banner and fired upon it with a shotgun. A soldier shot at the mounted assailant, killing the horse and wounding the man, who escaped.

At Sedalia, Mo., a child was singing campaign songs and holding a flag in her hands. The flag was seized by a man of the opposing party and thrown upon a bonfire, and its destruction applauded by companions.

Clubs of oppositional political parties met at the railway station at Janesville, Wis., with the result that the national flag was rotten-egged and torn.

A procession marched through the streets of Lafayette, Ill., bearing the red flag at the front and trailing the American flag after it through the filth of the street.

We want the flag protected from all insults. We appeal to loyal Americans to stand by the DAR in this crusade.

REBEKAH W. P. NULKELEY, JULY 3, 1898

SONG SHEET

THE FOURTH IN PHILADELPHIA

4:37 a.m. Sunrise Salute to Old Glory. Battery A, Nat'l Guard, 44 guns.
9 a.m. Celebration: Invocation, Reading of the Declaration, Oration.
10 a.m. Sham Battle, First Brigade, Penna. National Guard. About 40,000 rounds of ammunition will be expended. Naval Battalion will add to the din by the discharge of boat howitzers.
1 p.m. Field Sports. A special feature will be an Exhibition by the German Turnvereins of Philadelphia.
2:30 p.m. Grand Balloon Ascension with 13 Hot-air balloons, symbolic of the original colonies.
2:30 p.m. – 6:00 p.m. Rowing Races.
8:30 p.m. Grand Pyrotechnic Display.

SOUVENIR PROGRAM

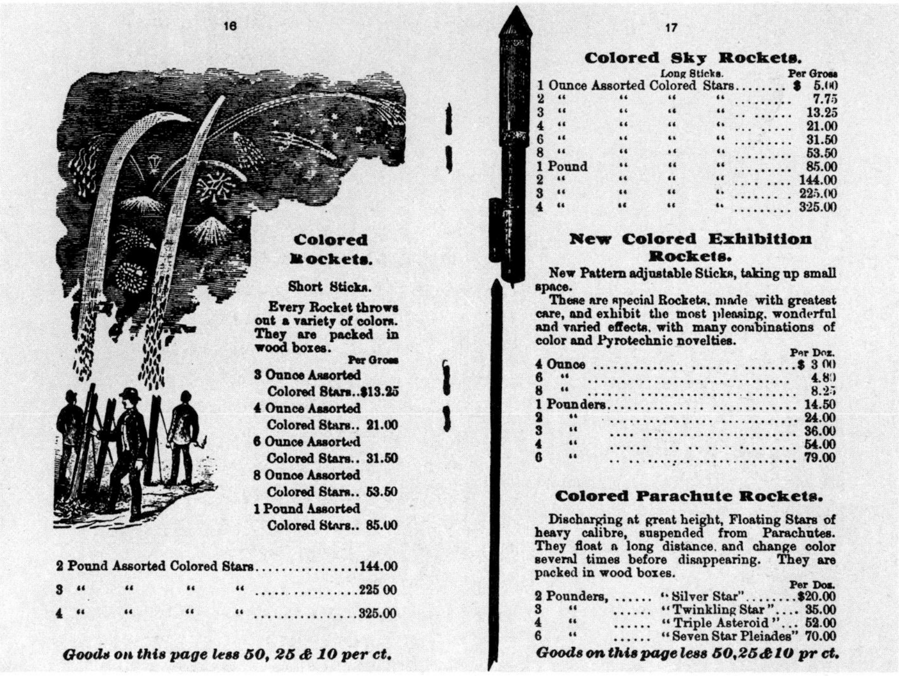

16

Colored Rockets.

Short Sticks.

Every Rocket throws out a variety of colors. They are packed in wood boxes.

	Per Gross
3 Ounce Assorted Colored Stars..	$13.25
4 Ounce Assorted Colored Stars..	21.00
6 Ounce Assorted Colored Stars..	31.50
8 Ounce Assorted Colored Stars..	53.50
1 Pound Assorted Colored Stars..	85.00
2 Pound Assorted Colored Stars................	144.00
3 " " " "	225 00
4 " " " "	325.00

Goods on this page less 50, 25 & 10 per ct.

17

Colored Sky Rockets.

Long Sticks.	Per Gross
1 Ounce Assorted Colored Stars........	$ 5.00
2 " " " "	7.75
3 " " " "	13.25
4 " " " "	21.00
6 " " " "	31.50
8 " " " "	53.50
1 Pound " " "	85.00
2 " " " "	144.00
3 " " " "	225.00
4 " " " "	325.00

New Colored Exhibition Rockets.

New Pattern adjustable Sticks, taking up small space.

These are special Rockets, made with greatest care, and exhibit the most pleasing, wonderful and varied effects, with many combinations of color and Pyrotechnic novelties.

	Per Doz.
4 Ounce	$ 3 00
6 "	4.80
8 "	8.25
1 Pounders............	14.50
2 "	24.00
3 "	36.00
4 "	54.00
6 "	79.00

Colored Parachute Rockets.

Discharging at great height, Floating Stars of heavy calibre, suspended from Parachutes. They float a long distance, and change color several times before disappearing. They are packed in wood boxes.

	Per Doz.
2 Pounders, ... "Silver Star"........	$20.00
3 " ...... "Twinkling Star"....	35.00
4 " ...... "Triple Asteroid"...	52.00
6 " ...... "Seven Star Pleiades"	70.00

Goods on this page less 50, 25 & 10 pr ct.

FIREWORKS CATALOG

PATRIOTIC DOLL

Chicago Historical Society

Halloween and Thanksgiving

STEREOPTICON SLIDE

MIRRORS OF LOVE

A quaint method of determining the faithfulness of lovers is to put three nuts upon the bars of stove grates, naming the nuts after the lovers. If a nut cracks or jumps the lover will prove unfaithful; if it begins to blaze and burn, he has a regard for the person making the trial. If the nuts named after the girl and her lover burn together, they will be married. The reading of the nuts may prove for many a lad and lassie a true prophecy.

Here is another device: Take three dishes, put clean water in one, foul water in another, leave the third empty. Blindfold a person and lead him to where the dishes are ranged; he or she dips the left hand—if by chance in the clean water, the future husband or wife will come to the bar of matrimony a bachelor or maid—if in the foul, a widower or widow; if in the empty dish it foretells no marriage at all. It is repeated three times and each time the arrangement of the dishes is altered. The old test of putting apple seeds on the eyes or cheeks and naming them after swains is another practice. The most faithful is he who sticks the longest.

But it is the maid with the stoutest heart who fears not her fate—and whose desires are great—who dares put it to the touch of the cellar stairs' visit at midnight. The proper form is for her to let down her back hair, then "dressed all in white" with uplifted candle, a la Lady Macbeth, in the left hand a mirror, she proceeds to wend her way slowly—and alone—down the stairs backward to the cellar; it is then when the final step is reached and the critical and dramatic moment arrives, that she will see the pictured face of her future husband in the mirror she carries in her left hand. It is only for those possessing great faith that the face in the mirror will materialize. If the maiden reading this doesn't believe in the efficacy of this special rite, let her try it for herself—seeing is believing.

THE LADIES WORLD, NOVEMBER 1892

CARDBOARD PARTY DECORATION

Americans of the ultrarespectable Victorian era thoroughly relished the old pagan holidays of Halloween and Thanksgiving. Halloween, which had begun as a druidic rite complete with moonlit blood offerings, by the late 1880s in the U.S. had turned into a young people's holiday. It still catered enthusiastically to superstition, but of a mild parlor variety, such as the quaint rituals at left, below, to indicate whether girl would get boy. Thanksgiving was America's version of the harvest festivals of the ancient Semitic tribes. The celebration was confined mainly to New England until 1863, when it grew into the all-American feasting day, complete with lavish dinner recipes and lavish reminders *(below)* about the tribulations of less fortunate folk and the virtues of both humility and generosity on this day of plenty.

THANKSGIVING POSTCARD

THANKSGIVING SERMON

Many men today, sitting in the darkness of great calamity, need some public summons to thanksgiving, lest they forget that they have anything to be thankful for. There are proud, rich men whose riches have gone down in disaster and they know not which way to turn, with families, reared in luxury, clinging to them for elegant support. And there are poor, working men, honest, sturdy, out of work, in rickety hovels and garrets with scanty fires, who go in tatters and eat the meat of charity or chance or none.

And there are women who, with sick and hungry children, tremble at the coming of brutal, drunken husbands. Ah, these days of thanksgiving are, to them, horribly misnamed—gloomy, gloomy days, and full of grim visions. And there is many a desolate work-girl, in our cities, weary, but not of labor, who shudders, standing near to hunger and there sees the smiling face of the tempter as he reaches out for her—how persuasively—furs and fires and food, comfort, luxury and sin. Can these give thanks just now at the behest of our proclamations? Yet let us hail this day with thanksgiving, remembering that though there is no perfect day this side heaven, there is no rayless night except beyond the grave.

THE REVEREND A. S. FISKE, SAN FRANCISCO

THANKSGIVING MENU

Raw Oysters.
Boiled Rockfish, Egg Sauce.
Potato Balls.
Roasted Turkey, Stuffing, Giblet Gravy.
Browned Sweet Potatoes. Baked Squash.
Cranberry Jelly. Sour Grape Jelly.
Moulded Spinach.
Venison Pasty.
Ham Baked in Cider, and Garnished.
Mince Pies. Pumpkin Pies. Fruit.
Coffee.
Hygeia Sparkling Lithia Water.

THANKSGIVING CAKE.—*Sift two pounds and a half of flour, in which mix three teaspoonfuls of baking powder, cream three pounds of sugar and one of butter together, add eighteen eggs and beat five minutes; add half a pound of blanched and chopped almonds, a teacupful of preserved lemon peel. Bake two hours.*

SHARE WITH OTHERS

As, with matronly pride, you survey your table's abundance, may it not suggest a possible paucity in the larder of some less fortunate neighbor to dispatch a well-filled basket to his humble abode, thus causing a ray of sunshine to enter there?

Then, with the ushering in of the Thanksgiving morn, throw dull care to the winds. Let the little ones romp, the cat purr by the fire, the man of the house smoke his cigar in the parlor.

THE LADIES WORLD, NOVEMBER 1892

CLASSROOM THANKSGIVING

Christmas

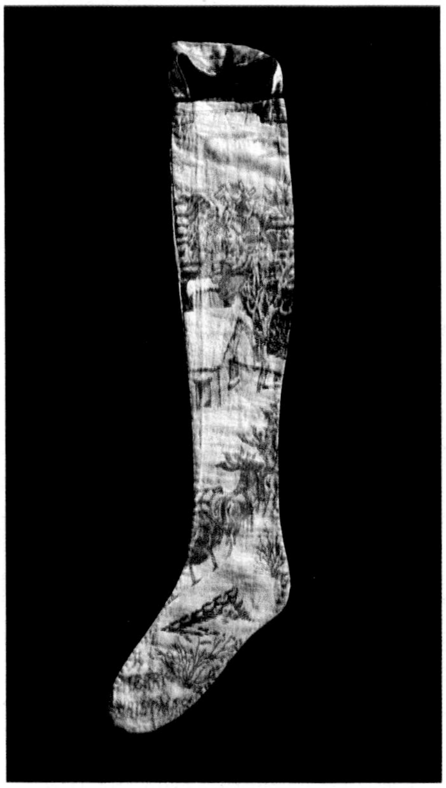

HANDMADE CHRISTMAS STOCKING

LANTERN SLIDE

A MERRY CHRISTMAS
Upon the earth the snow lies drear,
Veiling the landscape all in white;
But in our homes shall be good cheer,
When Christmas comes, with its delight.

CHRISTMAS CARD

CHRISTMAS STICKER

"An occasion of literally delirious joy" was Teddy Roosevelt's description of Christmas in the 1870s. T. R.'s comment was in keeping with the refulgent style of the Victorian Christmas. But equally in keeping with the spirit of Victorian times was the counterpoint to all this opulence—an overdose of morality that directed eyes to the meaning of Christmas, with references to the deserving poor and the widow's mite. The English author Charles Dickens' moralistic *A Christmas Carol* swept the nation; and when Dickens read his *Carol* on one of his several visits to the U.S., he reported afterward that "one girl burst into a passion of grief about Tiny Tim and had to be taken out."

BEST FOR THE LAUNDRY.
MADE ONLY BY
THE N.K. FAIRBANK COMPANY,

TRADE CARD

THE GREEDY WIFE

"Would you have me steal to provide you with the means of gratifying your desire to make expensive presents?" a young man only three years married asked his wife last Christmas. "I would have you support me in the manner to which I have been accustomed," was the unwifely rejoinder. That night the young man went out. The next day he could not be found but later he was escorted to his home by his broken hearted father who found him in some out of the way place recovering from his first alcoholic spree. "This is your work," the old man said to his daughter-in-law and never were words more deserved. It was her work that her husband cares no more for her; her work that she is unhappy; her work that her husband's ambition is dead. It was impossible to satisfy her when he did his best; consequently further effort was useless. Reflect upon these things.

THE LADIES WORLD, DECEMBER 1892

May your CHRISTMAS both happy and merry be.
Three dainty little maids from school,
Where all is managed by line and rule,
To wish you the blessings of peace and content,
And the happiest Christmas you ever have spent.

CHRISTMAS CARD

CANDY BOX

TASTEFUL GIVING

It takes common sense and independence to accept a costly present from a rich friend, without making any return.

If you have money to spend on presents, do not waste on people richer than yourself, but on those poorer.

Above all, in sending presents do not send articles that cost money and are vulgar and tawdry. A piece of music, a note written on Christmas Day, wishing many happy returns, or a few flowers, entail no obligation, require no work, and do their own work of love as well as costly gifts, and show a delicacy of breeding.

THE LADIES WORLD, DECEMBER 1892

More rapid than eagles
his coursers they came.
And he whistled,
and shouted,
and called them by name-
Now, Dasher! now, Dancer!
now, Prancer and Vixen!
On, Comet! on, Cupid! on,
Dunder and Blitzen!

ON THE CHIMNEY TOP

THE NIGHT BEFORE CHRISTMAS BY CLEMENT MOORE

A GENTLE REMINDER

CAST: *Little Girl. Santa Claus.*
S.C. *My work done, now my goal*
Is north of the north pole!
L.G. *Neither in stocking nor on tree*
Has any present been left for me!
I can't see the reason why
We poor are oftenest passed by.
S.C. *'Tis done for a curious reason*
Suggested by the Christmas season:
Should I make gifts to those who need,
'T become a time of general greed,
All would think "What'll we get?"
"What shall we give?" they'd forget.
Then I leave some poor ones out
That the richer may find,
as they look about
Their opportunities near at hand
In every corner of the land.
My token to those who in plenty live
Is a gentle reminder, meaning Give!

ST. NICHOLAS MAGAZINE, JANUARY 1891

TRADE CARD

CHRISTMAS ORNAMENTS AND FAN

CHRISTMAS TOY

CHILD'S SCRAPBOOK

The Frontier

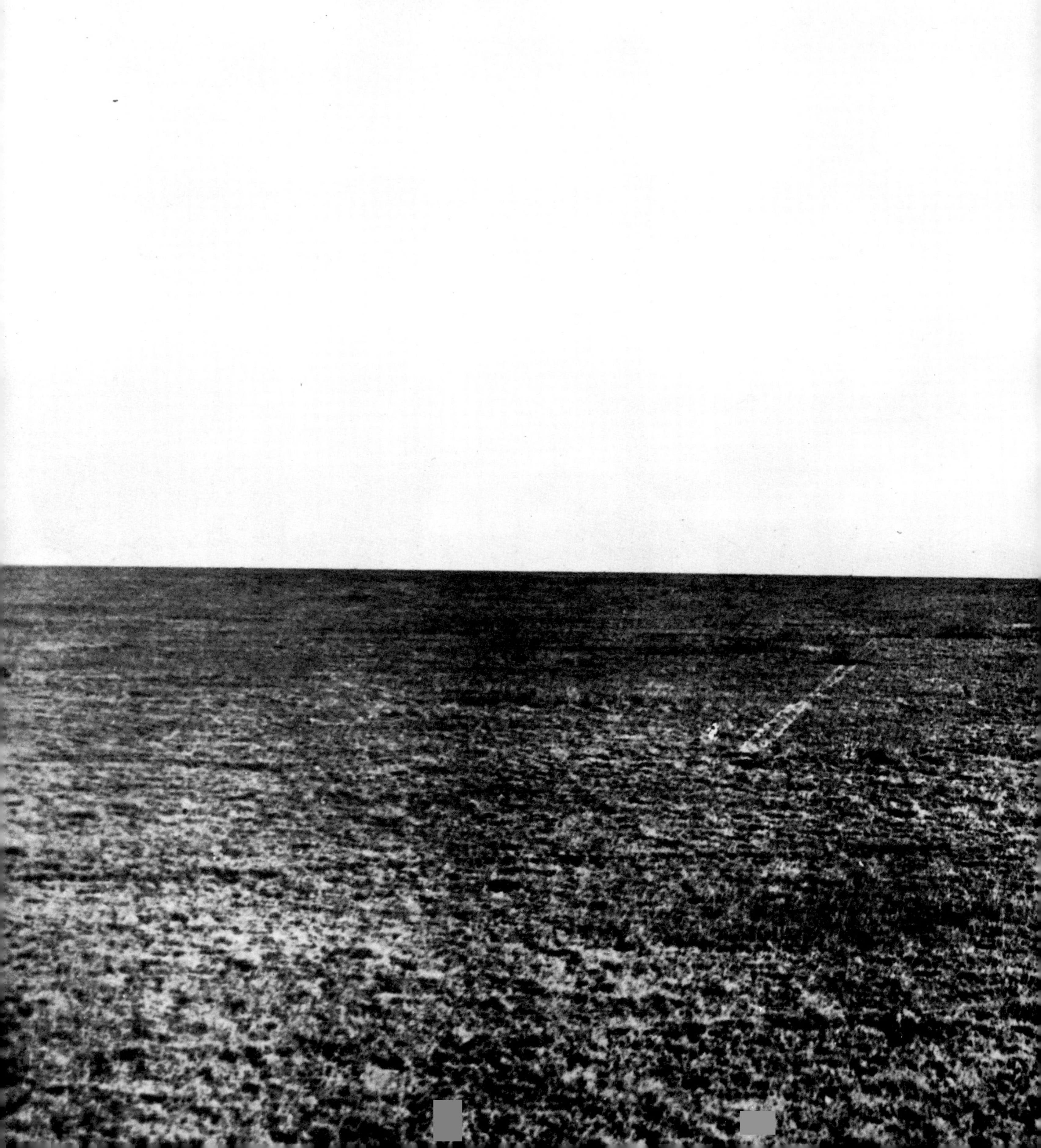

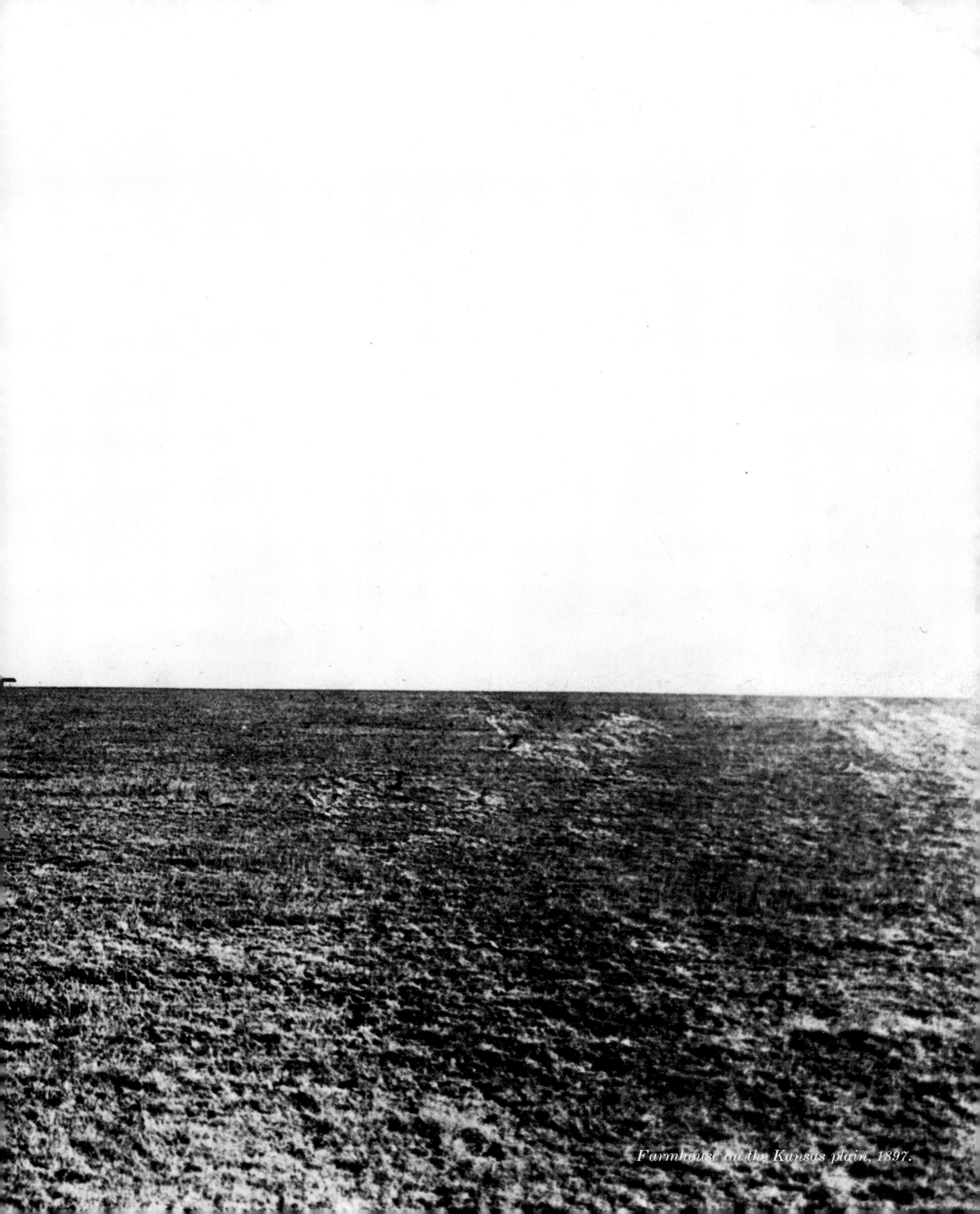

Farmhouse on the Kansas plain, 1897.

The Promised Land

Thoughts stray back to the comfortable homes we left behind and the question arises, is this a good move? The wagon train is divided, some want to turn back; others favor going on. A decision is reached at noon; the train is to move on.

DIARY OF MRS. LUCY A. IDE, 1878

War whoops of Indians attacking settlers. The crack of Winchesters as the cavalry canters to the rescue. Shootouts in Dodge City. Masked cowpunchers clubbing sheep to death. Custer's yellow mane fluttering as he coolly awaits the oncoming Sioux at Little Big Horn. Gunfight at the OK Corral. Calamity Jane, Bat Masterson, Billy the Kid, Buffalo Bill, Wyatt Earp, Wild Bill Hickok. Nothing else in the entire American pageant matched the sweep and excitement of the Wild West. Yet all this flamboyance tended to obscure the central fact that the real frontier story was the story of plain people struggling for land.

During the Civil War, the trans-Mississippi Great Plains were opened up by the Union government to free homesteading. An Act of Congress gave 160 acres of land to anyone willing to work it—making an egalitarian dream come true. In England the workers crammed into their slums had put the dream to song: "To the west, to the west, to the land of the free/ Where mighty Missouri rolls down to the sea/ Where a man is a man if he's willing to toil/ And the humblest may gather the fruits of the soil/ Where the young may exult and the aged may rest/ Away, far away, to the land of the west."

Now it was actually happening. "Here," said a Dakota Legislative Committee in 1869, "is a place for a man to rebuild his fortune again; here there need be no destitute, for all that work there is abundance." It was a chance for a new start and between 1870 and 1890 the greatest migration in American history increased the population of the trans-Mississippi west from fewer than seven million to more than 16 million. They were all kinds: boys in blue who had dreamed around wartime campfires of homesteading on the prairies; boys in gray who had fled the South's postwar anarchy to start anew; scoundrels seeking a fast buck; Mennonite immigrants smuggling the fabulous Turkey Red wheat out of the Crimea into the Dakotas; native Americans quitting overcrowded, worn-out family farms for "oceans of land, ready for the plow, good as the best in America, yet lying without occupants."

Jouncing west in her covered wagon, Jane Grout wrote in her diary: "Farther we go, better I like it." But for most emigrants, the farther west they went, the closer they came to the reality of the frontier, where the simple act of existing often turned into a bitter struggle. The land of opportunity was also one of plagues, drought, storms and epidemics, fierce extremes of heat and cold. In 1870 a visiting businessman described the plains as an "expanse

Homesteaders rest by their covered wagon in Colorado in the 1870s. The trip from Ohio or Indiana—1,100 miles—took about two months.

teeming with milk and honey"; in 1875 the Army was distributing two million rations in order "to prevent starvation." And along with the quiet struggle to stay alive, another more visible battle was shaping up with land speculators, cattlemen and Indians.

The Great Plains so coveted by the newcomers belonged for the most part to the Indians. President Rutherford Hayes, a righteous man, said so himself in his annual message in 1877: "The Indians were the original occupants of the land we now possess." Successively dispossessed and pushed westward, they had been solemnly deeded most of the Great Plains by 1840, a time when the region was universally and inaccurately called the Great American Desert. It was to take another third of a century and 928 officially recorded clashes—27 a year—to force the Indians from their desert.

The Sioux uprising of 1876 epitomized the process. One of the trans-Mississippi areas that the Sioux had received in perpetuity was the Dakota Black Hills, a region so forbidding that Washington thought the settlers never would covet it. But early in the 1870s came rumors that there was gold in the hills. Once more, pressured by land seekers, Washington asked the Sioux to move. When the Indians refused, the government announced that whites could enter the Black Hills at their own risk.

Predictably, 15,000 fortune seekers invaded the Sioux territory, and just as predictably the Sioux rose under Chiefs Crazy Horse and Sitting Bull. They annihilated a cavalry force of 246, incautiously led by the glory-hunting General George Custer. Then, four months later, tired of running, the Indian war party surrendered. Bayoneted in captivity, the dying Crazy Horse called to the soldier who had wounded him: "Let me go, my friend, you have hurt me enough." Sitting Bull, who had fled to Canada, returned in 1881, and several years later, while being put under precautionary arrest, was also killed.

The Indians were defeated, but the conflict over the Western lands had just begun. From the moment it became apparent that the Great Plains was not a desert but a treasure, all manner of Americans began to fight over the prize. The railroads grabbed the largest share—181 million acres of land, six times the size of Pennsylvania—for building half a dozen rail links with the West; and in consequence they became the largest landholders in the country.

The cattlemen, in their usual style, simply took for grazing huge chunks of public domain, generally an average of 30 to 40 square miles apiece, and waved off with cocked guns newcomers who questioned their title. Land speculators built holdings of up to 600,000 acres apiece, using a bagful of tricks: they falsified dates of occupancy, stole choice sites from the original settlers by legal chicanery, filed for free homesteads in different states under different names. One man built a doll-sized house, then swore he had fulfilled the Homestead Act requirements for a "twelve by fourteen dwelling," failing to specify that he had counted by inches, not feet. Overall, half a billion acres of U.S. land went to major landholders and only 80 million to homesteaders; despite the national commitment to give free land to the masses, probably only one acre in nine was thus disposed of.

The real rulers of the prairie were the cattle ranchers. Raising their low-cost livestock on free land that was so rich in grass that, according to one rancher, it could "make the dollars crawl right into yer jeans," the cattlemen dominated the West until 1885. In 1880 a British Parliamentary Commission reported that a 33 per cent profit could be anticipated in American ranching—whereupon belted earls and others dispatched $17 million in sterling to be invested in cattle. "Cotton was once crowned king," crowed a livestock man, "but grass is now."

Then in the mid-1880s, the undisciplined cattlemen overreached themselves. Rocketing prices brought overproduction; prices dropped 40 per cent, and the *Daily Drovers Journal* warned: "If you have steers, prepare to shed them now." A summer of drought and one of the worst winters in history completed the rout; spring revealed that nearly 90 per cent of the animals on the range were dead. Hundreds of ranch owners pulled out (among them Theodore Roosevelt, who turned over his Dakota holdings to his hands and took the train back East). The cattleman's hegemony over the prairie was broken; and from now on the Western lands would belong to those who had been promised them in the first place—the homesteading farmers.

Unlike the cattlemen in their bonanza years, the sodbusters who came West in their wagons found no natural compatibility with their environment, but had to tame it—or bend to it—from the start. To a newcomer who said "This would be a fine country if we just had water," an oldtimer snorted, "Yes, so would hell."

At times even hell might have seemed more comfortable. The family's first shelter was usually a sod-faced dugout cut into a hillside, so small, said one settler, that "we had to put the bed outside in the daytime and the table at night." Corn meal, salt pork and sorghum were the food staples. Cut-down gunnysacks became men's pants; and calico, bought during rare visits to town, was made up into a year's wardrobe of two dresses. Snakes, mice and bedbugs flourished in the sod-house; so did disease. Cholera, smallpox, typhoid fever and diphtheria came in epidemics; and malaria was so common that sufferers said, "That's nothing, we only have the ager."

250 miles to the nearest post office; 100 miles to wood; 20 miles to water; 6 inches to hell. God bless our home! Gone to live with wife's folks.

SIGN ON EMPTY CABIN, TEXAS PANHANDLE, 1886

For the women, frontier life was hardest of all. Childbirth was a dread; the doctors were far away, usually ill-trained and quite often drunkards. The first law passed in the Dakotas relating to doctors was a statute specifying that a physician must be tried for manslaughter if he poisoned a patient while intoxicated.

Every day brought a grinding succession of the most primitive chores—making soap and candles, drawing water, feeding livestock, struggling to keep a dirt house clean or spending half a day softening the harsh alkali water to wash the family clothes. But it was simple loneliness that seemed hardest to bear. The endless, monotonous space, the silence broken only by the constant keening of the wind, drove some to depression and occasionally to madness. One farm woman, discovering a dandelion growing, carefully cultivated it and saved the seeds, explaining that "I felt less lonely." Another, Mrs. James McClure, who had not seen a white woman for a year, heard that at last one had come to live miles away. Taking her two small children, she walked across the prairie until she reached the other's cabin. The women stood looking at each other and then—utter strangers—threw their arms around each other and wept and laughed.

There was, in addition, constant danger from plagues, blizzards, prairie fires, tornadoes and, at first, from Indians. In 1874 grasshoppers swarmed across the central plains, hiding the sun, devouring the greenery, mosquito netting, clothes, even plow handles, and leaving, said one farmer, "nothing but the mortgage." On another day in January 1888, the School Children's Storm swooped down while the children were still in school or starting home, freezing to death more than 200 youngsters.

Some families quit and turned back East, their wagons defiantly bearing such signs as "In God we trusted, in Kansas we busted." Most settlers stayed, however, and between 1870 and 1900 they tamed 430 million acres of the tough earth. By 1890 the Report of the Census Bureau announced a historic change: "There can hardly be said to be a frontier line."

Though the physical frontier had all but vanished, the frontiersman's hunger for land had not. There was still one piece of Indian land left in an area soon to be called Oklahoma, the last of the old-time permanent Indian territory assigned by the federal government and still held by 22 tribes. Now, once more, the land seekers besieged Washington. Once more the Indians were told to move aside. At noon, April 22, 1889, pistol shots opened 1.92 million virgin acres to 100,000 eager men lined up and waiting on the border—on foot, on horse, in carts and in 15 overflowing Santa Fe trains. By that night, Guthrie and Oklahoma City were established, every last acre had been claimed and men sat with guns and guarded their land.

Blackfoot women and children sit in front of their tepee in the Montana Territory in 1881. By then almost all the fighting bands had been pushed

onto reservations, and the end of the nomadic Indian civilization was near: "When we sit down, we grow pale and die," mourned a Kiowa chief.

1,000 lbs. flour, 400 lbs. bacon, 4 gallons vinegar, 200 lbs. sugar, 150 lbs. beans, 2 gallons pickles, 100 lbs. dried beef, 50 lbs. salt, 2 doz. boxes of matches, 50 lbs. coffee, 40 lbs. dried fruit, 1 coffee mill, 30 lbs. rice, 25 lbs. soap, 3 camp kettles, 10 lbs. pepper, 8 lbs. tea, 50 lbs. lead for bullets, 6 lbs. cream tarter, 3 lbs. soda, 1,000 gun caps.

SIX MONTHS' PROVISIONS FOR FOUR PROSPECTORS

Prospectors camp in the Colorado Rockies. "I do not see," said one miner, "how any young man can content himself working for wages."

Surveyors pause before descending a bluff near Silverton, Colorado. "If anyone thinks it is fun, let him try it, that's all," wrote a surveyor.

Hoo-oo! My children, my children. In days behind I called you to travel the hunting trail or to follow the war trial. Now those trails are choked with sand; they are covered with grass, the young men cannot find them. Today I call upon you to travel a new trail, the only trail now open—the White Man's Road.

WOVOKA, PAIUTE CHIEF, 1891

Nineteen days after U.S. troops fired into an encampment of Sioux at Wounded Knee, South Dakota, killing 62 women and children, General

Nelson Miles and his staff inspect the vanquished tribe. On this day, January 16, 1891, the Sioux surrendered, ending America's Indian wars.

Railway tracks reach west through the flatlands of Montana in 1887.

Track-laying is a science. A light car, drawn by a single horse, gallops up to the front with its load of rails. Two men seize the end of a rail and start forward, the rest of the gang taking hold by twos. They come forward at a run. At a word of command the rail is dropped in its place. Less than thirty seconds to a rail for each gang, and so four rails go down to the minute! Close behind come the gaugers, spikers and bolters, and a lively time they make of it. It is a grand Anvil Chorus that those sturdy sledges are playing across the plains.

WILLIAM A. BELL, *NEW TRACKS IN NORTHERN AMERICA*

A rail crew building the Northern Pacific link between Washington Territory and Minnesota pauses on a mountain trestle in 1885.

Like many towns built on railroads to lure settlers, Green River, Wyoming Territory, on the Union Pacific, waits in 1871 for arrivals.

Ho for the West! The truth will out! The best farming and stock raising country in the world! Not too hot or too cold. The large population now pouring into this region, consists of shrewd and well-informed farmers, who know what is good, and are taking advantage of the opportunities offered. The opportunities offered to buy B. & M. R.R. lands on long credit, low interest, twenty percent rebate for improvements, low freight and fares, free passes to those who buy, &c,&c, can never again be found. There are plenty of lands elsewhere but they are in regions which can never be largely prosperous. Southern Nebraska, with its fine soil, pure water, and moderate climate is the right country for a new home. Go and see for yourself. I will sell tickets from Grinnell to Lincoln and return for $12.75, and the fare is refunded to those who buy.

BURLINGTON AND MISSOURI RIVER RAILROAD AGENT

Between January 15 and 16 we had a terrible snow storm, which claimed a life among us Norwegians, namely the second oldest son of Tollef Medgaarden, Ole, who froze to death out on the prairie. He was as close to the nearest house as the distance from Tollef Hagene to your farm when they found him. At the burial banquet a Jew functioned as cook, and he managed very well, in the American manner, of course.

LETTER HOME FROM OLE NIELSEN, ESTHERVILLE, IOWA, 1870

Swedish immigrants to Kansas, like those shown here, quickly founded their own city of Lindsborg, complete with a college.

Russian peasants such as these in the Dakota Territory generally settled in the northern reaches, which resembled their native steppes.

My husband I pity he is wasting his life
To obtain a scant living for his children and wife.
The Sabbath which once was a day of sweet rest
Is now spent toiling for bread in the west.
After five years hard toiling with hopes that were in vain
I have such despair on this desolate plain.

SONG BY MRS. A. M. GREEN, GREELEY, COLORADO, 1887

A pioneer family poses in front of its sod house on the Kansas prairie. The sods for such dwellings were turned up in long strips by steel plows,

then chopped into short sections and laid atop each other like bricks, making an insulated house that was warm in winter and cool in summer.

Dakota farm women take a rare break from their chores to get together in a neighbor's house and exchange gossip at a quilting bee.

A Montana farm wife milks her cow in a muddy corral.

Out in the midst of level stretches of prairie even to cook and eat the very limited variety that the table affords is a task that makes heavy demands upon the weary woman with her family to care for, the garden-patch to cultivate, the cows to milk, and the plow-handles to hold in the intervals. Yet she accomplishes it all—and more.

THE OUTLOOK, JANUARY 6, 1894

Against snow-shrouded Old Baldie in the northern Rockies, children and their teacher play Ring-a-Rosie in their schoolyard. Pioneer settlers

gave high priority to educating youngsters; only a few days after a new settlement had been established, the men would join to build a schoolhouse.

The best seat in a stage is the one next to the driver. If the team runs away — sit still and take your chances. If you jump, nine out of ten times you will get hurt. Don't smoke a strong pipe inside the coach — spit on the leeward side. Don't lop over neighbors when sleeping. Never shoot on the road as the noise might frighten the horses. Don't discuss politics or religion. Don't grease your hair, because travel is dusty.

TIPS FOR STAGE RIDERS, *OMAHA HERALD*, 1877

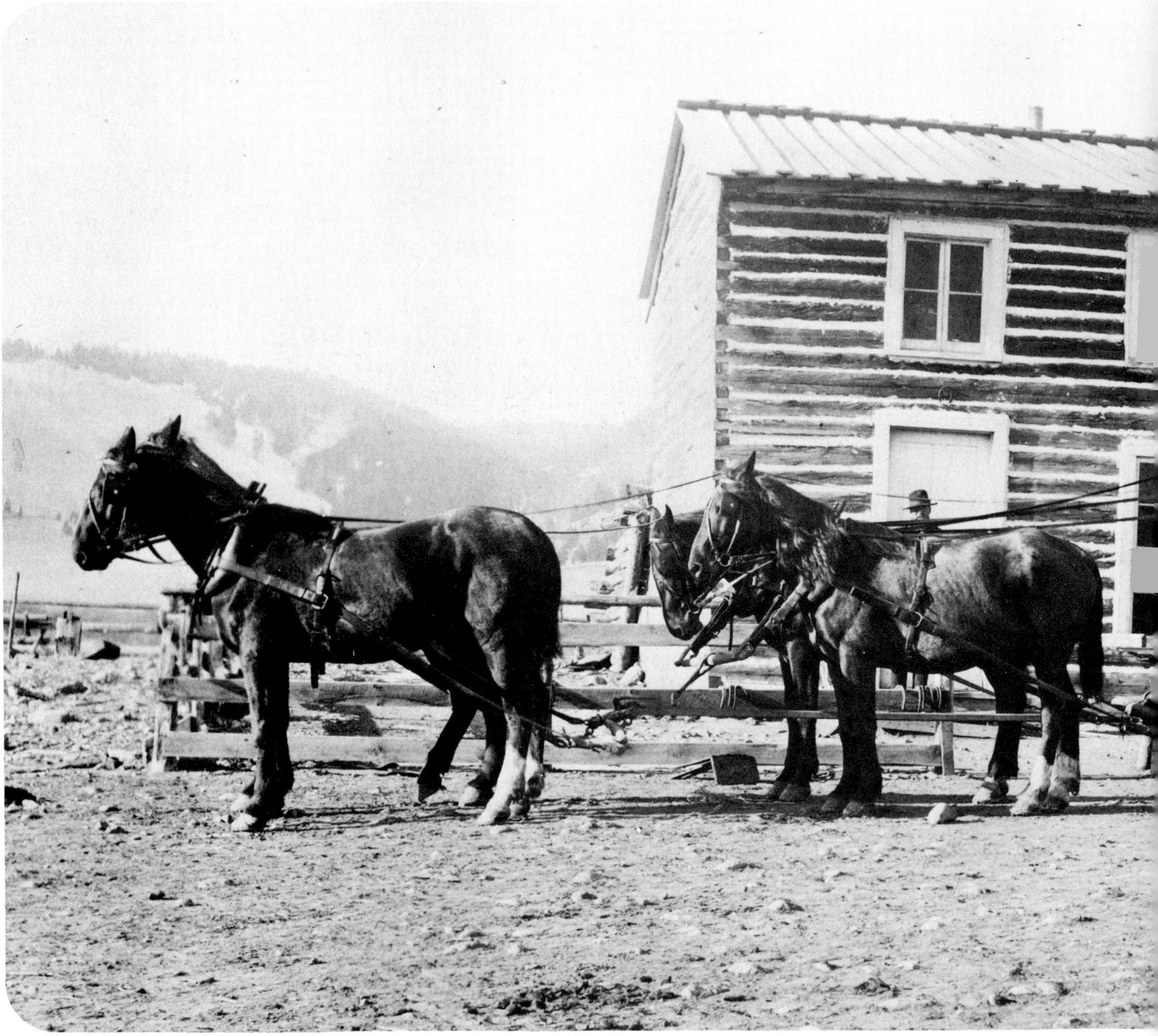

An Overland stage heads out from its station at Calvin, Montana. The six-horse teams covered the 10 miles between regular stations in about an

hour; then fresh teams were harnessed up. Every fourth or fifth stop was a home station, where passengers could get grub, whiskey and a bed.

Eastern sportsmen and their wives, hunting from their private rail car, "City of Worcester," pause during a safari onto the Great Plains.

In the early days of the first Pacific Railroad, and before the herds had been driven back from the tracks, singular hunting parties were sometimes seen on the buffalo range. These hunters were capitalists connected with the newly-constructed roads; and some of them now for the first time bestrode a horse, while few had ever used firearms. These were amusing excursions where a merry party of pleasant officers from a frontier post, and their guests, a jolly crowd of merchants, brokers and railroad men from the East start out to have a buffalo hunt. With them go the post guide and a scout or two, the escort of soldiers, and the great blue army wagons, under whose white tilts are piled all the comforts that the post can furnish—unlimited food and drink, and many sacks of forage for the animals. Here all was mirth and jest and good fellowship, and the hunters lived in as much comfort as when at home. The killing of the buffalo was to them an excuse for their jolly outing amidst novel scenes.

SCRIBNER'S MAGAZINE, SEPTEMBER 1892

The boom town of Creede, Colorado, sprouts in a canyon so narrow there is room for only one main street. After a prospector found silver in the

Owned by the Henry Ford Museum

area in 1890, Creede grew by some 150 to 300 people daily. But in 1893 the silver market collapsed; by 1900 Creede was almost a ghost town.

Cowboys take some red-eye in an Indian Territory saloon in 1889.

These women are expensive articles and come in for a share of the money wasted. In daylight they may be seen gliding through the streets carrying fancy derringers slung to their waists.

Inside the city soldiers, herdsmen, teamsters, women, railroad men are dancing, singing, or gambling. I believe that there are men here who would murder a fellow creature for five dollars. Not a day passes but a dead body is found.

JOURNALIST HENRY M. STANLEY, NEBRASKA TERRITORY

The sporting ladies of Paradise Alley in Dawson throw a whiskey party on a rare warm afternoon in the Klondike goldfields, circa 1900.

A tent city sprawls across the prairie at Guthrie, Indian Territory, only five days after the opening of the Oklahoma region to white settlers. On

April 22, 1889, the first day, 15,000 people from 32 states swarmed in to stake claims. By the end of the first week Guthrie had 50 saloons.

Cycling

Florida wheelmen on the road near Tallahassee.

America Goes A-Wheeling

We claim a great utility that daily must increase;
We claim from inactivity a sensible release;
A constant mental, physical, and moral help we feel,
That bids us turn enthusiasts, and cry, "God bless the wheel!"

POET WILL CARLETON, CIRCA 1890

In 1876, when Philadelphia put on its dazzling Exhibition *(pages 24-31)* to celebrate the 100th birthday of the United States, the millions of people who came to gaze at the scientific wonders displayed there gave only passing notice to the one creation that would have the most immediate effect on their lives: a bicycle displayed by the British firm of Smith & Starley. After all, bicycles had been around in one form or another through most of the century. And to the visitors at Philadelphia, Smith & Starley's "ordinary English bicycle"—called the ordinary for short—with a saddled front wheel 5 feet high and an 18-inch rear wheel for balance, did not seem all that different.

Yet in the America of 1876, the bicycle was clearly an idea whose time had come. At least so it appeared to a few sharp Yankee manufacturers who learned of the ordinary at Philadelphia and could smell the money in it. One such was a Bostonian named Colonel Albert A. Pope, who far-sightedly converted his air-pistol factory into a pioneering bicycle works, and then saw his business quickly climb above a million dollars per annum. Within eight years there were 50,000 cyclists wheeling around the U.S.; races and touring clubs flourished in every major city; and 29-year-old Thomas Stevens of California pulled off the astounding feat of circling the globe on his cycle in two years, eight months and 13 days from 1884 to 1887.

For all its sporting appeal, the ordinary was no simple vehicle to master. To make riding easier, inventors contrived more easily balanced multi-wheel, two- and three-seaters, hoping they might appeal both to ladies and to those gentlemen who could not ride a bicycle "on account of age, timidity, or excessive weight." Then, in 1885, the British produced a second cycling coup by introducing their low-wheeled "safety," a bicycle that balanced handily on two smaller, equal-sized wheels. Almost anybody could learn to ride a safety and, overnight, almost everybody did. During the whole decade of the 1890s perhaps 10 million Americans took to the wheel, from clergymen on their rounds to young ladies clad in skirts that rose scandalously above the ankle to make pedaling easier. By 1896 bike manufacturing was a $60 million business in the U.S., with the Pope Manufacturing Company turning out a cycle a minute at an average price of $100. Riders spent another $12 million a year for spare parts and fancy extras—lamps, bells, cyclometers and that ultimate in accessories, according to an ad in *Bicycling World*, "A Good Thing for Bicycle Rider; Iver Johnson Cycle Revolver."

Elegant cyclist Maurice Aron shows off the costume that won him the first-place wreath in the New York Evening Telegram's 1896 parade.

High Wheels and High Fashion

One of the favored diversions of the 19th Century cyclists was touring. Around Boston, for example, where the first cycling club was organized in the 1870s, scarcely a weekend passed without groups of strong-legged wheelmen taking a century tour, that is, 50 miles out on Saturday, and 50 miles back on Sunday. Ladies toured in a more leisurely fashion, traveling on tandem tricycles or quadricycles with husbands and beaux providing a good deal of the motive power. Besides being splendid exercise, these mixed outings afforded an opportunity for a stylish young matron to display her sportiest fashions on a kind of freewheeling *concours d'élégance.*

A typical tour-cum-fashion-show was the Ladies' North Shore Tricycle outing from Malden to Gloucester, Massachusetts, which began on October 6, 1887, and encompassed four pleasure-filled days. An account of the gala send-off, along with a preview of the tour itself, appeared *(below)* in the Malden, Massachusetts, *Evening Mail.*

Malden, Oct. 6:—This morning the third annual ladies' tricycle tour was started. By the appointed time, the tricyclists had assembled on Salem Street in front of the Public Library, where a large number of people had gathered to see the start. The lady tricyclists looked very "nifty," in their natty costumes and tourist caps, and

were the objects of admiring glances from the lookers-on. Following is the program.

First day, Thursday, Oct. 6—Leave Malden Square at 9:30 a.m., ride to Salem (11 1-2 miles), dinner at Essex House at 12 M. Leave Salem at 1:30 and ride to Gloucester, around Cape Ann (15 1-2 miles), supper and lodging at Pavilion. Ride of first day, 27 miles.

Second day, Friday, Oct. 7—Start at 9 a.m. around Cape Ann. A picnic lunch will be served on the rocks at Pigeon Cove. Six o'clock dinner and lodging at Pavilion. Ride of second day, 17 miles.

Third day, Saturday, Oct. 8—Start at 9 a.m. Ride to Magnolia (4 1-2 miles) and visit Rafe's Chasm, Norman's Woe, etc. Dinner at Willow Cottage. Ride to Salem (13 1-2 miles). Supper and lodging at Essex House. Ride of third day, 17 1-2 miles.

Fourth day, Sunday, Oct. 9—Leave Essex House at 9 a.m. Ride to Marblehead Neck and Nahant, stopping a short time at each place. Dinner at Nahant, 12 M. The homeward run to suit the pleasure of the party. Ride of fourth day, 10 miles.

A musical and literary program has been arranged for Friday evening at the Pavilion in Gloucester, where professional and amateur talent will entertain the company. Pleasure will be the order of the day and riding will be done in easy stages, giving time to enjoy nature's beauties.

Many wheelmen and ladies will undoubtedly run down Saturday night or Sunday morning to meet the party and participate in the homeward run.

Mr. and Mrs. William Quinnell of Chelsea, Massachusetts, wore matching blue and white, Mr. Quinnell in velvet knickers with blue socks.

Spectators swarm around the starters of the 1894 Martin Road Race, a 25-mile amateur event held in Buffalo, New York.

Cycling magazines reported on racing.

Days at the Races

In 1875 a small English cycling magazine called *Ixion* announced a two-wheeler race meet. Prizes were offered —for professionals, 20 pounds; for amateurs, 12 guineas. Like the cycle itself, bike racing and bike magazines soon caught the sporting fancy of America.

In the fall of 1883, Springfield, Massachusetts, staged the first recorded U.S. cycling championship—in which one G. M. Hendrie outpedaled W. G. Rowe for the title. By the time the decade ended, crowds of 25,000 were watching outdoor races like the one at left in Buffalo. Indoor ovals in Philadelphia, Chicago and New York annually outdrew the local major-league ball clubs with special speed trials and six-day endurance contests from which the winners took home purses of as much as $15,000 a year. By 1897 racing had become such a craze that it prompted the rage of many a God-fearing man. That year one national magazine scolded: "The question of Sunday bicycle-racing is again being agitated. It should be prohibited. The spectators of Sunday bicycle-racing are not the class which stands for law and order."

But no one paid much attention. In fact, the nation's fascination with cycling speed reached its peak two years later when slim, wiry Charles Murphy went roaring down a board track behind a railroad train filled with newsmen to become the first human to cycle a measured mile in less than 60 seconds. At the finish, Murphy collapsed, gasping, "Carry me back to where my wife is." Instead he was taken to the waiting crowd, which hailed the newly crowned "Mile-a-Minute Murphy" as a sportsman to rank with Gentleman Jim Corbett among contemporary U.S. heroes.

With a steadying hand from three natty gentlemen, Woman's Temperance leader Miss Frances E. Willard faces her first cycling lesson.

Ode to Gladys

In 1892 Miss Frances Willard, formidable founder of the Woman's Christian Temperance Union, succumbed to the temptation of cycling. At age 53, she announced she would learn to ride a bicycle, partly to silence friends who said she was too old for such sport and partly to encourage all those sinful menfolk to forsake saloons for the wholesome pleasures of pedaling on the highroad.

Miss Willard went about the project with characteristic energy and flair. She named her bicycle Gladys, and in a detailed journal of her adventure described the machine as her "silent steed so swift and blithesome." The entire project took three months of daily 15-minute practice sessions, or as the meticulous Miss Willard noted, "13 hundred minutes," less than one full day "as the almanac reckons time." From the very first unsteady moment *(left)* until the triumphant day of the first solo, Gladys assumed the personality of a skittish horse. Reported the temperance leader, grandly switching genders, "To hold his head steady and make him prance to suit you is no small accomplishment." Some of Miss Willard's other reflections on her travels with Gladys—together with the meaningful life lessons to be drawn therefrom—appear below.

I learned the bicycle precisely as I learned the a-b-c. When I set myself, as a stint, to mount and descend in regular succession anywhere from 20 to 50 times, it was on the principle that we do a thing more easily the second time than the first, the third time than the second, and so on, until it is done without any conscious effort whatever. This was precisely the way in which my mother trained me to tell the truth, and my music-teacher taught me that mastership of the piano keyboard which I have lost by disuse.

Gradually, item by item, I learned the location of every screw and spring, spoke and tire, and every beam and bearing that went to make up Gladys.

This was not the lesson of a day, but of many days and weeks, and it had to be learned before we could get on well together. To my mind the infelicities of which we see so much in life grow out of lack of time and patience thus to study and adjust the natures that have agreed in the sight of God and man to stand by one another to the last. Indeed, I found a whole philosophy of life in the wooing and the winning of my bicycle.

In many curious particulars, the bicycle is like the world. When it had thrown me painfully once, and more especially when it threw one of my dearest friends, then for a time Gladys had gladsome ways for me no longer, but seemed the embodiment of misfortune and dread. Even so the world has often seemed in hours of darkness and despondency; its iron mechanism, its pitiless grind, its on-rolling gait have oppressed to melancholy. I finally concluded that all failure was from a wobbling will rather than a wobbling wheel. I felt that indeed the will is the wheel of the mind—its perpetual motion having been learned when the morning stars sang together. When the wheel of the mind went well then the rubber wheel hummed merrily.

January 20th will always be a red-letter bicycle day because, summoning all my force, I mounted and started off alone. From that hour the spell was broken; Gladys was no more a mystery. Amid the delightful surroundings of the great outdoors, and inspired by the bird-songs, the color and fragrance of a garden, in the company of devoted and pleasant comrades, I had made myself master of the most remarkable, ingenious, and inspiring motor ever yet devised upon this planet. Moral: Go thou and do likewise!

A WHEEL WITHIN A WHEEL, 1895

The Press Climbs Aboard

By 1896, with four million Americans already riding bicycles and 300 factories churning out a million new cycles a year, magazines and newspapers turned over more and more space to cycling, with an eye toward raising both readership and advertising revenue. Highbrow publications like *Harper's Weekly* were filled with bicycle advertising *(right)*. The prestigious *Literary Digest*, noting solemnly that "Bicycle literature has become a feature of almost every journal, so important is the wheel as a factor in progressive civilization," ran bicycle stories week after week in 1896. The *Digest* excerpted newsworthy items from major publications all over the world; below is a sampling of reports from that year, suggesting just how pervasive—and controversial—the bicycle had become.

There is a psychic and moral void in city life which the "bike" goes farther toward filling than any other single institution. With his wheel at hand, there is no hard-driven clerk who may not look forward each day to a comforting flight from the demnition grind. Fat Germans, with their fatter fraus, leave the sweltering heat of East-side tenement rows and skim gayly through the park, along the Hudson, and away into pleasant country places. Nothing else can compare to the wheel as a leaven for the heavy lump of joylessness in our streets.

SCRIBNER'S

Not only the book trade, but all other trades that have been interviewed on the subject claim to suffer from the bicycle epidemic. It does not seem unreasonable to assume, when confronted with the report that nearly $20,000,000 are invested in the manufacture of bicycles in and near New York city alone, and that nearly 200,000 persons in the same locality are already addicted to wheeling, that the "wheel" does affect retail trades in general, and noticeably the book trade, which depends on sedentary rather than perambulatory habits. However, there seems to be some hope left. We note the proposal of a bookseller, that the book trade add bicycles and their concomitants to its stock, and so bind [its customers] to the habit of buying at a book-store. Let the booksellers help to set the world on wheels.

THE PUBLISHER'S WEEKLY

In cases of breakdown of the nervous system from overwork and anxiety, cycling will be found a most valuable adjunct to the rest which is necessary for recovery, and numerous brain-workers now consider a daily ride indispensable if their work is to remain at concert pitch. Many sufferers from sick headache, neuralgia, and hysteria have reaped much benefit from regulated cycle-riding, and many cases of so-called palpitation have been cured. Lastly, insomnia has frequently been found to yield to the proper use of the bicycle when every other soporific had been defied, and many cases of persistent nocturnal cramp have been relieved.

THE BRITISH MEDICAL JOURNAL

The alarmingly pessimistic view of the bicycle question is not justified by the facts. It is doubtless true that many young women ride to excess. It is also doubtless true that to the woman of impure life the wheel may offer a convenient means for facilitating the execution of immoral designs, but that the pastime itself has a tendency to degrade or demoralize is a proposition too absurd for a moment's consideration. A woman who will violate the decencies and proprieties of life while wheeling will violate them on other occasions. Where one woman rides to destruction on the wheel a thousand maintain all the decorum, modesty, and circumspection that characterize the well-bred, self-respecting women from the ideal American homes.

CHICAGO TIMES-HERALD

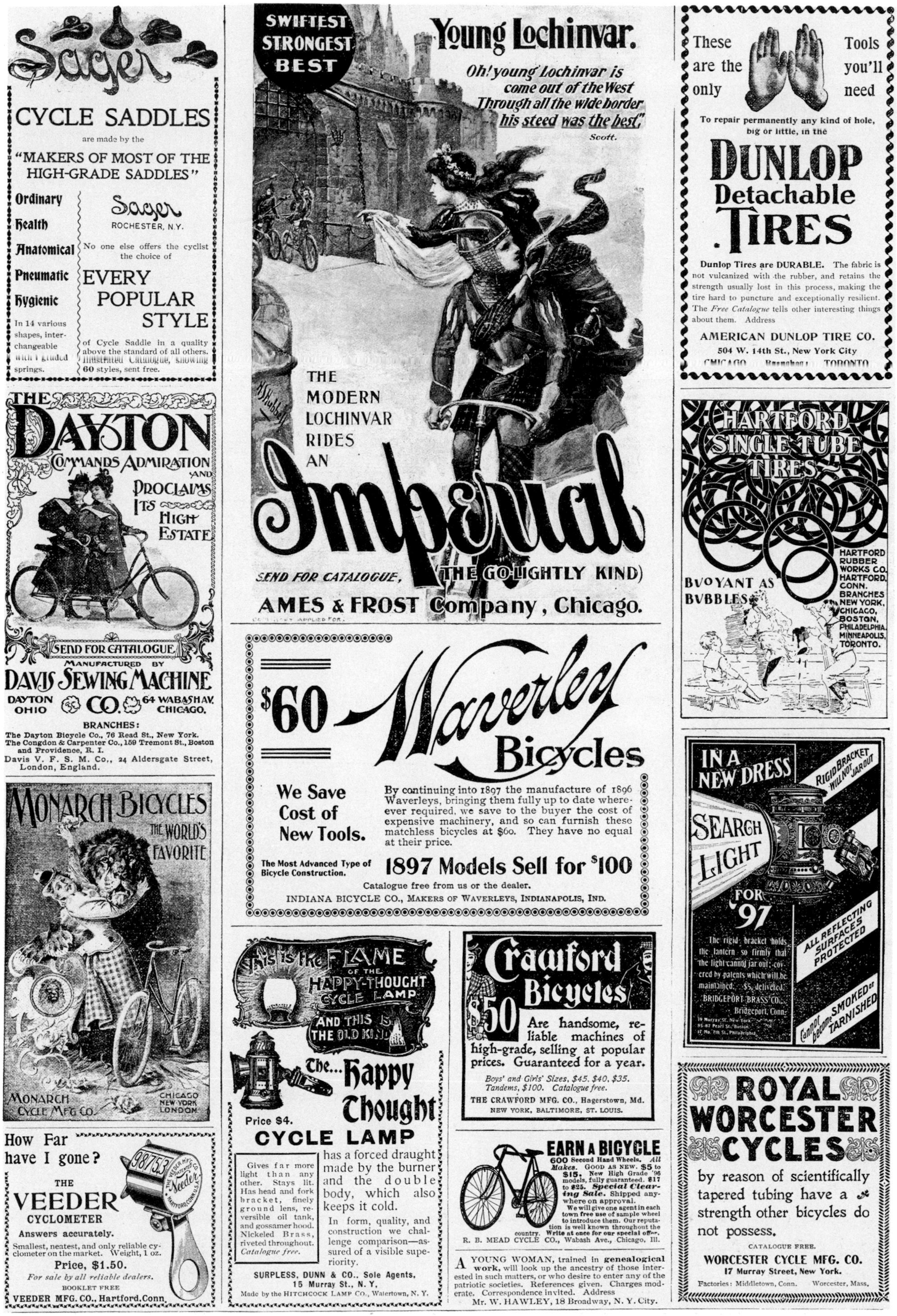

Sager
CYCLE SADDLES
are made by the
"MAKERS OF MOST OF THE HIGH-GRADE SADDLES"
Ordinary
Health
Anatomical
Pneumatic
Hygienic
In 14 various shapes, interchangeable with graded springs.
Sager
ROCHESTER, N.Y.
No one else offers the cyclist the choice of
EVERY POPULAR STYLE
of Cycle Saddle in a quality above the standard of all others. Illustrated Catalogue, showing 60 styles, sent free.

THE DAYTON
COMMANDS ADMIRATION AND PROCLAIMS ITS HIGH ESTATE
SEND FOR CATALOGUE
MANUFACTURED BY
DAVIS SEWING MACHINE CO.
DAYTON OHIO
64 WABASH AV. CHICAGO.
BRANCHES:
The Dayton Bicycle Co., 76 Read St., New York.
The Congdon & Carpenter Co., 159 Tremont St., Boston and Providence, R. I.
Davis V. F. S. M. Co., 24 Aldersgate Street, London, England.

MONARCH BICYCLES
THE WORLD'S FAVORITE
MONARCH CYCLE MFG. CO.
CHICAGO NEW YORK LONDON

How Far have I gone?
THE VEEDER CYCLOMETER
Answers accurately.
Smallest, neatest, and only reliable cyclometer on the market. Weight, 1 oz.
Price, $1.50.
For sale by all reliable dealers.
BOOKLET FREE
VEEDER MFG. CO., Hartford, Conn.

SWIFTEST STRONGEST BEST
Young Lochinvar.
Oh! young Lochinvar is come out of the West
Through all the wide border his steed was the best."
Scott.
THE MODERN LOCHINVAR RIDES AN
Imperial
(THE GO-LIGHTLY KIND)
SEND FOR CATALOGUE,
AMES & FROST Company, Chicago.

$60 Waverley Bicycles
We Save Cost of New Tools.
By continuing into 1897 the manufacture of 1896 Waverleys, bringing them fully up to date wherever required, we save to the buyer the cost of expensive machinery, and so can furnish these matchless bicycles at $60. They have no equal at their price.
The Most Advanced Type of Bicycle Construction.
1897 Models Sell for $100
Catalogue free from us or the dealer.
INDIANA BICYCLE CO., MAKERS OF WAVERLEYS, INDIANAPOLIS, IND.

This is the FLAME OF THE HAPPY-THOUGHT CYCLE LAMP
AND THIS IS THE OLD KIND
The... Happy Thought
Price $4.
CYCLE LAMP
has a forced draught made by the burner and the double body, which also keeps it cold.
Gives far more light than any other. Stays lit. Has head and fork bracket, finely ground lens, reversible oil tank, and gossamer hood. Nickeled Brass, riveted throughout. *Catalogue free.*
In form, quality, and construction we challenge comparison—assured of a visible superiority.
SURPLESS, DUNN & CO., Sole Agents, 15 Murray St., N. Y.
Made by the HITCHCOCK LAMP CO., Watertown, N. Y.

Crawford Bicycles
$50
Are handsome, reliable machines of high-grade, selling at popular prices. Guaranteed for a year.
Boys' and Girls' Sizes, $45, $40, $35. Tandems, $100. Catalogue free.
THE CRAWFORD MFG. CO., Hagerstown, Md.
NEW YORK, BALTIMORE, ST. LOUIS.

EARN A BICYCLE
600 Second Hand Wheels. *All Makes.* GOOD AS NEW. $5 to $15. New High Grade '96 models, fully guaranteed. $17 to $25. ***Special Clearing Sale.*** Shipped anywhere on approval.
We will give one agent in each town free use of sample wheel to introduce them. Our reputation is well known throughout the country. Write at once for our special offer.
R. B. MEAD CYCLE CO., Wabash Ave., Chicago, Ill.

A YOUNG WOMAN, trained in **genealogical work,** will look up the ancestry of those interested in such matters, or who desire to enter any of the patriotic societies. References given. Charges moderate. Correspondence invited. Address
Mr. W. HAWLEY, 18 Broadway, N. Y. City.

These are the only Tools you'll need
To repair permanently any kind of hole, big or little, in the
DUNLOP Detachable TIRES
Dunlop Tires are DURABLE. The fabric is not vulcanized with the rubber, and retains the strength usually lost in this process, making the tire hard to puncture and exceptionally resilient. The *Free Catalogue* tells other interesting things about them. Address
AMERICAN DUNLOP TIRE CO.
504 W. 14th St., New York City
CHICAGO TORONTO

HARTFORD SINGLE TUBE TIRES
BUOYANT AS BUBBLES
HARTFORD RUBBER WORKS CO. HARTFORD, CONN.
BRANCHES NEW YORK, CHICAGO, BOSTON, PHILADELPHIA, MINNEAPOLIS, TORONTO.

IN A NEW DRESS
RIGID BRACKET WILL NOT JAR OUT
SEARCH LIGHT FOR '97
The rigid bracket holds the lantern so firmly that the light cannot jar out; covered by patents which will be maintained. $5, delivered.
BRIDGEPORT BRASS CO., Bridgeport, Conn.
19 Murray St., New York.
85-87 Pearl St., Boston.
17 No. 7th St., Philadelphia.
ALL REFLECTING SURFACES PROTECTED
Cannot become SMOKED or TARNISHED

ROYAL WORCESTER CYCLES
by reason of scientifically tapered tubing have a strength other bicycles do not possess.
CATALOGUE FREE.
WORCESTER CYCLE MFG. CO.
17 Murray Street, New York.
Factories: Middletown, Conn. Worcester, Mass.

Ads for bikes and extras cover a typical page in Harper's Weekly—which claimed to be A Journal of Civilization.

Occupations

Puddlers and water boys at an Ohio steel mill.

The Many Roads to Riches

Work has sometimes been called worship, and the dusty, smoky workshop a temple; because there man glorifies the great Architect by imitating him in providing for the wants of his creatures. CHRONICLER FRANKLIN WILSON, 1874

During the enormous geographical and economic expansion in the decades after the Civil War, Americans found before them the greatest array of job opportunities in the history of any nation. Not only was there the better part of a rich continent to subdue, but the climax of the industrial revolution had opened up thousands of jobs in whole new areas of technology.

In 1870, for example, there was no such thing as a telephone. But by 1900 there were 19,000 telephone operators. The booming U.S. iron and steel industry had put more than a million people to work turning out nearly half the world's supply of structural metals. And clothing factories, expanded during the Civil War to turn out soldiers' uniforms, converted so successfully to the mass production of civilian clothes that at century's end 1.45 million people were employed in the business.

It did not seem to bother many people that most of this labor was for coolie wages: seven out of 10 industrial workers earned no more than 10 cents an hour. For in keeping with the stern ethics of the era, most Americans willingly lived by—and even echoed—the work philosophy of Franklin Wilson *(above)*. "Honor lies in honest toil," intoned Grover Cleveland as he accepted the Democratic Presidential nomination in 1881. Another future President, William McKinley, added: "We glory in the fact that in the dignity and elevation of labor we find our greatest distinction among the nations of the earth." Besides, in the laissez-faire business atmosphere of the day, there was the chance for any kid to do as Andrew Carnegie had done; starting as a bobbin boy at age 13 in a textile mill, he had wound up as the richest steelman on earth.

Ladies, too, were seizing new opportunities en masse; by 1890 some 3,704,000 of them were in the U.S. labor force. Even more significantly, seven out of every 10 colleges had gone coeducational by the turn of the century, and they had graduated 7,500 woman doctors, 3,000 ministers and 1,000 lawyers.

The lack of child-labor laws also meant that some 1.75 million kids under 15 were out scratching in mines and tobacco fields for as little as 25 cents a day. But this, too, was thought good and proper, according to a slogan of the day: "The factories need the children and the children need the factories." For this was America's greatest time of growth. Anybody could see that by looking around. And an observer could see, too, by the prideful bearing of the workers, that what Americans wanted was to get on with the job.

The Noble Face of Labor

POLICEMAN

NURSE

SOLDIER

OCCUPATION	MALE	FEMALE
AGRICULTURAL PURSUITS		
Dairymen, dairywomen	16,161	1,734
Farmowners, overseers	5,055,130	226,427
Hired hands (farm)	2,556,958	447,104
Lumbermen	65,838	28
Nurserymen, gardeners, florists	70,186	2,415
Wood choppers	33,665	32
PROFESSIONAL SERVICE		
Actors	23,200	4,583
Architects, designers, draftsmen	17,134	327
Artists, art teachers	11,681	10,815
Clergymen	87,060	1,143
Dentists	17,161	337
Engineers, surveyors	43,115	124
Journalists	20,961	888
Lawyers	89,422	208
Musicians, music teachers	27,636	34,519
Literary, scientific persons	8,453	2,764
Officials (government)	77,715	4,875
Physicians, surgeons	100,248	4,557
Teachers, college professors	101,278	246,066
DOMESTIC AND PERSONAL SERVICE		
Barbers, hairdressers	82,157	2,825
Bartenders (hired)	55,660	146
Lodging-house keepers	11,756	32,593
Hotel keepers	38,800	5,276
Janitors, sextons	23,730	2,808
Launderers, laundresses	31,831	216,631
Nurses, midwives	6,190	41,396
Restaurant keepers	16,867	2,416
Saloon keepers	69,110	2,275
Servants, waiters	238,152	1,216,639
Watchmen, policemen, detectives	74,350	279

OCCUPATION	MALE	FEMALE
TRADE AND TRANSPORTATION		
Bankers, brokers	35,458	510
Boatmen, sailors	76,823	51
Bookkeepers, accountants	131,602	27,772
Company executives	39,683	217
Draymen, hackmen, teamsters	368,265	234
Hostlers, stablemen (hired)	54,014	22
Hucksters, peddlers	56,824	2,259
Livery-stable owners	26,710	47
Messengers, office boys	48,446	2,909
Salesmen, saleswomen	205,943	58,451
Railroad employees	460,771	1,442
Stenographers, typewriters	12,148	21,270
Telegraph, telephone operators	43,740	8,474
MANUFACTURING AND MECHANICAL PURSUITS		
Bakers	57,910	2,287
Blacksmiths	209,521	60
Bookbinders	12,298	11,560
Brewers, maltsters	20,294	68
Broom, brush makers	8,949	1,166
Cabinet makers	35,891	24
Carpenters, joiners	618,044	198
Confectioners	17,577	5,674
Coopers	47,438	48
Dressmakers	836	292,668
Fishermen, oystermen	59,899	263
Harness, saddlemakers	42,647	833
Millers	52,747	94
Miners, quarrymen	386,872	376
Paper hangers	12,315	54
Photographers	17,839	2,201
Tailors	123,516	64,509
Wheelwrights	12,855	1

This census excerpt shows that in 1890 America's eight million farm workers still outnumbered jobholders in all other industries.

A Sailor *pauses by the shrouds of his merchant vessel. In 1870, of 4.25 million tons in America's commercial fleet, 56 per cent were sail. By 1900, the figure was only about 25 per cent.*

Farmers *in Oregon pose on a pile of wheat after stacking it beside their steam thresher. This massive device, together with other farm machinery that was invented during the era, helped double the production of American corn and wheat between 1860 and 1880; the total doubled again by the end of the century.*

The Cowboy *tended and drove to shipping centers the vast herds of cattle raised on the Western plains in the last third of the 19th Century. Some 40,000 of these hard-riding nomads, of whom 5,000 were Negroes like this man, drove their beef great distances —often more than 1,000 parched, dangerous miles—to the meat markets in Kansas City and Chicago, where the cattle were sold and slaughtered. By 1890 the railroad was taking over the cowboy's job of moving cattle long distances. Whereupon many of the blacks took new jobs with the competition—as Pullman porters.*

A Newspaper Publisher, *Colonel John P. Jackson, shown here with a folded copy of his own San Francisco Daily Evening Post, was one of hundreds of journalistic entrepreneurs who profited from the nation's growth. With the extension of the railroad and the settling of the West, between 1880 and 1890 the number of daily newspapers jumped from 971 to 1,610, and total U.S. circulation of papers went from 3.6 million to 8.4 million.*

A Sheep Herder *displays the pelts of coyotes he shot with his 1873 model Winchester rifle in his effort to shield his Montana flock from predators. Sheep raising in Victorian America was big business—and very good business, too. In 1870 there were no fewer than 80 sheep to every 100 humans in the whole population. Any young man with a few dollars could get a start at raising sheep: a pair could be bought for $3.74, and a healthy pair could be expected to proliferate fast. Two men in California who began with a herd of 13,900 in 1866 had 58,000 ten years later.*

A Surveyor, *this man was one of the many who went all over the U.S. with their transits in the last third of the century. They laid out sections and properties in the eight new states, totaling 733,676 square miles, that were admitted to the Union. Surveyors also ran lines for 64,186 miles of railroad put down in the same period.*

TABLE
BOARD

Waitresses *(above) line up outside the Pine Street Dining Room in Manchester, New Hampshire. Some 107,000 women and men worked in the nation's restaurants in 1900.*

Housemaids–*four out of a working force of a million and a quarter female domestic servants–gather for a portrait outside the Massachusetts boardinghouse where they live.*

Telephone Linemen *in the Connecticut River Valley in New England festoon one of the millions of poles erected during the last three decades of the century. In 1876 there were only 3,000 telephones in all the nation; by 1900 there were 1.4 million.*

Miners *emerge at day's end from their tunnel leading into a vein of silver at Sutro, Nevada. This digging was part of the rich Comstock Lode, which yielded more than half a billion dollars in silver and gold in the years between 1859 and 1900.*

Hops Pickers *show off their abundant harvest on an upstate New York farm in the 1880s. About half a pound of hops went into the making of a*

barrel of beer, the favorite drink of the American male. In 1900 national consumption totaled 34.3 million barrels, or 16 gallons per capita.

Wagoners *transported virtually every kind of short-haul load in the U.S.—and before the nation's rail network was substantially completed, they moved a great deal of the long-distance freight as well. In 1884 the country had 15.4 million horses and as these pictures show, they brought the day's supply of milk, they carried furniture across town, they delivered meat in refrigerated wagons and sometimes they transported ailing horses from the barn to the veterinarian's hospital. Even the heaviest commodities moved by horse-power; it took two tons of coal to keep a moderate-sized house warm for a few months in winter, and wagons like the one below delivered it right to the cellar door.*

INS COAL Co.
20

The Blacksmith *and his backhander—an aide or apprentice who stood behind the smith and handed over tools as needed—were essential members of every community. In 1900 some 226,477 of them throughout the U.S. shod the horses that transported Americans and their goods. In addition, blacksmiths manufactured nails, scythes, harness fastenings, pots and pans, plowshares and sometimes even swords.*

Education

Grade-school classroom at Valley Falls, Kansas.

There are flowers in the garden.
The girls jump rope.
The boys play ball.

The Ladder of Learning

Just see, wherever we peer into the first tiny springs of the national life, how this true panacea for all the ills of the body politic bubbles forth—education, education, education.

ANDREW CARNEGIE, *TRIUMPHANT DEMOCRACY*, 1886

A buoyant belief in the power of education sprang up in post-Civil War days and swept all segments of the country. Plutocrats like Andrew Carnegie, small-town farmers, city dwellers and professional educators all felt that their personal versions of the American dream would come true just as soon as the blessing of learning was available to anyone at any level. In the three decades after the war, 31 state legislatures saw to it that little children received this blessing, whether they wanted it or not, by passing laws making attendance compulsory at elementary schools. As a result, by 1898 some 15 million youngsters were in school learning their bedrock three R's—plus an occasional so-called Expression Subject such as music or art. And urged on by the unspared rod of straight-eyed schoolmarms and masters, they also learned the rules and rewards of decorous classroom behavior *(page 149)*.

As the youngsters moved upward, they created a heavy demand for more public high schools, which were sometimes called people's colleges. "The high school," one educator pontificated, "is the institution which shall level the distinction between the rich and the poor," thus allowing the laborer's boy to "stand alongside the rich man's son." Between 1870 and 1900 the number of these levelers for the laborer's boy burgeoned from about 500 to 6,000.

Higher education as well was undergoing a period of growth. In 1862 Congress passed the Morrill Act, giving enormous federal tracts to each state for the establishment of colleges of agricultural and mechanical arts. By the end of the century, there were 977 colleges of all kinds serving 238,000 students. It was at the college level, too, that the wealthy industrial barons were most involved, for sound practical reasons that glared unmistakably through the soft glow of philanthropy. Carnegie, for one, was certain that the best way to sustain the workers' faith in the capitalistic system was to provide "ladders upon which the aspiring can rise." And what better ladder, asked Carnegie, than a college education?

Putting his money where his morality was, Carnegie handed out $20 million to various fresh-water colleges, and in 1900 spent $2 million to start Pittsburgh's Carnegie Institute of Technology. Other tycoons fell in step, among them Baltimore banker Johns Hopkins, Western Union founder Ezra Cornell, California railroad-builder Leland Stanford, and oil baron John D. Rockefeller, who underwrote a Baptist university the church fathers called Chicago when the tycoon forbade them to name it after him.

A Cornell graduate dons his mortarboard, armed with the college degree that one in 400 Americans had in 1900.

Practice Makes Perfect

For Victorian children, grade school was a robot parade-ground for the mind; virtually everything was drilled into young heads through interminable repetition. One approved method for teaching arithmetic required that the pupils spend the entire first year working only on the numbers 1 through 10—counting, adding, multiplying—before they were permitted to advance to the lofty plateau of 11 through 20. Reading and spelling *(overleaf)* were much the same. And even handwriting was turned into a mechanistic nightmare, with drill books that told precisely where the pupil must place his thumb, fingers and even his feet before he was permitted to start.

PENMANSHIP

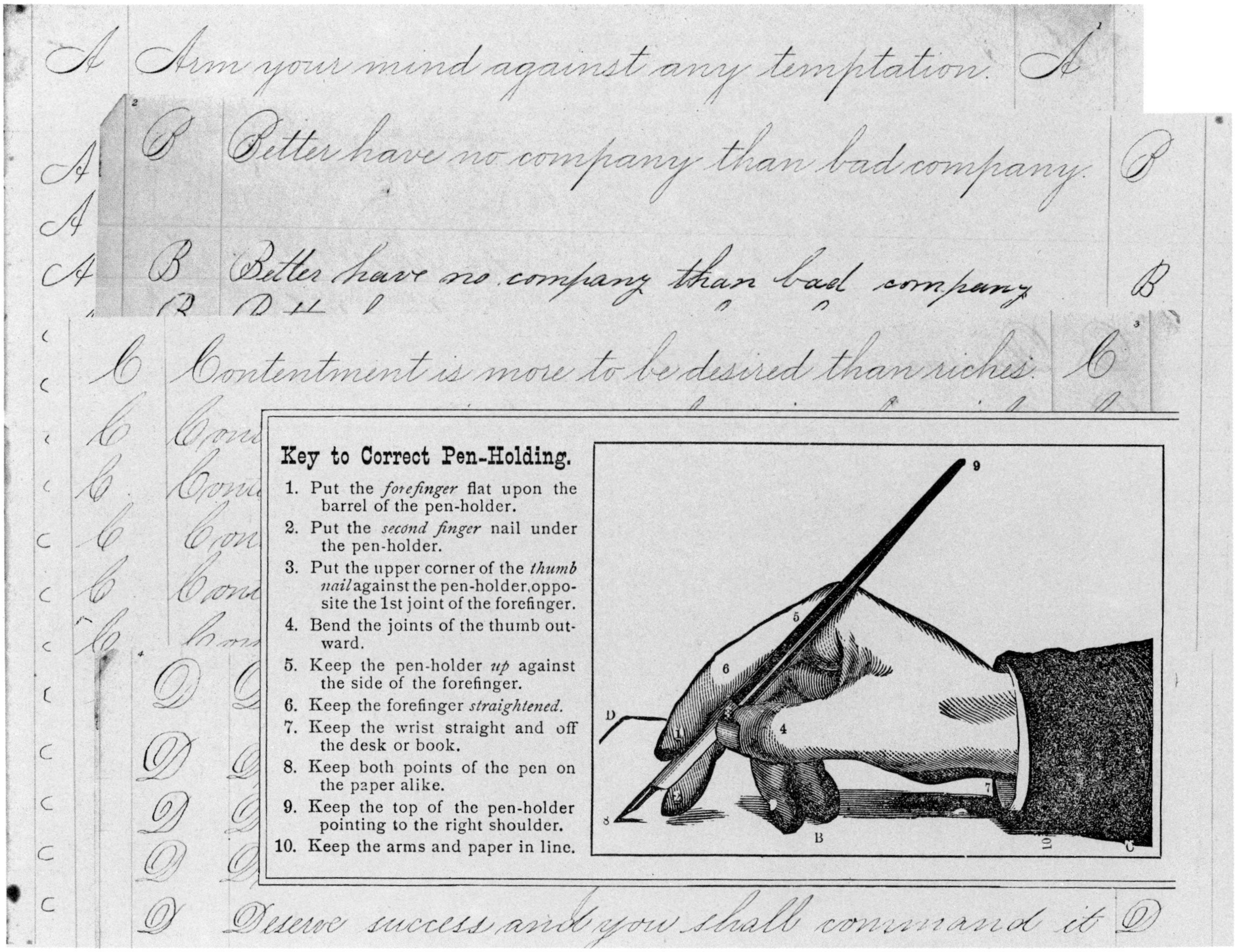

A Arm your mind against any temptation. A
B Better have no company than bad company. B
B Better have no company than bad company B
C Contentment is more to be desired than riches. C
Key to Correct Pen-Holding.
1. Put the *forefinger* flat upon the barrel of the pen-holder.
2. Put the *second finger* nail under the pen-holder.
3. Put the upper corner of the *thumb nail* against the pen-holder, opposite the 1st joint of the forefinger.
4. Bend the joints of the thumb outward.
5. Keep the pen-holder *up* against the side of the forefinger.
6. Keep the forefinger *straightened.*
7. Keep the wrist straight and off the desk or book.
8. Keep both points of the pen on the paper alike.
9. Keep the top of the pen-holder pointing to the right shoulder.
10. Keep the arms and paper in line.
D Deserve success and you shall command it D

Military precision in all aspects of penmanship was emphasized in illustrations (right) from the top-selling instruction books of an Ohio clerk named Platt Rogers Spencer. His jealous imitators hewed to the same principles and the same lettering forms; for example, one copybook (inset above) advertised "75 percent more practice than Spencerian," a point much in the imitator's favor.

FRONT POSITION

RIGHT-SIDE POSITION

ARITHMETIC

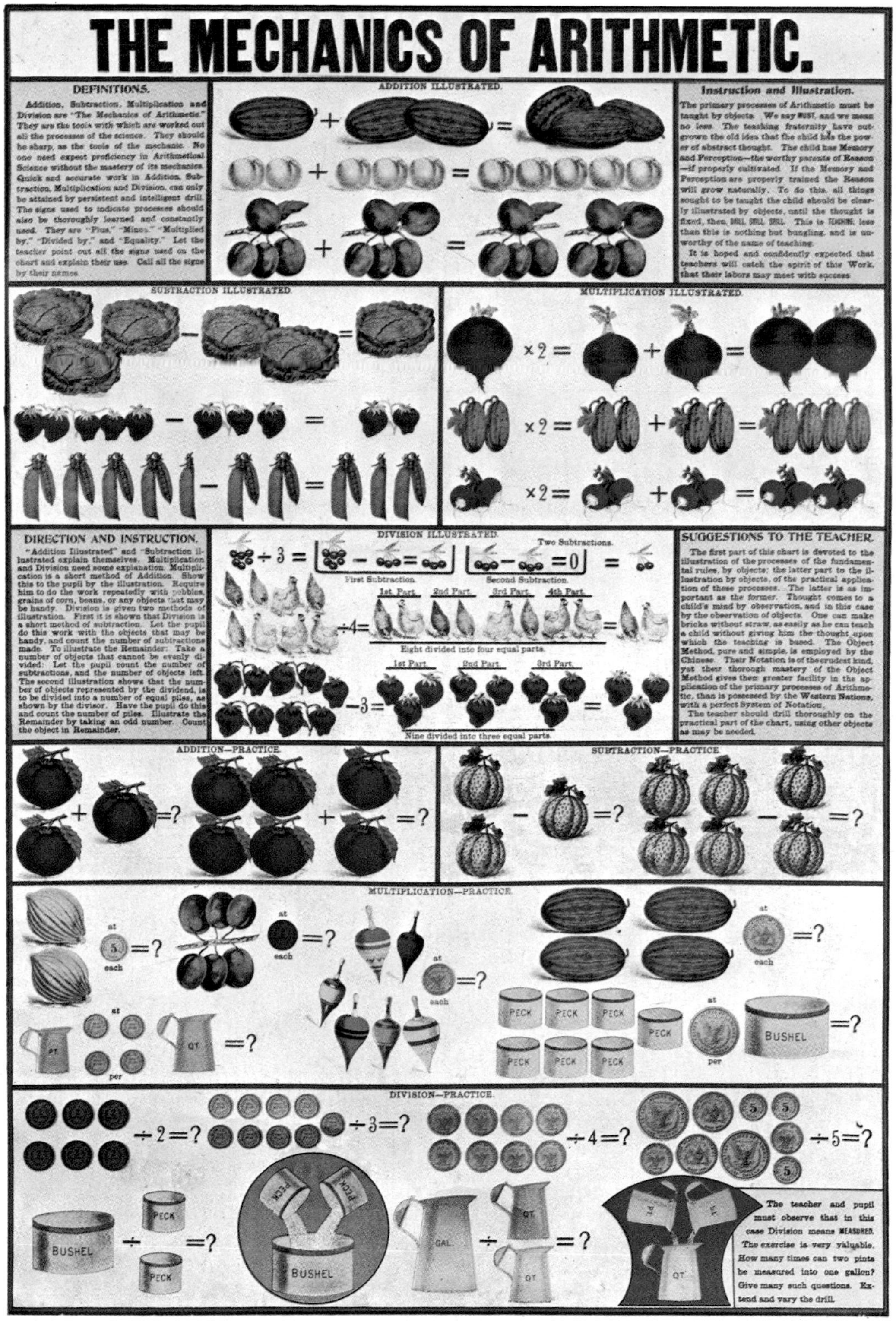

This arithmetic chart, one of a series offered by a Minneapolis publisher, taught elementary math using objects that were most familiar to school kids in an America where farming was still the major occupation. One Kansas pupil remembered "a teacher who explained common fractions by an apple neatly cut into segments. I really understood fractions for the first time that day." Nevertheless, most kids still hated arithmetic. Small wonder. Added to the innate horrors of basic math were exhortations like the one on the chart above: "DRILL, DRILL, DRILL."

SPELLING

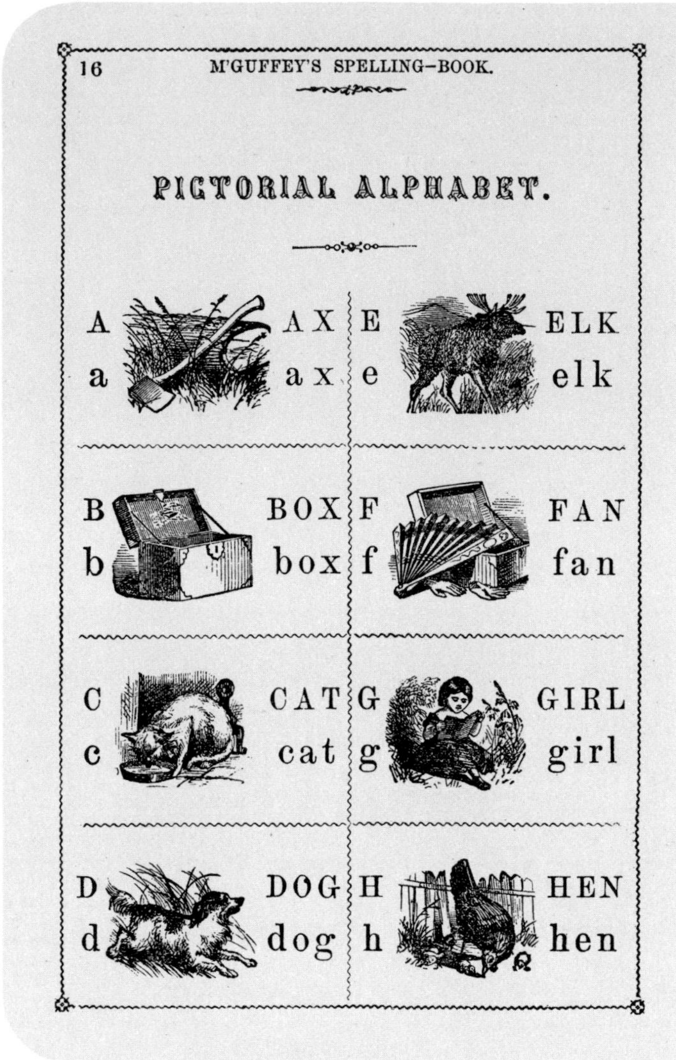
16 M'GUFFEY'S SPELLING-BOOK.

PICTORIAL ALPHABET.

A a	AX ax		E e	ELK elk	
B b	BOX box		F f	FAN fan	
C c	CAT cat		G g	GIRL girl	
D d	DOG dog		H h	HEN hen	

America's best-selling schoolbooks, McGuffey's Readers, sold over 60 million readers and spellers from 1870 to 1890. The skills taught were strongly stressed in a semi-literate society. One old pupil remembered losers in a spelling bee at his grammar school "shuffling downwards, with eyes on their toes."

READING

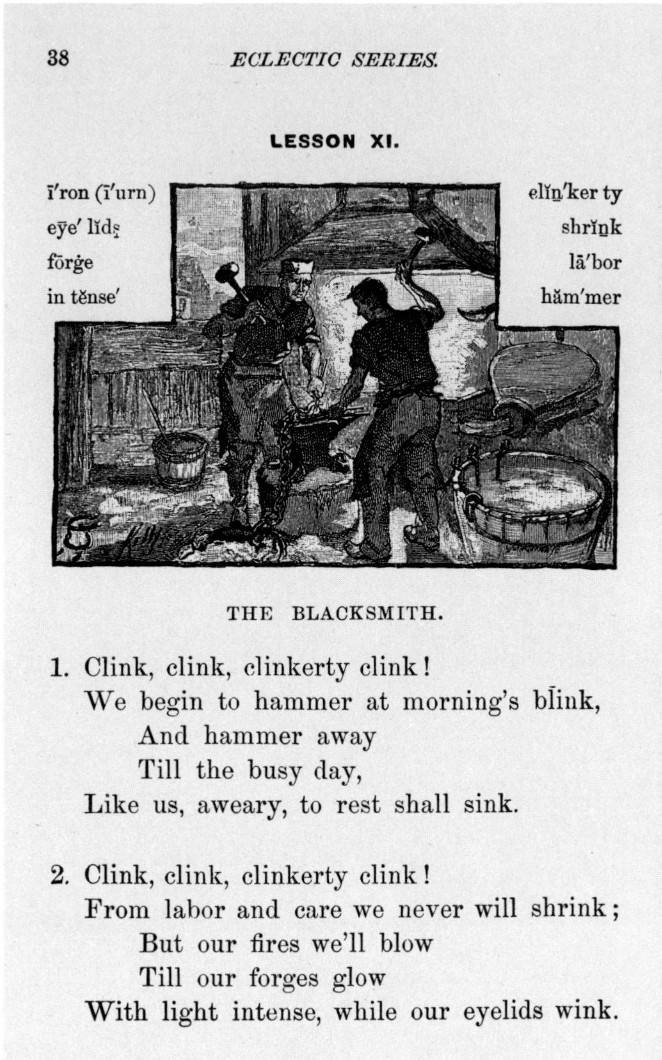
38 ECLECTIC SERIES.

LESSON XI.

ī'ron (ī'urn)
eȳe' lĭds
fōrge
in tĕnse'
clĭnk'er ty
shrĭnk
lā'bor
hăm'mer

THE BLACKSMITH.

1. Clink, clink, clinkerty clink!
We begin to hammer at morning's blink,
And hammer away
Till the busy day,
Like us, aweary, to rest shall sink.

2. Clink, clink, clinkerty clink!
From labor and care we never will shrink;
But our fires we'll blow
Till our forges glow
With light intense, while our eyelids wink.

As early as 1887 McGuffey's publisher put out a series of revised editions that featured attractive illustrations. Engravings like the one above, from the Third Eclectic Reader, typified this effort to give schoolbooks visual appeal. But the style of accompanying prose remained cheerily, drearily the same.

ELOCUTION

"LOOK THERE!"

"THE FATAL BLOW"

"OH, DESPAIR!"

"LIFTETH TO HEAVEN"

"THIS VAST GALAXY"

GEOGRAPHY

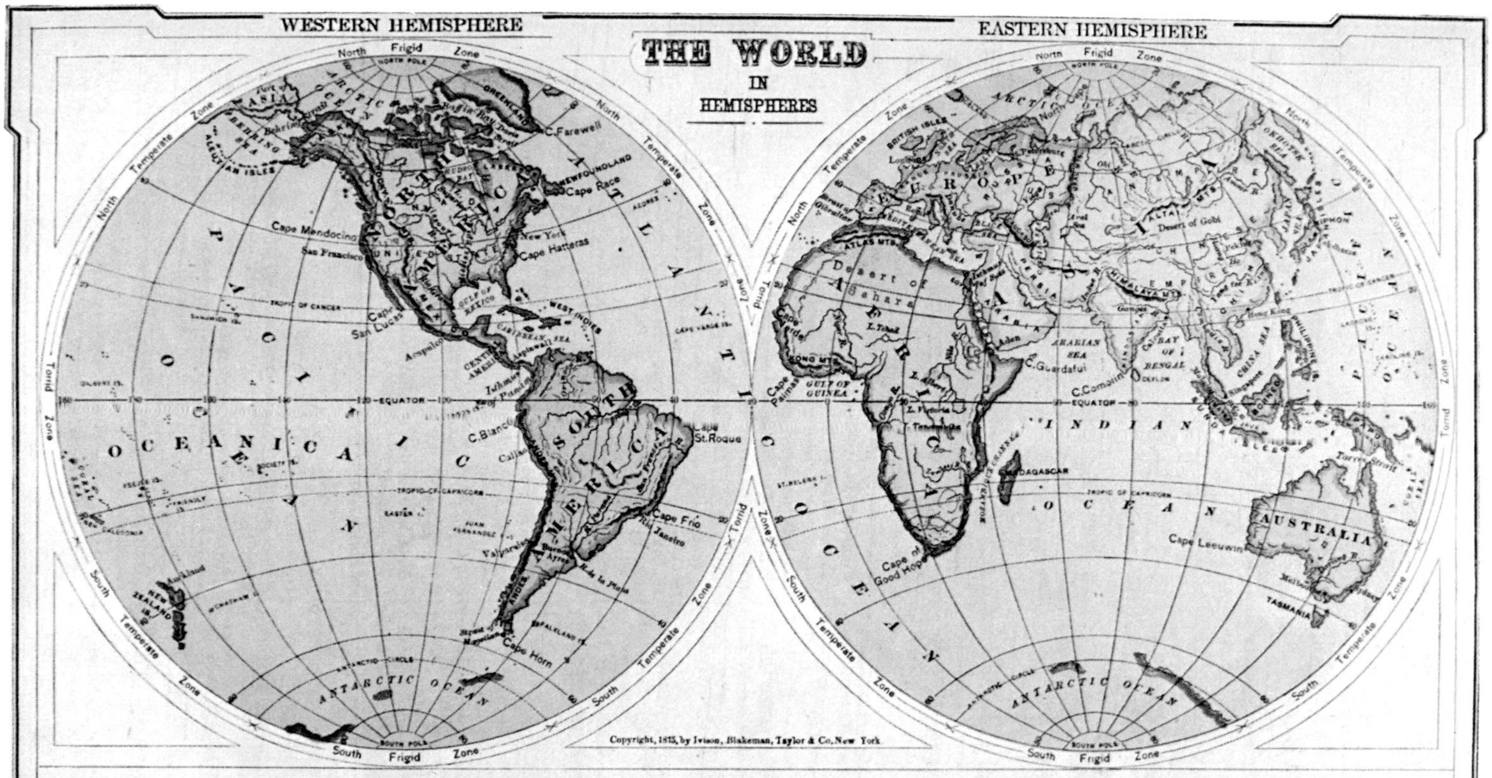

STUDIES ON THE HEMISPHERE MAP.

I. Grand Divisions.

1. What two grand divisions of land are in the Western Hemisphere?—what three in the Eastern? 2. What division of America is crossed by the Equator? 3. In which hemisphere is North America? 4. What part of South America is crossed by the Tropic of Capricorn? 5. In what zone is most of North America?—most of South America? 6. What Isthmus joins North and South America? 7. By what oceans are the two Americas surrounded? 8. What is the direction of Europe from Asia?—of Africa from Asia? 9. What grand divisions are wholly in the Northern Hemisphere? 10. In what three zones is Asia? 11. In which zone is most of Europe? 12. What oceans surround the Eastern Continent?

II. Islands.

1. What island off the northeast coast of North America? 2. What group of islands between North and South America? 3. What large island in the Pacific Ocean is crossed by the 40th parallel? 4. What line of isles south of Behring Sea? 5. What isles off the west coast of Europe? 6. What isles off the east coast of Asia? 7. Describe these islands:—Newfoundland;—Iceland;—Madagascar;—Borneo.

III. Capes.

1. What cape at the southern extremity of Greenland?—at the eastern point of South America?—at the southern point of Africa? 2. Describe the following capes:—Hatteras;—Frio;—St. Lucas;—North Cape;—Verde.

IV. Coast Waters.

1. What great inbreaking of the Atlantic Ocean in the northern part of North America?—in the southern part of the United States? 2. Describe the following:—Hudson Bay;—Caribbean Sea;—Behring Sea. 3. Where is the North Sea? 4. Describe the Mediterranean Sea. 5. What large gulf west of Africa? 6. What sea between Arabia and Hindostan? 7. Where is the Bay of Bengal? 8. Describe the following:—Red Sea;—China Sea;—Japan Sea.

V. Mountains.

1. What great mountain system in North America?—in South America? 2. In which grand division are the Alps? 3. What mountains in North Africa? 4. Where are the Himalaya Mountains?

VI. Rivers and Lakes.

1. What river flows into the Gulf of Mexico? 2. Where is Lake Superior? 3. What South American river has its mouth near the Equator? 4. Describe the Orinoco. 5. Describe two great European rivers. 6. What is the largest river of Africa? 7. Where is Lake Albert?—Victoria? 8. What great rivers of Asia flow northward?—southward? 9. What large rivers in China?

VII. Latitude and Longitude.

Vessels were spoken in the following latitudes and longitudes: in what waters were they? Lat. 40° N., long. 60° W.?—Lat. 20° N., long. 120° W.?—Lat. 40° S., long. 140° E.?—Lat. 60° S., long. 80° W.? Lat. 40° S., long. 0°?—Lat. 40° S., long. 180° W.?

In an 1875 grade school, Manhattan youngsters studied the world from this map in Swinton's A Complete Course in Geography.

ISEST, BRIGHTEST" "MEANEST OF MANKIND" "HEIR OF GLORY" "FRAIL CHILD OF DUST!"

In the 1870s oral reading developed—or deteriorated—into a posturing form of expression called elocution. This bizarre exercise concentrated on dramatic presentation of the written word, using a spectrum of set-piece poses to emphasize various phrases in a memorized passage. An 1874 manual for high-school speakers (left) showed some of the various positions that were de rigueur for public recitations; Mark Twain scornfully described them as "the painfully exact and spasmodic gestures which a machine might have used."

HISTORY

Jefferson reading the Declaration in Committee.

THE DECLARATION OF INDEPENDENCE

Congress began to think of renouncing allegiance to the crown. In June, Richard Henry Lee introduced a resolution: "That these united colonies are, and of right ought to be, free and independent states; and that their political connection with Great Britain is, and ought to be, dissolved." A committee of five was appointed to draft a formal Declaration of Independence. This document was written by Thomas Jefferson, and received a few alterations from John Adams and Franklin, of the committee. It was presented to Congress July 1st, and after being carefully considered and amended was passed on the 4th of July —ever since observed as the birthday of American freedom. The bell of the old state-house, in which Congress was assembled, rang out the glad tidings. The people, south and north, hailed the news with delight, kindling bonfires, illuminating their houses, and receiving the Declaration, as read by their orators, with heart-stirring acclamations.

The story of the Declaration of Independence was told with un-Victorian simplicity in G.P. Quackenbos' American History for Schools (above), published in 1877. But Custer's Last Stand is described in the same book with the more familiar hyperbole: " 'The White Chief' undauntedly defended himself with his sword, until a bullet laid him in the dust."

MUSIC

When the music reader above was published in 1888, rote singing as a form of stiff-necked classroom recreation was giving way to an effort to teach sight-reading of sheet music as part of a more flexible elementary-school curriculum.

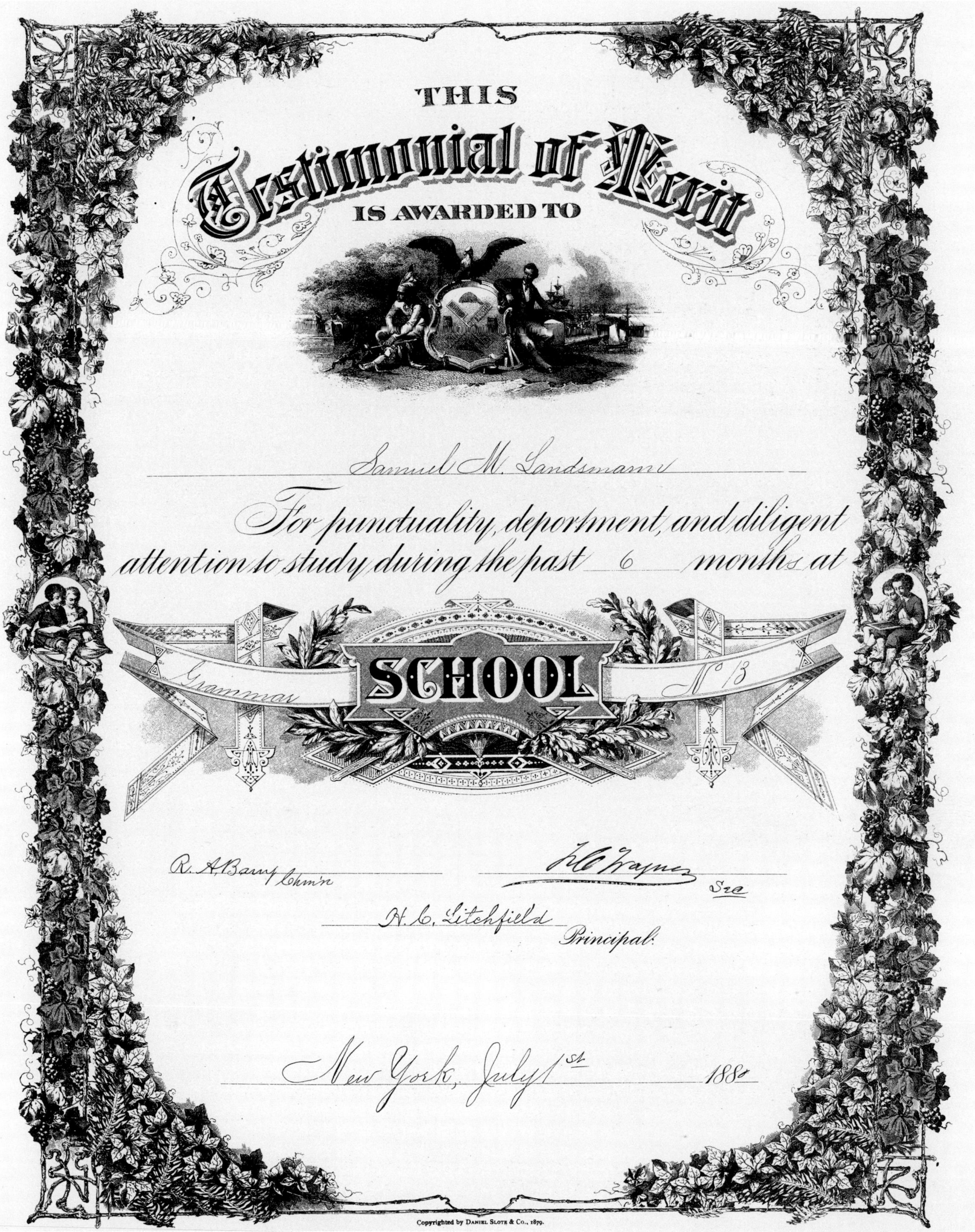

THIS
Testimonial of Merit
IS AWARDED TO

Samuel M. Landsmann

For punctuality, deportment, and diligent attention to study during the past 6 months at

Grammar SCHOOL No. 13

R. A. Barry Chm'n

H. C. Wayne Sec

H. C. Litchfield Principal.

New York, July 1st 1880

Copyrighted by Daniel Slote & Co., 1879.

Having stoically and decorously endured another school year of rote and routine, a 10-year-old New Yorker came home with this reward.

9 + 5 = 14
6 + 5 = 11
Work
play
That

Against a blackboard display of handwriting and arithmetic, grade schoolers in Keota, Iowa, celebrate the last day of school.

Something for Everyone

In 1865 telegraph tycoon (and New York state senator) Ezra Cornell found himself with "about half a million dollars more than my family will need." A self-made man who had never lost his pride in his humble origins, Cornell decided to use the money to help found a technical college where other poor but gifted boys could get an advanced education. With fellow senator Andrew White, he pushed a bill through the legislature to establish a state college within the provisions of the federal land-grant act; and he pledged to donate a site in Ithaca, along with the gift of his surplus $500,000. During the next three years Cornell super-

CORNELL CAMPUS

vised the building of a campus on a hilltop overlooking Cayuga Lake. White, a former professor who later became the new college's first president, persuaded him to take the radical step of adding liberal arts courses to the usual vocational fare of the land-grant institutions. And when Cornell University opened in October 1868 (tuition: $10 a trimester), it provided classes in everything from classical Greek to Spanish and Danish and veterinary science. Two years later, in an even more radical departure, Cornell admitted its first woman student, and by 1872 the board of trustees had voted to make the University entirely coeducational.

Only two buildings had been completed by Cornell's opening day in 1868, and Professor James Law, who taught veterinary science, conducted his first classes in open fields and barns. Not until 1894 did the trustees pry $50,000 from the state legislature to build a handsome veterinary college for Dr. Law *(below)*. The state came across with another $50,000 for an up-to-date dairy-husbandry facility *(right)*. Some departments were less favored: over the years physics accumulated excellent equipment—but got no new building to house it. By 1900 students could hardly move around the crowded old lab without bumping into apparatus.

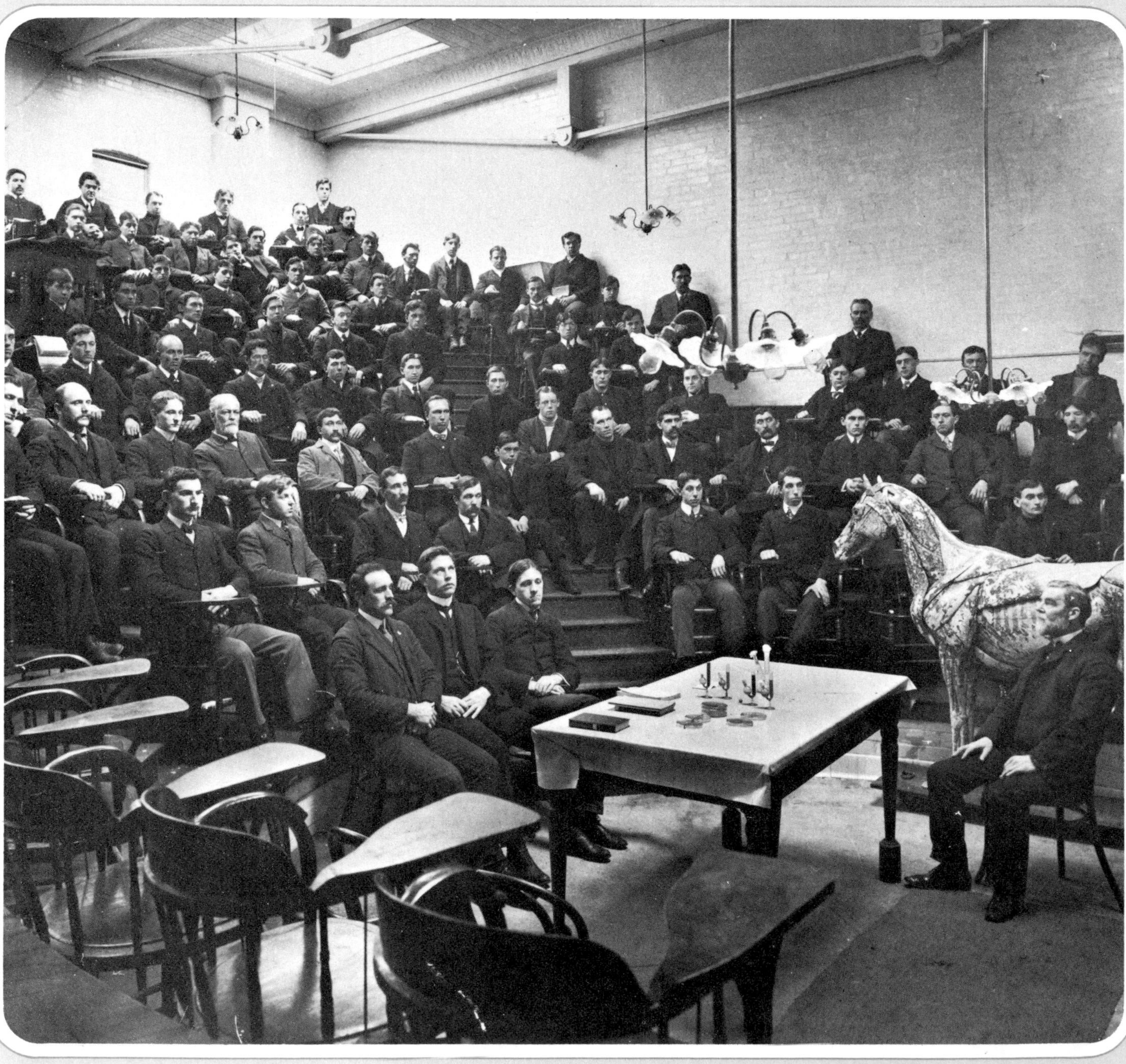

VETERINARY CLASS

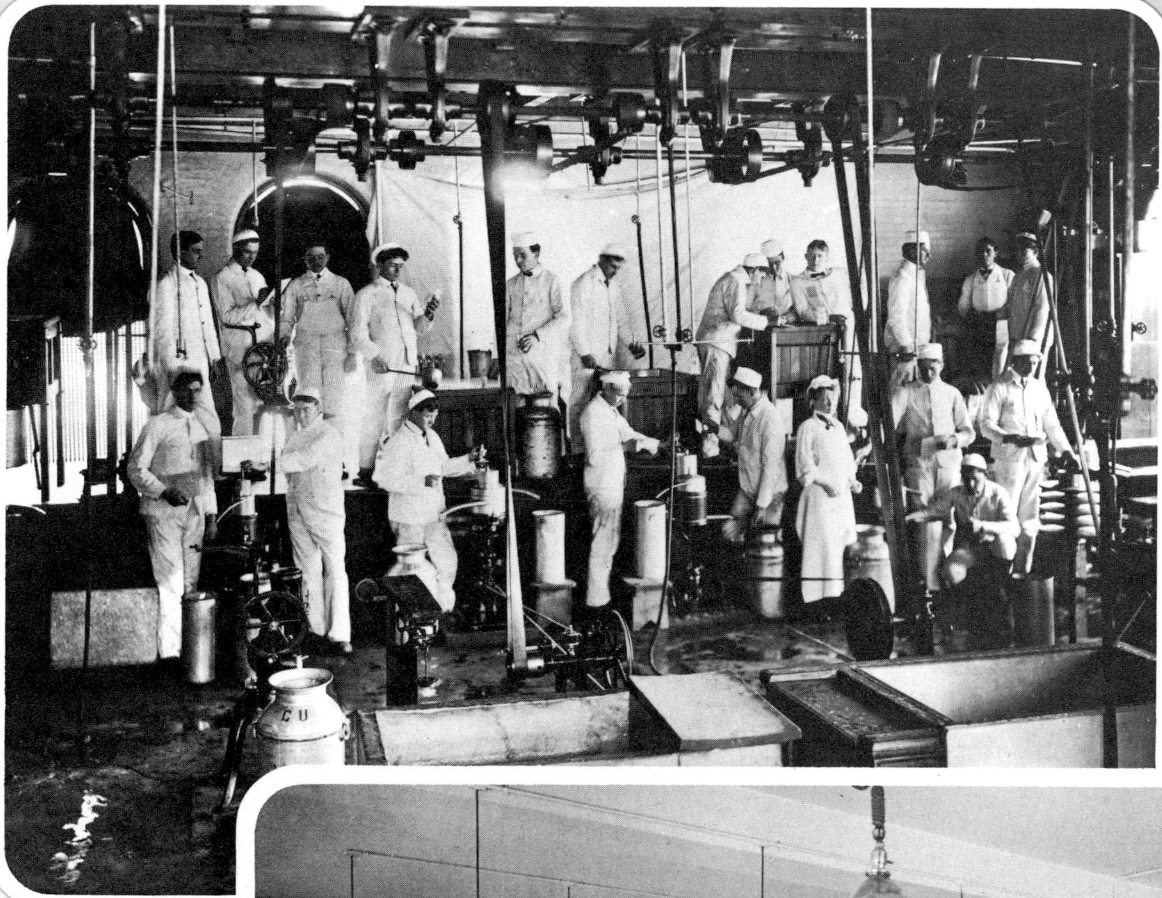

DAIRY LABORATORY

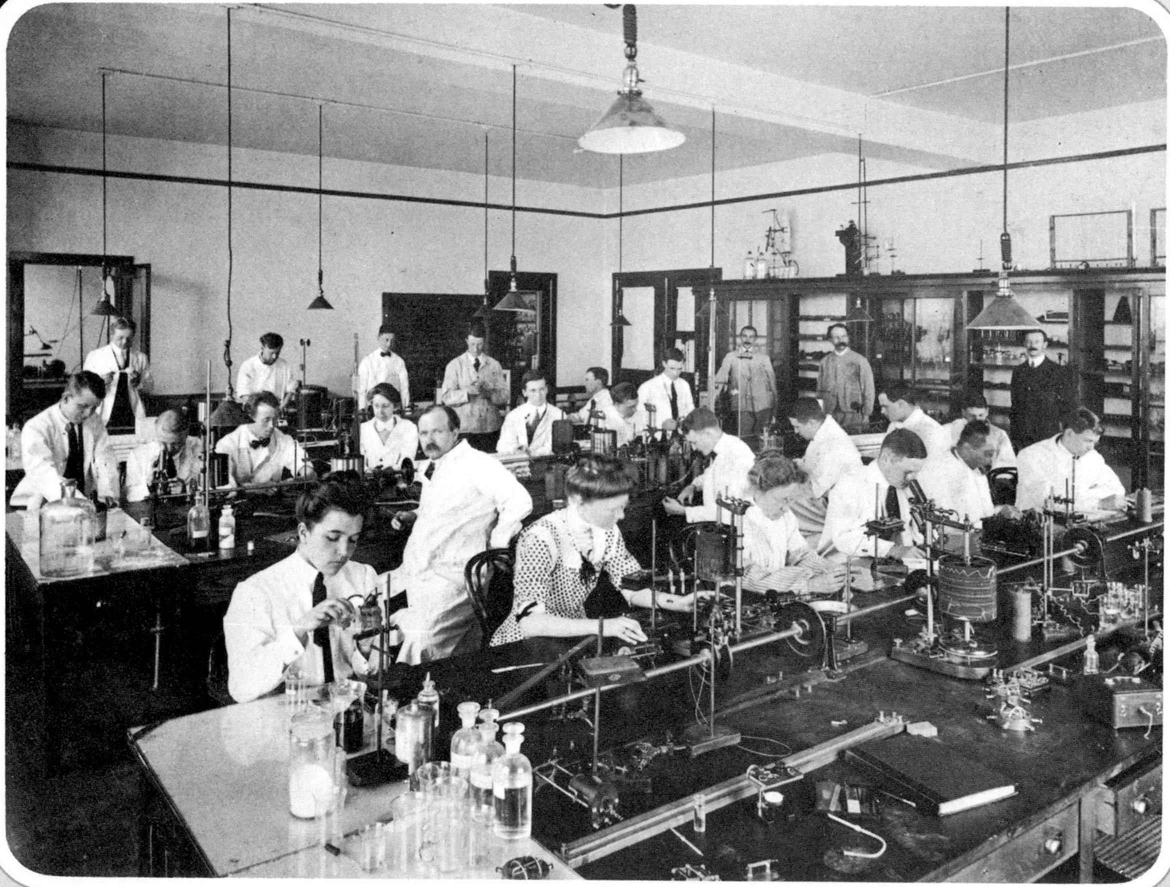

PHYSICS CLASS

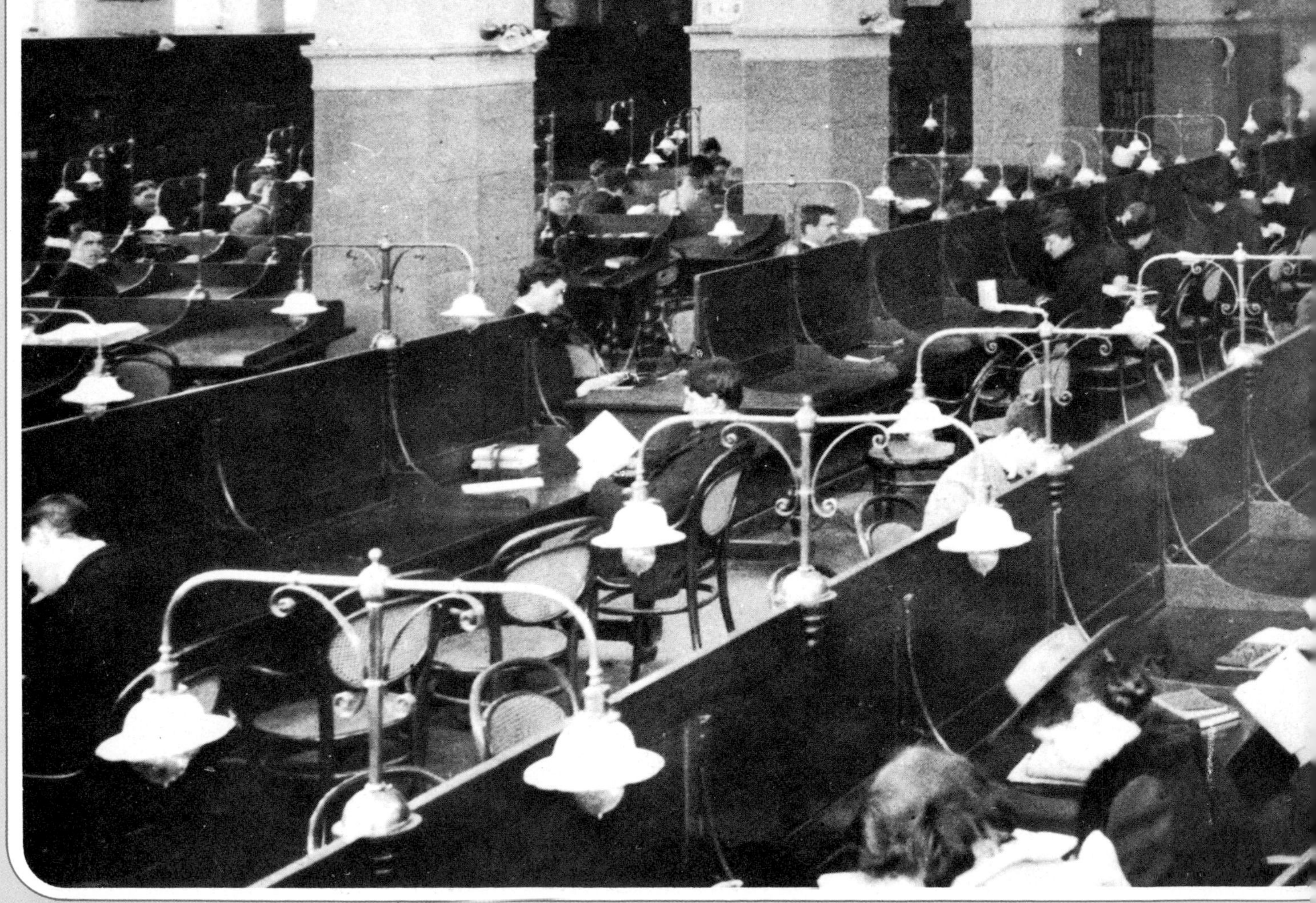

UNIVERSITY LIBRARY

STUDENT'S ROOM, ITHACA BOARDINGHOUSE

COLLEGE MEN AT EASE

In the '90s, the life style of many Cornell undergraduates still reflected the spare, no-nonsense tastes of the school's founder. Most coeds were housed within the confines of Sage dormitory. The men all lived off-campus, a number in spartan rooms rented for a dollar or less per week. Yet the sons of the rich—and the gay spirit of the '90s—had infiltrated the Ithaca campus. By 1900 affluent dudes like those above had moved into opulent quarters, like the $35,000, Neo-Gothic mansion complete with lookout towers Chi Psi bought its members.

FRESHMAN CREW

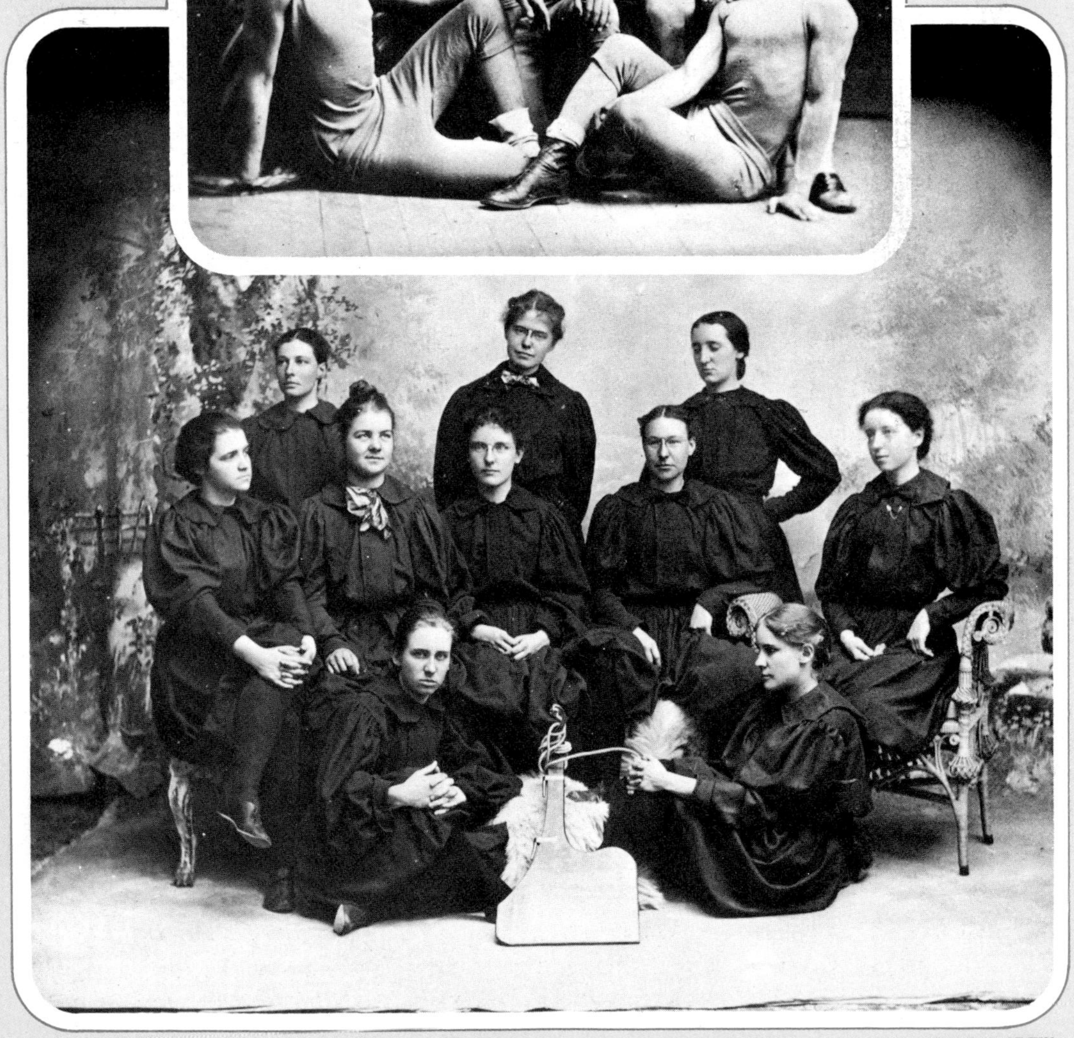

WOMEN'S CREW

VARSITY CREW

In 1873 Cornell took its first unsteady step into intercollegiate sport by hiring a rowing coach, who promptly horrified his fledgling crewmen by decreeing that each one lose 25 pounds. Following a regimen of starvation diets and practice drills on Cayuga Lake, the grim-faced oarsmen *(above)* struggled home fifth in their formal debut at Springfield, Massachusetts. Next season, the coach was replaced by a senior who believed in more food and more rowing victories. The crew got both; in the following year the freshman *(above, left)* and varsity crews became collegiate champions. Rowing dominated the sports scene at Cornell from then through the end of the century, with even the women's crew *(left)* getting a boathouse of its very own in 1896.

In 1873 a group of students asked whether they could play a football game in Cleveland—and received the blast below. President White loathed the sport, which he considered barbaric. And in fact, the special brand of football then developing at Cornell was so lethal that in 1876 both Harvard and Yale refused to play the Ithaca school. The game remained an intramural activity until 1886, when a new president, Charles K. Adams, decided that a cleaned-up brand of intercollegiate football might be good for the university after all. Under his guidance, Cornell's athletes gave up their free-for-all style; by 1892

I refuse to let forty boys travel four hundred miles merely to agitate a bag of wind.
CORNELL PRESIDENT ANDREW D. WHITE, 1873

Cornell was a legitimate grid power, losing only to Harvard, 20 to 14. In 1894 the faculty began passing new resolutions against the game, and the university's team reverted to the lackluster depths of de-emphasis. By 1895 the effects were evident: that year's heroes, at right, though they formed a handsome tableau, proved all too vincible on the field, where they lost four games, tied one and won only three.

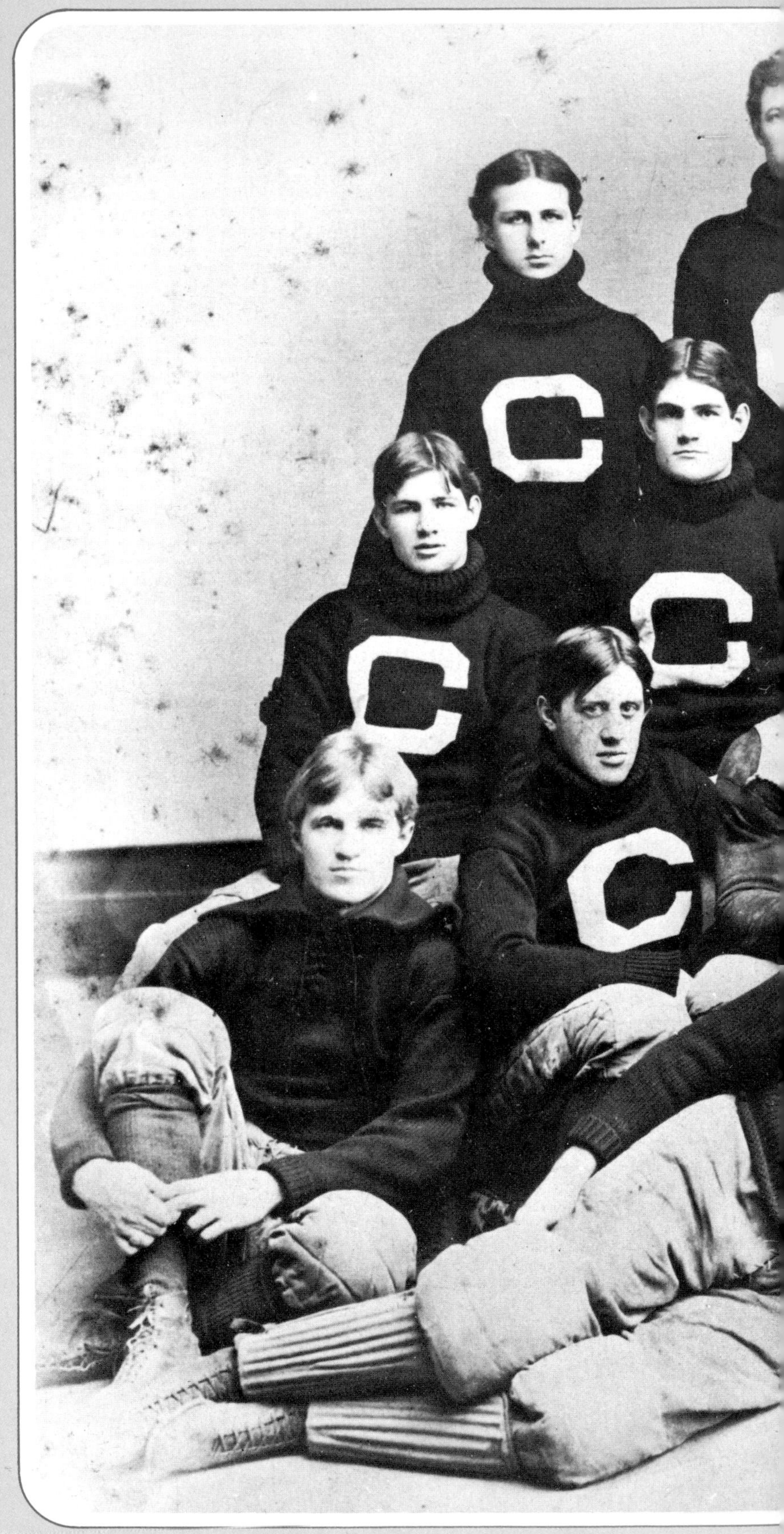

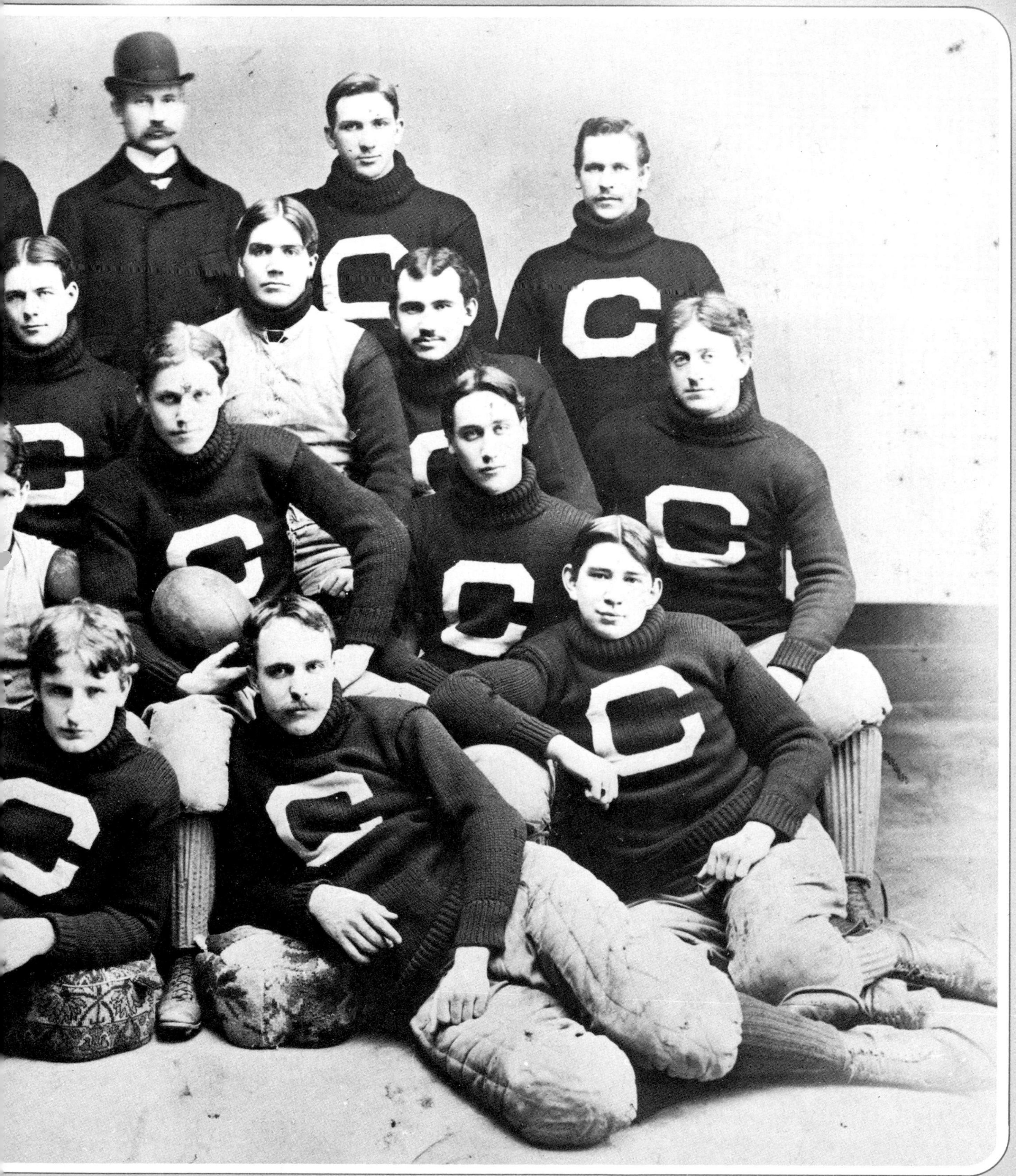

FOOTBALL TEAM

New York's Newspaper Row during the Spanish-American War, 1898.

The Press

TRIBUNE BULLETIN.
THE JOURNAL
A LANDING IN CUBA.
ARMY TO THE FRONT
WASH 1 PM 20,000 VOLUNTEERS HAVE BEEN ORDERED TO CHICKAMAUGA FROM THESE STATES.
N.Y.
OHIO.
A SPANISH DISASTER.
1130 AM-LONDON:-900 SPANIARDS HAVE BEEN KILLED IN A FIGHT WITH INSURGENTS. PLACE NOT GIVEN. THIS A SPECIAL DISPATCH FROM HAVANA TO LONDON.
TRIBUNE WAR ATLAS
25 CENTS A COPY
CUBA: WEST INDIES.
PHILLIPINES.
MANY OTHER COUNTRIES
FLAGS OF ALL NATIONS
— FOR SALE IN —
TRIBUNE OFFICE.

From Good Gray to Dirty Yellow

Accuracy! Accuracy is to a newspaper what virtue is to a woman.
JOSEPH PULITZER TO HIS STAFF

In 1883 Hungarian born Joseph Pulitzer, aged 36, came to the big city from St. Louis and bought the New York *World*, which did not seem to be much of a bargain—its circulation was only 15,000 and it was losing $40,000 a year. But Pulitzer did not seem to be much of a bargain himself—six feet, two and a half inches tall, thin as a rake, with a large bladelike nose, a receding chin and such poor eyesight that he would soon need a keeper. It would have taken a perceptive man to recognize Pulitzer for what he was: the best journalist of the 19th Century.

When Pulitzer emerged on the New York scene the traditional American newspaper, dull in appearance and rarely selling more than 200,000 copies a day, was being drastically remodeled. In part the change was taking place because 1870 to 1900 was a bully time for news, much of it of the terrible sort that publishers relish—the assassination of President Garfield, the Johnstown flood, Custer's annihilation, the Charleston earthquake, the Spanish-American War. Events of that caliber stimulated the headline writers—some of them clung to the narrow, many-decked old style *(opposite)* that, because of its visual effect, was called a tombstone. But by 1898, on the day after the American defeat of the Spanish fleet at Manila Bay, the *New York Journal* splattered a single word, "SURRENDERS!", across all seven columns of its front page. While headlines were burgeoning, so was technology: innovations such as typewriters, telephones, teletypesetting machines, photogravure and high-capacity rotary presses all helped to speed up and to expand the business of bringing people the news. However it was mainly the impact of the powerful personalities of Joseph Pulitzer and his competitors that changed the American press.

In 1883, on his first day as owner of the *World*, Pulitzer assembled the staff and said, "Gentlemen, heretofore you have all been living in the parlor and taking baths every day. Now I wish you to understand that, in future, you are all walking down the Bowery." Although several of the editors misunderstood him and resigned, Pulitzer meant that he had brought a strong social conscience to a city that lacked one. Himself an immigrant and an earnest believer in democracy, he saw that the millions of other immigrants crammed into the slums of New York had no paper to speak for them. They were poor and economically oppressed. (When a bill was introduced in the New York Assembly to reduce the work day of horsecar drivers to only 12 hours, young Assemblyman Theodore

THAT FUND IS GROWING! SEND YOUR MITE AT ONCE FOR THE Poor Babies' Free Doctors TO THE EVENING WORLD.

The World.

CIRCULATION GUARANTEED Greater Than That of Any Two Other American Newspapers Combined.

CIRCULATION BOOKS OPEN TO ALL

Circulation Per Day During the Month of May, 1889, 345,808 Copies.

THREE STEPS UPWARD.

AVERAGE DAILY CIRCULATION DURING THE LAST THREE MAY MONTHS:

1887	218,173
1888	290,336
1889	345,808

VOL. XXIX., NO. 10,149. 12 PAGES. NEW YORK, MONDAY, JUNE 3, 1889. 12 PAGES. PRICE TWO CENTS.

THE VALLEY OF DEATH

Horrors Growing Hourly at the Stricken City of Johnstown.

TEN THOUSAND PEOPLE DEAD.

Suffering Among the Survivors Who Are Encamped Amid the Hills.

HUMAN MONSTERS WHO ROB THE CORPSES.

The Great, Broad River Alone Is Calm, Silent and Serene.

PATHETIC PLIGHT OF THE VILLAGE BELLE.

Relief Schemes Everywhere Taking Practical Shape—One Million Dollars Needed at Once.

A typographical desert but the Garden of Eden for the morbid, a Pulitzer page has a single subject and uses "death" or "dead" 21 times.

Roosevelt objected. The idea was communistic, he said.)

These newly arrived poor, together with the old established poor, were Pulitzer's constituency, as he made plain in his opening editorial. "There is room in this great and growing city for a journal that is not only cheap [two cents] but bright, not only bright but large, not only large but truly democratic—dedicated to the cause of the people rather than to that of the purse potentates—devoted more to the news of the New than the Old World—that will expose all fraud and sham, fight all public evils and abuses—that will serve and battle for the people."

Although he was very fond of a dollar himself, there was no doubt of Pulitzer's sincerity when he attacked the purse potentates. One colleague wrote of him: "When J. P. was dictating an editorial upon some favorite topic, such as Collis P. Huntington's extremely ill-gotten wealth, Jay Gould's infamous railroad-wrecking or Cyrus Field's income, his speech was so interlarded with sulphurous and searing phrases that the whole staff shuddered. He was the first man I ever heard who split a word to insert an oath. . . . His favorite was 'indegoddampendent.' "

Pulitzer's editorial page soon became the profession's noblest. He advanced a 10-point program: "Tax luxuries; tax inheritances; tax large incomes; tax monopolies; tax privileged corporations; a tariff for revenue; reform the Civil Service; punish corrupt officers; punish vote buying; punish employers who coerce employees in elections."

Pulitzer scrupulously printed the important news and played it straight. He also printed sharp, bitter stories of life in the slums calculated to provoke honest wrath: "She had lain down in the cellar to sleep, and the sewer that runs under the house overflowed and suffocated her where she lay. No one will ever know who killed Kate Sweeny. No one will ever summon the sanitary inspectors. Nobody seems to have thought it worth an investigation." There were other items in the *World's* news columns, however, that did not appear to have been published by the same man. Pulitzer, who was not a great innovator but a master synthesist, had observed that other papers had been quite successful with snappy copy. In 1875, when four murderers made some pious comments just before being hanged, the *Chicago Times* ran the immortal headline, "JERKED TO JESUS." Pulitzer followed suit. He stopped running such stupefying *World* heads as "AFFAIRS AT ALBANY" and "BENCH SHOW OF DOGS" and led off with "MADDENED BY MARRIAGE" and "SCREAMING FOR MERCY."

Freely acknowledging the contrast between his angelic editorial page and his steamy heads and tales of sex and crime, Pulitzer cited what he said was journalistic necessity. The best a publisher could do was to "go for your million circulation, and when you have got it, turn the minds, and the votes, of your readers one way or the other at critical moments."

As he went for his million Pulitzer revealed his genius at turning minds and selling papers simultaneously—as for example, when he helped shove Grover Cleveland into the Presidency in 1884. Cleveland and Pulitzer, Democrats, belonged to a party that had been out of office for 24 years and had only modest prospects of getting back in. The Republicans, backing James G. Blaine, appeared securely in the lead throughout the campaign. A few days before the election, however, Blaine exposed his jugular. He came to New York and allowed himself to be greeted by a group of Protestant clergymen. An eager old preacher among them blurted out that the opposition party, the deplorable Democrats, had its roots in "rum, Romanism and rebellion," a wildly impolitic remark that the inattentive Blaine failed to disavow. That evening, although there was serious economic hardship in many parts of the country, Blaine compounded his folly by speaking of "Republican prosperity" to a dinner audience of millionaires including Jay Gould and John Jacob Astor.

Next morning Pulitzer slashed Blaine's throat. The front page of the *World* was devoted to the mindless slogan, "rum, Romanism and rebellion" and Blaine's "insult" to Catholics, a notion that had never crossed poor Blaine's mind. No doubt he had known in waking moments that New York was full of Irishmen but had momentarily forgotten it. There was also a very large cartoon, "THE ROYAL FEAST OF BELSHAZZAR—BLAINE AND THE MONEY KINGS,"

Pulitzer in his prime was professorial and "indegoddampendent."

depicting the Republican candidate and his friends guzzling Gould Pie, Lobby Pudding and Monopoly Soup while a poor family begged vainly for leftovers. Pulitzer's smashing front page (the paper sold more than 100,000 copies) cannot have failed to influence several thousand votes—and as it turned out, New York State went Democratic by a tiny swing of less than 600, throwing its 36 crucial electoral votes to Grover Cleveland and barely squeezing him into the White House.

Pulitzer was delighted with the outcome, but that did not prevent him from jostling Cleveland fairly soon—particularly when newspaper circulation could be increased. In 1886, to the bemusement of a good many citizens, the 50-year-old President took to wife a 24-year-old girl. On the morning after that event Cleveland glanced out of the bridal chamber window and was outraged to discover the flower of Washington journalism clustered nearby, taking notes. In an age so prim that books by male and female authors were still occasionally segregated on library shelves, it seemed to Cleveland that the press had become far too aggressive. Pulitzer sympathized completely—not with Cleveland, but with the reporters. The bon mot of fellow journalist Charles A. Dana, editor of the New York *Sun*, also expressed Pulitzer's view: "I have always felt that whatever the Divine Providence permitted to occur, I was not too proud to report."

Pulitzer was also happy to follow the examples of Dana and others in developing promotional stunts and crusades. As early as 1871 the *New York Herald* had sent its reporter Henry M. Stanley to find the long missing Dr. David Livingstone in Africa. In 1881 the *New York Tribune* began its fresh-air fund for slum children. In 1885 Pulitzer saw that there was a profitable cause in the Statue of Liberty. When a suspicious Congress refused to appropriate money for a pedestal for the statue, which had been given to the U.S. by the citizens of France, Pulitzer appealed to the *World's* readers and raised the necessary $100,000. More than 120,000 people chipped in while Congressmen blushed and papers sold at an admirable pace. Pulitzer became permanently attached to the flashy, unusual device for building circulation—in 1890 to 1891 he sent Elizabeth Cochran, a girl reporter who worked under the name Nellie Bly, dashing around the globe; and during 1894 he launched in the Sunday *World* the first newspaper comic page.

Within a year of Pulitzer's takeover the *World's* circulation passed 100,000—a number far short of his goal of a million but well worth celebrating. He had a 100-gun salute fired in City Hall Park and bought tall silk hats for all his employees. (As a rule he rewarded initiative with cash bonuses, once handing one of his men a bag containing $1,000 in $20 gold pieces.) By the late 1880s the *World*, whose morning and evening editions were rich in advertising and sold more than 300,000 copies combined, had

Text continued on page 172.

Manufactured News *was a favorite method of selling papers. In perhaps the most spectacular of these promotional stunts, Pulitzer sent dashing lady reporter "Nellie Bly" (her real name was Elizabeth Cochran) around the world for the World. Racing against the record of the fictional Phileas Fogg in Jules Verne's novel Around the World in Eighty Days, Nellie traveled by ship, sampan, jinricksha, burro and train. The World kept its readers in a constant swivet with a storm of stories, pictures and games, including the shake-the-dice race below. When Nellie came panting back to New York, she had been on the road for only 72 days, 6 hours, 11 minutes and 14 seconds and had become far more famous than the notorious slowpoke, P. Fogg.*

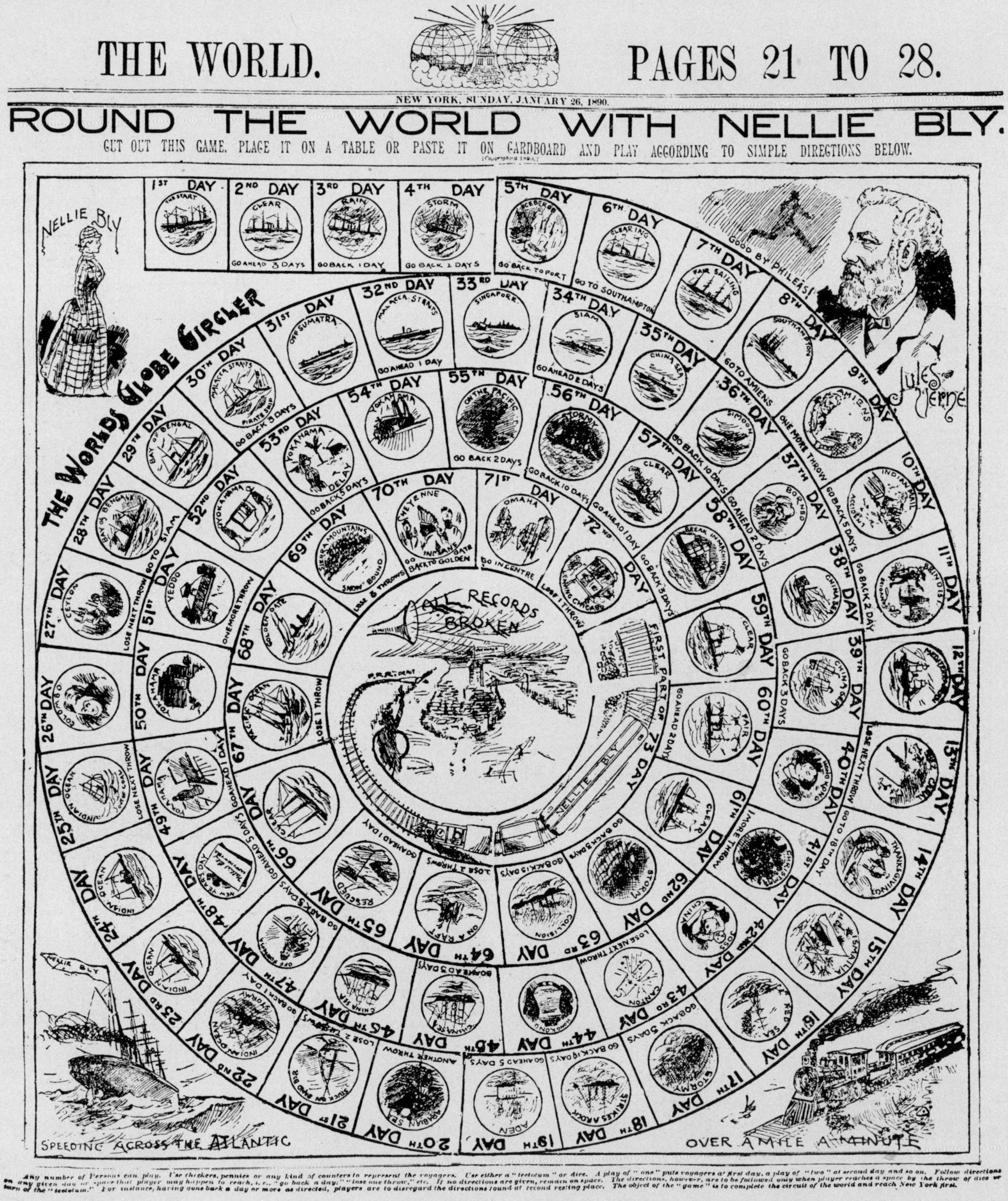

"Yellow Journalism," *the opprobrious term for the excesses generated by Pulitzer and Hearst, had the most innocent of origins. Pulitzer created the first Sunday comic section, whose most popular character was a nameless urchin christened The Yellow Kid, after the color of his costume. In January 1896, Hearst stole the illustrator who created The Yellow Kid from Pulitzer, and for a time there were competing versions in the two papers. Since both publishers were then engaged in reckless journalism, yellow came to be the word for it. The panel below takes off on the America's Cup races of 1895, in which Lord Dunraven's British challenger Valkyrie III was defeated by the American yacht Defender, skippered by Captain Hank Haff of Maine.*

become the most profitable newspaper ever published. Pulitzer's income was about one million dollars a year, and he spent it on a yacht and houses in Maine, the Riviera and New York—still stoutly maintaining on his editorial page that luxuries and large incomes ought to be taxed.

Pulitzer's expenditure of energy cost him dearly. Although his physical courage was unquestionable, he suffered from nerves—the noise of crumpling paper, even the sound of someone eating a piece of toast, drove him into agonies—and was treated for asthma, diabetes, headaches, insomnia, dyspepsia and rheumatism. His eyesight became so poor that he began to stroke the faces of his wife and children as though trying to memorize them. On his doctors' advice he ceased the editing of the *World* and went abroad for a rest. In Constantinople in 1889, standing on a ship, he remarked, "How quickly it grows dark in this latitude." His companion said, "But it is not dark," and Pulitzer replied, "It is for me." He had gone blind.

Joseph Pulitzer had been born to well-to-do parents in Hungary and educated by private tutors. He left home at 17 in 1864 and fell in with an American recruiting agent who signed him up for the Union Army and sent him to America in steerage. After a few uneventful months as a cavalryman, Pulitzer was honorably discharged and made his way to St. Louis. One day in 1868, when he was playing chess in the game room of that city's Mercantile Library, his dashing style impressed Carl Schurz, German-American Civil War general, politican and part-owner of the *Westliche Post*, a German-language newspaper. Schurz offered Pulitzer a job as a reporter.

He learned his profession exceedingly fast. He was something of a comic figure as he dashed near-sightedly across town covering his stories—his competitors, mimicking his accent, called him "Choe Bulitzer." They soon had reason to respect his shrewdness. When a tiny local paper went bankrupt, Pulitzer bought it for a token sum. What he realized—while others did not—was that the paper owned an Associated Press franchise, a difficult thing to obtain, that entitled it to receive and print telegraphed

French Scientist and Explorer Discovers a Race of Savages with Well-Developed Tails.

NEW YORK, SUNDAY, DECEMBER 15, 1895.—COPYRIGHTED BY THE PRESS PUBLISHING CO. 1895.

The Missing Link.

THE HUMAN MAN-MONKEY WITH A TAIL, DISCOVERED BY A FRENCH EXPLORER.

Sunday Supplements *pioneered by Pulitzer had many trumped-up features. This creature was reported found by an explorer who was quoted in English and French to establish credibility—"to be certain that I was not the plaything of an illusion, I felt his tail (l'appendice caudal)."*

news. Pulitzer took the franchise around the corner the next day and sold it to another paper for $30,000.

As he accumulated money and knowledge Pulitzer bought for $2,500 another bankrupt paper, the *St. Louis Dispatch,* and merged it with the feeble *St. Louis Post.* Within five years, crusading, employing bright men and pitting them against one another (whoever lost, Pulitzer won), he built the *Post-Dispatch* into a wonderful newspaper worth perhaps $500,000. There was no place for him to go then but to the center of journalistic action, New York. Retaining ownership of the *Post-Dispatch,* he went.

The blind publisher had no difficulty in continuing his control of the *World.* He merely went on with his old policy of arranging battles among editors. He required his top men to send him detailed, confidential reports on one another, creating a sharkish situation that, according to one man who survived it, "drove at least two editors to drink, one into suicide, a fourth into insanity, and another into banking." Nonetheless the reports kept Pulitzer informed and firmly in charge.

After 1889 the publisher, voyaging repeatedly to Europe, spent little time in New York. Contrary to his doctors' orders he continued to work. He managed the paper by cable, having each issue read to him and firing off detailed critiques. ("Get the facts—bank robber described as short—what is short? Four feet? Five feet? Be exact.") For personal services, general information and conversation, he relied upon a staff of male secretaries—he preferred highly cultivated, soft-voiced Englishmen—who accompanied him everywhere. Among other duties they had the task of reading the master to sleep for his afternoon nap. On command the secretary on duty would start to read in a loud, clear voice and would continue until Pulitzer said *Leise* (softly). Then the secretary would lower his voice until it became a monotonous, soothing drone. *Ganz Leise* (very softly), Pulitzer would say, and the secretary would reduce his volume still further, until it became only an indistinct mumbling. When Pulitzer fell asleep the secretary would have to continue mumbling for as long as two hours—and if he once changed his tone, sneezed or coughed, Pulitzer would awaken and berate him for a full 15 minutes.

At dinner the secretaries were obliged to furnish a constant flow of bright, informative talk. Pulitzer was merciless in his demands. When one hapless man professed some familiarity with Shakespeare, Pulitzer insisted that he recite the plots of all 38 plays. When the man had finally gotten through this ordeal, assisted by notes passed to him under the blind man's nose by the other secretaries, Pulitzer snapped, "Well, go on, go on! Haven't you read the sonnets?"

In 1895 Pulitzer, whose vigor seemed only to increase with his illnesses, took a direct hand in U.S. foreign policy. A boundary dispute arose in South America between Venezuela and British Guiana (and hence England herself) concerning a tract of howling jungle that had been only vaguely surveyed. Citing the Monroe Doctrine, President Cleveland virtually demanded that the dispute be resolved on U.S. terms. He spoke of a menace to the peace and safety of the United States and "the integrity of our free institutions," adding that "in making these recommendations I am fully alive to the responsibility incurred and keenly realize all the consequences that may follow." In mundane prose, Cleveland was talking about war.

A lust for battle arose everywhere in the nation—the New York *Sun,* the *World's* rival, said that anyone who did not want to fight England was "an alien or a traitor" and foresaw glorious naval engagements "in the British Channel and the Irish Sea." Theodore Roosevelt, by that time Police Commissioner of New York, wrote, "If there is a muss I shall try to have a hand in it myself!" and looked forward enthusiastically to "the conquest of Canada."

Joseph Pulitzer, in one of the best hours in American journalism, stood up boldly against the general sentiment for war: "Does the determination of a boundary line in South America threaten . . . 'our distinctive form of government'? Merely to ask such questions is to expose the . . . preposterously inadequate nature of the war-threat which the president has fulminated. It is an insult to the un-

ZOLA'S "WIFE BEATERS"----READ IT TO-DAY.

NIGHT SPECIAL. NEW YORK JOURNAL NIGHT SPECIAL.

EVENING

NO. 5,566—P. M. NEW YORK, FRIDAY, FEBRUARY 11, 1898. PRICE ONE CENT.

EXTRA

BABIES KILLED BY SCORE

Twenty Bodies Have Been Recently Found in the Streets of Harlem.

POLICE AFTER SLAYERS.

Direct Attention to Midwives and Already One Arrest Has Been Made.

SHE IS HELD WITHOUT BAIL.

ALLOWS $605,237 FOR THE TEACHERS.

Board of Estimate Fixes the Amount for Salaries and Other Expenses for January.

The Board of Estimate and Apportionment this afternoon allowed $605,237 for the Board of Education, covering expenses and salaries for January.

THE DE LOME QUESTION

Washington, Feb. 11. — Will Hale sail?

BELIEVED TO BE TROLLEY ROBBERS.

Four Men Arrested on Suspicion of Having Murdered a Philadelphia Motorman.

LIGHT ON DREYFUS PLOTTING

Colonel Picquart Tells of Disregarded Evidence Against Esterhazy.

HANDWRITING RECOGNIZED

Zola Feelingly Replies to a Reflection of General Pellieux Amid Great Excitement.

WHAT M. BERTILLON DISCOVERED.

THIGH OF THE BODY FOUND.

NEW CLEW TO THE EAST RIVER MYSTERY.

$1,000 REWARD FOR SOLUTION.

Evening Journal Will Pay This for the Clearing Up of the Crime.

Questions to be answered and detective clews up to date:

WHO WAS HE?

Jean Lancreal? George Farrell? C. Swartschild? Peter Smith? T. Abrahamson? ——? Wm. McGarigle?

WHY WAS HE SLAIN?

For Money? By a Woman? For Revenge? In a Quarrel? For Jealousy? By a Maniac?

WHO KILLED HIM?

Nothing Known of the Identity of the Murderer.

HOW WAS HE KILLED?

Choked? Crushed? Shot? Dismembered?

WHERE WAS HE KILLED?

Not more than a week ago. No one knows, but somewhere in the limits of New York.

A man's thigh was found floating in the East River at the foot of Pacific street, Brooklyn to-day.

Careful measurements taken by the Evening Journal showed at once that the limb was a part of the body of the murdered man whose trunk was at the Morgue.

These measurements were confirmed by Coroner's Physician Donlin and other experts when the thigh was brought to the Morgue this afternoon.

About thirty contusions were found, proving beyond doubt that the murdered man had engaged in a fierce struggle.

The body had apparently been dis-jointed by the use of a hatchet, pounded with a hammer.

The bone in the thigh was complete. The joints were disarticulated. The flesh was hacked. Then the joints were twisted and torn from the sockets.

The finding of the thigh has added a new and thrilling interest to the great murder mystery. For information leading to its solution the Evening Journal will pay $1,000 reward.

Part of Leg Belonging to Mutilated Body Found in the River To-day.

DISCOVERY DRE WA CROWD.

PARTS FIT PERFECTLY.

EXTRA.

(BY WIRE TO THE EVENING JOURNAL PRESS.)

DANGER OF RIOT IN PARIS

REDMOND AMENDMENT OVERWHELMINGLY DEFEATED.

EDGEMONT SMELTING COMPANY GOES UP.

MR. ASTOR GETS HIS TAXES REDUCED.

MORE MEN WALKED THE PLANK.

WANTS TO RENT PIER

RACING AT SINGERLY.

THIRD RACE—Earn, Crown, Wexford.

FOURTH RACE—Harry Bennett, Hack Jr., Quilla.

Twenty Murdered Babies Found in Harlem Streets.

ABSOLUTE DIVORCE FOR F. L. COLWELL.

He Is Also Given the Custody of His Children—A $50,000 Verdict for Damages.

This Woman the Police Call a Second Mrs. Nack.

$1,000 REWARD!

The Evening Journal will pay $1,000 reward for information, given to it exclusively, that will lead to the identification of the body found in the East River on Tuesday, and the conviction of the supposed murderer or murderers.

DISJOINTED WITH A HATCHET.

BODY TO BE PRESERVED.

OTHER PARTS WILL BE FOUND.

Continued on Sixth Page.

To build circulation Hearst treated the mystery of a dismembered corpse as a game with a prize. Later, his reporters caught the murderers.

derstanding of an intelligent American schoolchild."

Pulitzer sent cablegrams to scores of British leaders, including the Prince of Wales, the Duke of York, and the members of Parliament, asking them to send him by return cable, collect, their thoughts concerning peace. On Christmas Day, 1895, the *World* ran a special front page headed "PEACE AND GOOD WILL" and featuring the British reply ("earnestly trust . . . warm feeling of friendship . . . so many years") in large type. At this, most war promoters across the nation commenced to feel ridiculous. However, Theodore Roosevelt offered to put Pulitzer in prison for having, as a private citizen, meddled with American foreign policy. There was not much support for the proposal.

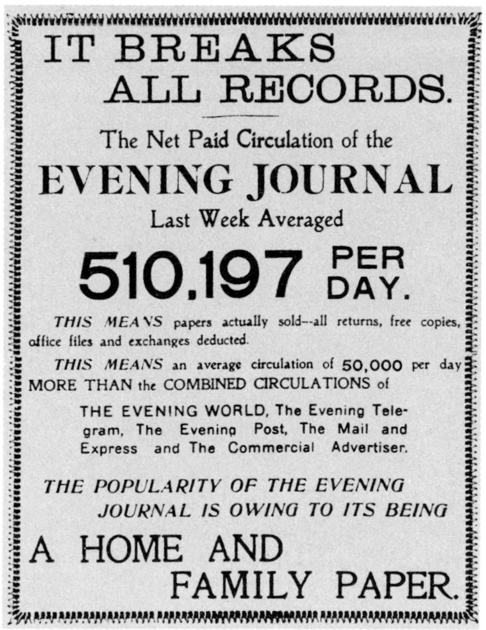
IT BREAKS
ALL RECORDS.
The Net Paid Circulation of the
EVENING JOURNAL
Last Week Averaged
510,197 PER DAY.
THIS MEANS papers actually sold—all returns, free copies, office files and exchanges deducted.
THIS MEANS an average circulation of 50,000 per day MORE THAN the COMBINED CIRCULATIONS of
THE EVENING WORLD, The Evening Telegram, The Evening Post, The Mail and Express and The Commercial Advertiser.
THE POPULARITY OF THE EVENING JOURNAL IS OWING TO ITS BEING
A HOME AND
FAMILY PAPER.

In the mid-90s Pulitzer was challenged by young William Randolph Hearst, who came to New York and bought the *Journal*. Hearst admired Pulitzer and imitated his tactics—indeed, in one piratical swoop he hired away the entire staff of Pulitzer's Sunday paper, who strolled in a body from the *World's* office to the *Journal's*. Pulitzer, cabling an offer of more money, persuaded them to walk back; Hearst offered still more and the staff took another stroll, this time remaining at the *Journal* for good. Pulitzer quickly assembled a new staff but realized that he was in a tangle with a most formidable competitor.

Almost immediately Hearst began to publish ghastly tales of butcheries in Cuba, where Spain was attempting to maintain her colonial rule. Hearst's stories were largely fabrications but the *Journal's* circulation began to soar and, apparently, Pulitzer lost his head. He set out to compete with Hearst in sensationalism and soon the *World* was printing: "The skulls of all were split to pieces down to the eyes. Some of these were gouged out. . . . The arms and legs of one had been dismembered and laced into a rude attempt at a Cuban five-pointed star. . . . The tongue of one had been cut out and placed on the mangled forehead. . . . The Spanish soldiers habitually cut off the ears of the Cuban dead and retain them as trophies."

Prose of that wild sort, repeated day after day by both papers, created an irreversible demand for war all across the nation. When the U.S. battleship *Maine* mysteriously exploded and sank in Havana harbor in February 1898 (a naval court of inquiry failed to fix the responsibility), Pulitzer and Hearst wasted no time in announcing *their* opinions: the wicked Spaniards had undoubtedly done it. When war was declared two months later, Pulitzer and Hearst were largely responsible for it, and both of them profited enormously. On the news of the *Maine's* sinking, the *World* and the *Journal* topped a million in daily sales, and when Spanish-held Manila fell to Admiral Dewey, both papers sold about 1.5 million. It was a triumph of sorts but the real verdict on this kind of journalism was passed by Edwin Godkin, the widely respected editor of the *New York Evening Post*, who said simply: "Nothing so disgraceful . . . has been known in the history of American journalism."

When the war ended, Pulitzer had repented of his attempt to scrimmage on Hearst's level. He summoned his editors and quietly discussed the state of the *World* with them. One of them summed up what the boss was feeling: "The great mistakes which have been made . . . have been caused by an excess of zeal. Be just as clever as you can. Be more energetic and enterprising than any other man if you can, but above all, be right." It was in this chastened mood that Joseph Pulitzer, having helped to create the new newspaper, saw the old century pass away.

The World's Greatest Circulation Record!

1,011,068 Per Week-Day April Average. GAIN in One Year - - 338,748

The World.

"Circulation Books Open to All."

1,011,068 Per Week-Day April Average. GAIN in Three Years - 461,205

VOL. XXXVIII. NO. 13,404. (Copyright, 1898, by the Press Publishing Company, New York World.) NEW YORK, MONDAY, MAY 2, 1898. PRICE ONE CENT in Greater New York and Jersey City. TWO CENTS outside of Greater New York and Jersey City and up ...

DEWEY SMASHES SPAIN'S FLEET

VICE-ADMIRAL MONTOJO.

The Defeated Commander of the Spanish Fleet.

Great Naval Battle Between Asiatic Squadron and Spanish Warships Off Manila.

THREE OF THE BEST SPANISH VESSELS WIPED OUT, OTHERS SUNK.

The Damage Done to the American Boats Engaged Only Nominal---Hundreds of the Enemy Slain in the Encounter.

COMMODORE DEWEY.

Winner of First Great Victory for New American Navy.

LISBON, Portgugal, May 1, 11 P. M.----The Spanish fleet was completely defeated off Cavite, Philippine Islands, according to trustworthy advices received here.

WASHINGTON, May 1, Midnight.---President McKinley expresses entire satisfaction over the reported battle between Commodore Dewey's squadron and the Spanish fleet. He accepts the news as true, but believes it is worse for the Spanish than they will admit. There has been no official confirmation of the news. Nothing official is expected for forty-eight hours.

THE THREE SPANISH CRUISERS COMPLETELY DESTROYED.

CASTILLA.

DON JUAN DE AUSTRIA.

SPANISH FLAG SHIP "REINA MARIA CRISTINA."

FLYING SQUADRON STRENGTHENED.

(Special to The World.)

FORT MONROE, May 1.—The recently converted yacht Scorpion, in charge of Lieut.-Commander Marix, joined the Flying Squadron in Hampton Roads at 1 P. M. to-day after a quick trip from New York. The Scorpion's arrival greatly pleased Commodore Schley, as the squadron, while strong in heavy fighting ships, is weak in swift, light-armed craft.

Chaplain Jones, the "fighting parson" of the Texas, preached a red-hot war sermon to-day to the officers and men of the battleship. He took his text from the thirty-second chapter of Deuteronomy, reading from the eighteenth to the forty-third verse, inclusive.

He said that if these verses had been written to order as an admonition to Spain, their appropriateness could not have been more emphatic, especially these:

"He said I will hide my face from them, I will see what their end shall be; for they are a very forward generation; children in whom is no faith.

"They shall be burnt with hunger and devoured with burning heat and with bitter destruction.

"For they are a nation void of counsel; neither is there any understanding in them.

"Oh, that they are wise; that they understand this; that they would consider their latter end."

Nothing is known as to when the squadron will start.

The work of laying mines and torpedoes in the harbor continued all day.

Pennsylvania Railroad Announces

Improved service between New York and Atlantic City daily except Sunday. Commencing Wednesday, May 4, the Atlantic City Express will leave foot of West 23d street 1.50 P. M., Cortlandt and Desbrosses streets 2.10 P. M., and arrive Atlantic City 5.20 P. M. Returning leave Atlantic City ... A. M., arrive New York, 23d street, 12.58 P. M. The train will not run into Camden.

ADMIRAL MONTOJO ADMITS HIS UTTER ROUT.

In His Report to Spain He Says Many Ships Were Burned and Sunk and the Losses in Officers and Men "Numerous."

MADRID (via Paris), May 2.—The time of the retreat of the American squadron behind the merchantmen was 11.30 A. M. The American squadron forced the port before daybreak and appeared off Cavite. Night was completely dark.

The Naval Bureau at Manila sends the following report, signed "Montojo, Admiral:"

"In the middle of the night the American squadron forced the forts, and before daybreak appeared off Cavite. The night was completely dark. At 7.30 the bow of the Reina Christina took fire, and soon after the poop also was burned.

"At eight o'clock, with my staff, I went on board the Isla de Cuba. The Reina Maria Christina and the Castilla were then entirely enveloped in flames.

"The other ships having been damaged retired into Baker Bay. Some had to be sunk to prevent their falling into the hands of the enemy. The losses are numerous, notably Capt. Cadarso, a priest, and nine other persons."

The Spaniards fought splendidly, the sailors refusing to leave the burning and sinking Don Juan de Austria. There is the greatest anxiety for further details.

MADRID'S FORLORN HOPE.

LONDON, May 2.—The Madrid correspondent of the Financial News, telegraphing this morning, says:

"The Spanish Ministry of Marine claims a victory for Spain because the Americans were forced to retire behind the merchantmen. Capt. Cadalso (or Cadarso), in command of the Reina Maria Christina, went down with the ship.

MADRID OFFICIAL REPORT ADMITS DISASTROUS DEFEAT

(Despatch Sanctioned by Spanish Government and Passed by the Censor)

MADRID, May 1, 8 P. M.---The following is the text of the official despatch from the Governor-General of the Philippine Islands to the Minister of War, Lieut.-Gen. Correa, regarding the engagement off Manila:

"Last night, April 30, the batteries at the entrance to the fort announced the arrival of the enemy's squadron, forcing a passage under the obscurity of the night.

"At daybreak the enemy took up positions, opening with a strong fire against Fort Cavite and the arsenal.

"Our fleet engaged the enemy in a brilliant combat, protecte

(Continued on Second Page.)

Trailing Hearst in circulation, Pulitzer splashed his front page with a banner headline and drawings of the winner and loser at Manila.

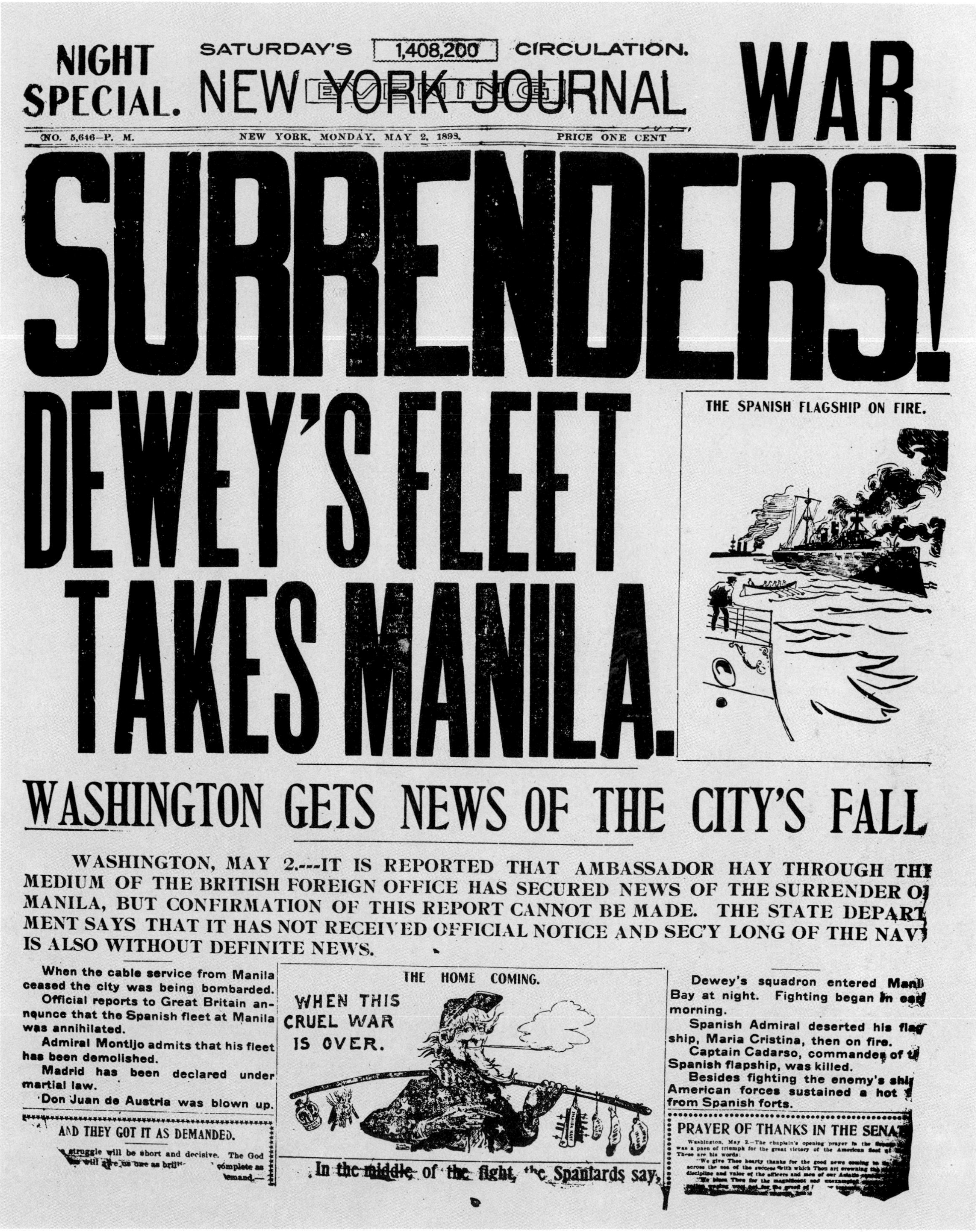

NIGHT SPECIAL.

SATURDAY'S 1,408,200 CIRCULATION.

NEW YORK JOURNAL

WAR

NO. 5,646—P. M. NEW YORK, MONDAY, MAY 2, 1898. PRICE ONE CENT

SURRENDERS!

DEWEY'S FLEET TAKES MANILA.

THE SPANISH FLAGSHIP ON FIRE.

WASHINGTON GETS NEWS OF THE CITY'S FALL

WASHINGTON, MAY 2.---IT IS REPORTED THAT AMBASSADOR HAY THROUGH THE MEDIUM OF THE BRITISH FOREIGN OFFICE HAS SECURED NEWS OF THE SURRENDER OF MANILA, BUT CONFIRMATION OF THIS REPORT CANNOT BE MADE. THE STATE DEPARTMENT SAYS THAT IT HAS NOT RECEIVED OFFICIAL NOTICE AND SEC'Y LONG OF THE NAVY IS ALSO WITHOUT DEFINITE NEWS.

When the cable service from Manila ceased the city was being bombarded.

Official reports to Great Britain announce that the Spanish fleet at Manila was annihilated.

Admiral Montijo admits that his fleet has been demolished.

Madrid has been declared under martial law.

Don Juan de Austria was blown up.

AND THEY GOT IT AS DEMANDED.

...struggle will be short and decisive. The God ... will give us one as brill... complete as ...emand.—

THE HOME COMING.

WHEN THIS CRUEL WAR IS OVER.

In the middle of the fight, the Spaniards say,

Dewey's squadron entered Manila Bay at night. Fighting began in early morning.

Spanish Admiral deserted his flagship, Maria Cristina, then on fire.

Captain Cadarso, commander of the Spanish flapship, was killed.

Besides fighting the enemy's ships American forces sustained a hot fire from Spanish forts.

PRAYER OF THANKS IN THE SENATE

Washington, May 2.—The chaplain's opening prayer in the Senate was a paen of triumph for the great victory of the American fleet at ... These are his words:

"We give Thee hearty thanks for the good news coming ... across the sea of the success with which Thou art crowning the ... discipline and valor of the officers and men of our Asiatic ...

"We bless Thee for the magnificent and unexampled ...

Hearst's version of the story led off with a screamer head of hand-drawn, four-inch letters that clearly topped Pulitzer's paper on the stands.

The Victorians

Porch done up in the late 19th Century style, Oakland, California.

Too Much Is Not Enough

Who knows how to be rich in America? Plenty of people know how to get money; but not very many know what best to do with it. To be rich properly is indeed a fine art. It requires culture, imagination and character. E. L. GODKIN IN *THE NATION*

In the long peace that followed the Civil War, the wealth of Americans multiplied prodigiously. Railroad builders, copper barons, ironmasters, gold miners, bankers, stockbrokers, public utilities operators and realty speculators joined war profiteers among the rich: by 1889, no fewer than 100 Americans could claim annual incomes of $1.2 million or more. In groping for culture to match their fortunes, many of these budding Brahmins fell victims to their untrained imaginations—and tastes. As a result, the era seemed for a time to be dominated by the conviction that nothing succeeds like excess.

In building new houses befitting their changed status, the Victorian rich hired architects who often mismated classic styles, endowing the offspring with cupolas, dormers, arches and gimcrackery, as in the house on the opposite page. Erected with no concern for cost, such structures conspicuously lacked grace, but they provided a satisfying degree of comfort for their owners.

The interiors were stuffed with settees, divans, ornate tables and armchairs. In these same rooms, the Victorians also tended to stuff themselves, giving elaborate dinner parties that ran 12 heavy courses or more. Eager to display their level of refinement, they strove to emulate the older civilization of Europe by punctuating their careful conversations with *au 'voirs* and *recherchés*, and avidly collected paintings and sculpture, good or bad, from abroad.

"People of our position would naturally be expected to have a Corot," Mrs. Potter Palmer, wife of the Chicago multimillionaire, was reported to have said in the 1880s. At about this same time Chicago novelist Henry B. Fuller had a fictional counterpart of Mrs. Palmer say: "We haven't got any Millet yet, but that morning thing over there is a Corot—at least, we think so."

This extravagance characterized almost every other phase of Victorian life. In the theater, every hero was a prodigy of courage and a paragon of virtue. In politics, every opponent was a black-hearted scoundrel. In manners and morals, every living move an American might make was carefully prescribed in eagerly read books of etiquette —and every dying move, too, for the arbiters of taste were very precise regarding the proper dress and attitudes at the era's elaborate funerals. Though some Americans found all this extravagant posturing to be nothing more than tiresome ego exercise, most would have agreed that Diamond Jim Brady epitomized the mood of the period when he said: "Hell, I'm rich. It's time I had some fun."

Typical of the ornate houses of the 1880s, this Portland, Oregon, residence is festooned with fretwork from porch steps to gable peak.

Ornate clutter fills a Minnesota living room (top), a Staten Island parlor (bottom) and a California girl's bedroom (right).

Like Nature herself, every prospering Victorian matron abhorred a vacuum in the living space of her own home. Accordingly, she stuffed every room from fanlight to floor with an eye-boggling collection of umbrellas and fans, plaster busts, wicker rockers, lamps and cushions, coat racks, china cabinets, small tables and countless other knickknacks. "Provided there is room enough to move about without walking over the furniture, there is hardly likely to be too much in a room," said one professional decorator. An amateur critic who thought otherwise was the novelist William Dean Howells, who acidly describes a typical furnished apartment in the excerpt below.

Everything had been done by the architect to save space, and everything to waste it by Mrs. Grosvenor Green. She had conformed to a law for the necessity of turning round in each room, and had folding-beds in the chambers; but wherever you might have turned round she had put a gimcrack so that you would knock it over if you did turn. Every shelf and dressing-case and mantel was littered with gimcracks. The front of the upright piano had what March called a short-skirted portière on it, and the top was covered with vases, with dragon candlesticks, and with fans. The floors were covered with filling, and then rugs, and then skins; the easy-chairs all had tidies, Armenian and Turkish and Persian; the lounges and sofas had embroidered cushions hidden under tidies. The radiator was concealed by a screen, and over the top of this some Arab scarfs were flung. There was a super-abundance of clocks. China pugs guarded the hearth. Some red Japanese bird-kites were stuck about in the necks of spelter vases, a crimson umbrella hung open beneath the chandelier, and each globe had a shade of yellow silk.

A HAZARD OF NEW FORTUNES, 1889

AN ORNATE DESIGN (Illus. No. 5)

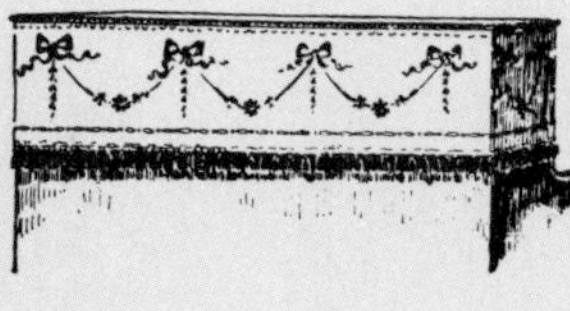

A SIMPLE DESIGN (Illus. No. 6)

THE BACK OF AN UPRIGHT PIANO

By James Thomson

WITH the prevailing fashion of placing the upright piano with its back toward the room has arisen the fashion of using drapery or some other method of decoration to adorn and beautify what otherwise would be a serious detriment to any parlor, no matter how artistic its other furnishing might be. As the adornment then of the back of the piano has become necessary, there are pre-

A FASHIONABLE DRAPERY (Illus. No. 1)

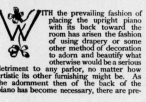

sented on this page several designs illustrative of such decoration; these designs will be found of simple and ornate fashion, and nearly all of them are made available by the use of any one of the many drapery fabrics sold at the art stores. Before describing the designs represented it may be well to state that whatever the method of decoration chosen, there should first be procured a pine board an inch in thickness, and in size a quarter of an inch larger than the upper ledge of the piano. This board may be padded on both sides, that its under side may not deface nor mar the piano lid. If economy is a consideration the board need only be padded where it will touch the polished surface. This board should then be covered with plush, velvet or any suitable material and will then be ready for the drapery, no part of which, it must be remembered, should be attached to the piano proper. By this method the board with the drapery attached may be removed at any time, and the piano will remain uninjured.

SIMPLE FESTOON DRAPE

THE effective design in Illustration No. 1 is a simple festoon drape, and will be found most effective when made up in the soft light goods such as China silk or satin damask. The heavier goods will not drape as gracefully in the small festoons and will look clumsy in comparsion. As may be seen this drapery can only be used when the piano has some sort of finished back. When the back must be entirely concealed a good plan is to attach at the top and bottom small brass sash rods, and to use China silk or any other soft material plaited or shirred on these.

ALMOST A SCREEN EFFECT (Illus. No. 2)

CONCEALING THE WOODWORK ENTIRELY

IN Illustration No. 2 will be found a design suitable for adoption where it is desired to conceal the woodwork altogether. The over-drapery may be omitted and the effect will still be pleasing. Heavier goods may be substituted for the under-drapery, and lighter material in harmonious coloring can be used for over-drapery. In making a choice of material particular attention should be paid to securing either a pleasing harmony or a judicious contrast of color, and in having these decorations conform as much as possible to the style, shape and furnishing of the music-room or parlor in which the piano is placed. The æsthetic yellows, olives, golden-browns, gray-blues, and dull reds or terra cottas will be found the most serviceable and useful tints to select, as they become less tiresome on long acquaintance than more vivid colors. In other words they are "better wearing" colors than most others.

UTILIZING A DIVAN

IN Illustration No. 3 is presented a very good scheme. By simply placing a small sofa or divan against the piano we have a very pleasing arrangement after the back has been suitably covered with drapery. This scheme can be carried out with any of the other designs.

A MIRROR BACK

A VERY effective design is shown in Illustration No. 4. A mirror in a plain frame is attached to the back of the piano, and a jardinière of flowers or plants is placed on the floor and against it. The effect of this reflected in the glass makes a most attractive feature. In any and all of these designs the edges of the board may be finished with gimp, cord-ball fringe, or studded with small brass nails in the design

A COZY ARRANGEMENT (Illus. No. 3)

of the fleur-de-lis, or star shapes. Pretty effects are in the form of valances, of which there are many variations, the designs shown in Illustrations No. 5 and No. 6 being examples. These are most suitable for ornamenting in embroidery or appliqué work.

DESIGN IN EMPIRE STYLE

ILLUSTRATION No. 7 shows a design in the Empire style. The ornaments here indicated are intended to be applied in gold and silver. These metal ornaments are made by machinery, are easily applied, and may be had in a great variety of designs, such as festoons, wreaths and harps; they also come in many different sizes.

CHOICE OF MATERIAL

THE choice of material for the covering of piano backs is not limited. Japanese leather, paper, cretonne or art silk, mohair plush, woolen reps or one of the pretty, changeable silks that are now so fashionable —even common burlap, plain or hand-decorated, will make a very good background indeed. A pile of gay floor cushions may be placed at the back of the piano. The colors chosen for them should, of course, correspond and harmonize with the back drapery. Then for additional drapery may be used one of the pretty silken scarfs, which may now be had at a moderate cost

MANY AND VARIED DESIGNS

THERE are many other arrangements similar to the designs here shown, such as placing a small screen, table or cabinet against the piano back, and arranging a drapery to conform. Palms make most effective aids in furnishing, and may be arranged in a great variety of ways. Another most effective object is a large brass peacock with plumage spread. This, placed against a suitable background, gives a most charming effect.

An open bookcase may be placed against the back of a draped piano. This will, perhaps, be found the most useful of all suggested backgrounds, although the bookcase cannot properly be considered as part of the furniture of the room in which the piano usually stands. But as books are always objects of interest, and as the upright piano is apt to be found in the family sitting-room, objection can hardly be made to its introduction on this score.

Upright pianos which are of necessity placed against a wall, should have a scarf,

AS IN A LOOKING-GLASS (Illus. No. 4)

at least a yard wide and three yards in length, of some soft, clinging material draped on them, and allowed to hang at the ends. Place pieces of bric-à-brac, which are sufficiently heavy to be steady, in effective groups on it; a bookrack, with a few musical books standing in it, will be effective, and a large portfolio, in which to lay loose sheets of music, most useful. And if possible, if you wish to preserve both the woodwork and tone of your instrument, have always a growing plant in the room with it.

SOME OTHER SUGGESTIONS

THE temperature of the room in which the piano is kept is one of the most important things to be considered. As moisture is absolutely necessary, see to it that the air in the room is not allowed to become too dry. The growing plant will prove a good test; if it thrives you may be sure that the atmosphere is such a one as your piano needs, and if, on the other hand, the plant does not thrive, it would be well to find out the reason. About seventy degrees is the proper temperature for the room in which the piano is kept. Do not allow it to stand where the sun's rays can shine directly upon it, and be careful to keep it closed and well covered while the sweeping and dusting of the room in which it stands are in progress.

To prevent the case of your piano from becoming smoky in appearance wipe a small portion at a time with a fine sponge wet in tepid water and a little Castile soap. Dry with a moistened chamois cloth which has been wrung until it is almost dry. When this has been done apply some reliable piano polish with a soft flannel cloth.

THE PRESENT RAGE (Illus. No. 7)

The piano so dominated every parlor that the Ladies' Home Journal of June 1893 gave three columns to dressing up the instrument. By 1899, the

75 million Americans owned a million pianos; pianos were increasing five times as fast as people, even adorning miners' tents in Colorado.

Monarch and His Domain

His wife called him Mister. His children, once they were out of swaddling clothes, addressed him as Sir. This was the American Father in the last Victorian decades, when the family was a microcosm of the state, and Father was its king, whether he sprawled with his feet and a drink on the table as at right or stood solemn and resplendent in frock coat, a heavy gold watch chain traversing his paunch. Every other member of the family had a role and a rank equally fixed by tradition.

But Father's head often lay as uneasy as any other that wears a crown. "The husbands are content to slave in business in order that their wives and families may live in ease and affluence," two English observers named Rivington and Harris reported in their *Reminiscences of America*, published as the '70s began. This was true at least of the upper middle class. Under the pressure to make money, Father worked as many as 10 or more hours a day, six days a week, so his wife managed not only the household, but frequently the family finances as well. The affluence he provided gave her servants and time to improve herself by reading and by studying the arts. Most husbands approved, unaware of the threats to their own supremacy. As the century moved on, women were less and less willing to accept their traditionally subservient role. Divorce, although far from respectable, increased from about 11,000 nationwide in 1870 to 55,751 in 1900 and served to restrain intolerably overbearing spouses.

The rights-for-women movement, too, began to flourish. Though most men found it amusing that women should want to vote, in the Wyoming Territory by 1869 they already could, and the idea was spreading. Women's insistence on a more emancipated role was also eliminating other manifestations of male dominance. Until 1882, for example, a husband owned even the clothing and jewelry he had given his wife; by 1900 women in a majority of states legally controlled their own property.

By century's end, it was all too clear to Father that the benevolent despotism he had exercised over family life was becoming, at an accelerated pace, a limited monarchy in which his wife was not only a consort but a queen.

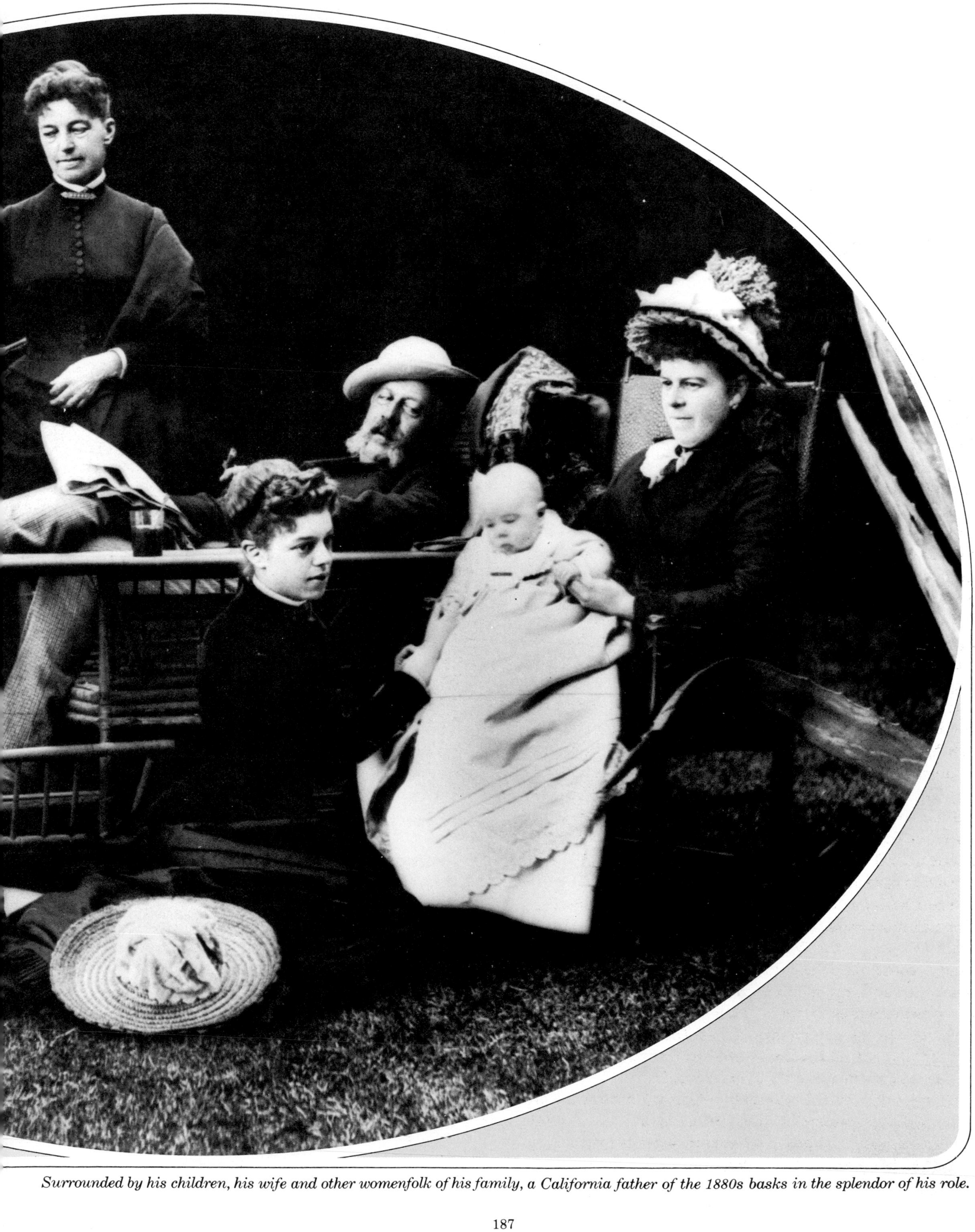

Surrounded by his children, his wife and other womenfolk of his family, a California father of the 1880s basks in the splendor of his role.

Though marriage was still the primary goal of the Victorian woman, an increasing number of females in the late 19th Century showed a willingness to wait a while before donning the bridal gown. New job opportunities opening in industry and the professions permitted modern women the luxury of choosing a $15-a-week job of their own or a $12-a-week husband. Such options, however, did not inhibit marriage: of 20 million women and girls over 14 in 1890, thirteen million wore wedding rings. "The very fact that marriage (with or without love) is not incessantly in the foreground of an American girl's consciousness probably makes the awakening all the more deep and tender," the Englishman James F. Muirhead wrote in his 1898 book, *The Land of Contrasts*. To keep it deep and tender, there was plenty of advice. Thomas E. Hill's *Manual of Social and Business Forms* recommended that the husband be "strong, brave and wise" and the wife, far from being emancipated, need only be "confident in his bravery, strength and wisdom."

The dark tones of an immigrant's old-country wedding gown contrast with the frothy white dresses of three native brides of the 1880s.

For the Victorian woman, elegance of appearance surpassed almost all other aspirations, and her hair and her gowns were the chief means by which she tried to achieve it. In a still religious America, she heeded the New Testament dictum that "if a woman have long hair, it is a glory to her"; she never cut it, but in this period of primness, she also never let it fall unfettered to her waist. Instead, she piled it on her head *(top)* in the 1870s, tortured it into ringlets *(bottom left and center)* in the 1880s and arrayed it to frame her face *(second row, right)* in the 1890s. In dress, she swathed her body in reams of silks and satins—up to 20 yards went into an afternoon gown like the one at right.

Bustles like this reigned in 1876 but eventually grew smaller, until the bicycle and the slim, athletic Gibson girl banished them altogether.

By the late 1890s, beards were waning again, but Eastern dudes like this still sported the handlebar mustache popularized by Westerners.

"The gods and heroes wear beards," proclaimed Robert de Valcourt, a Victorian. And the late Victorian man, determined to look both god and hero, sprouted an infinite variety of facial adornment. This hairiness was a marked departure. No Founding Father sported a beard; Uncle Sam wore none until 1858. Then beards and mustaches suddenly bloomed everywhere. Gold prospectors and fast-shooting marshals made them a mark of virility. Distinguished thinkers like Carl Schurz gave them an air of intellectuality. Finally, Abe Lincoln, growing a beard after a little girl said it might help his looks, established facial hair as a male status symbol of the era.

For small boys, the period posed a problem of identity and occasionally of self-defense. By nature, the normal youngster saw himself as a Tom Sawyer. And in fact he often was; Mark Twain had drawn his hero from memory. But the mothers of many small boys preferred to recast their offspring as Little Lord Fauntleroy, a fictional, golden-curled goody-good *(below)* who called his mamma "Dearest," wore spotless velvet suits and precociously discussed world affairs with the grocer. As a result of the motherly fascination with the doll-like Fauntleroy, many unfortunate sons had to face the streets coifed and dressed in the styles at right. Naturally there were hoots and sneers from youngsters who had escaped such maternal excesses. And just as naturally, there were some hard-knuckled confrontations from which many a Fauntleroy emerged looking and feeling much more like the good, tough Tom Sawyer he really was in his heart.

He started in life with a quantity of soft, fine, gold-colored hair, which curled up at the ends, and went into loose rings; he had big brown eyes and long eyelashes and a darling little face. His manners were so good, for a baby, that it was delightful to make his acquaintance. When he was old enough to walk out with his nurse, wearing a short white kilt skirt, and a big white hat set back on his curly yellow hair, he was so handsome and strong and rosy that he attracted every one's attention, and his nurse would come home and tell his mamma stories of the ladies who had stopped their carriages to look at and speak to him. His childish soul was full of kindness and innocent feeling.

LITTLE LORD FAUNTLEROY BY FRANCES HODGSON BURNETT, 1886

Reluctant Fauntleroys were stuffed by their mammas into fur-trimmed velvet, fancy shirtwaists and starched white suits they abhorred.

The personification of sugar and spice, 19 little girls in California treat their dolls to a tea party on a lawn in 1887. Such frolics were regarded

us sound training for an era when most girls married young and spent the rest of their lives managing households that averaged five people.*

In proper hat and floor-length skirt of 1898, a visitor stiffly takes tea in a Michigan parlor while the hostess sits on an overstuffed couch.

Doing the Right Thing

In the boom times of the late 19th Century, many newly prospering Americans were not at all sure how to handle themselves in company. So they tended to live by rigid rules of etiquette. A typical Victorian matron, determined never to commit a faux pas which might disgrace her or her family, might buy half a dozen of the numerous books of social rules that were published, telling her just how to behave on a picnic or how to give a proper birthday party or how and when to pay a simple call on a friend.

"Where lunch is served at one o'clock, and dinner at six or seven o'clock, the calling hours are from two to five," Mrs. H. O. Ward counseled such social-minded ladies as the tea drinkers opposite, in her 1878 volume, *Sensible Etiquette of the Best Society.* One never left the spoon in the cup, Mrs. Ward added. The innocents who bought such books wanted to know, too, whether mashed potatoes should be eaten with a knife or a fork, and whether napkins (yes) and finger bowls (no) were correct at breakfast.

Mature single ladies turned to Mrs. John Sherwood, whose *Manners and Social Usages,* published in 1884, ruled on such subtler issues as the propriety of an "elderly girl of 35" visiting an artist's studio alone. Said Mrs. Sherwood, "There is in art itself an ennobling and purifying influence which should be a protection"; but the book went on to warn the adventuring spinster that "it would seem wiser that she should be attended by a friend or companion" to avoid "even the remotest appearance of evil." Could the same girl go unchaperoned to the theater with a man? Yes. Should she allow him to pay for her ticket? No! "In permitting a gentleman to expend money for her pleasures, a lady assumes an obligation to him which time and chance may render oppressive."

As a result of all this advice and moralizing, an occasion such as the Washington, D.C., afternoon call that Mark Twain describes below could become a social exercise that slid beyond propriety into paralyzing boredom.

The ladies entered the drawing-room in full character; that is to say, with Elizabethan stateliness on the part of the dowager, and an easy grace and dignity on the part of the young lady that had a nameless something about it that suggested conscious superiority. The dresses of both ladies were exceedingly rich, as to material, but as notably modest as to color and ornament. All parties having seated themselves, the dowager delivered herself of a remark that was not unusual in its form, and yet it came from her lips with the impressiveness of Scripture:

"The weather has been unpropitious, Miss Hawkins."

"It has indeed," said Laura. "The climate seems to be variable."

"It is its nature, here," said the daughter—stating it apparently as a fact, and by her manner waving aside all personal responsibility on account of it. "Is it not so, mamma?"

"Quite so, my child. Do you like winter, Miss Hawkins?" She said "like" as if she had an idea that its dictionary meaning was "approve of."

"Not as well as summer—though I think all seasons have their charms."

"It is a very just remark. The general held similar views. He considered snow in winter proper; sultriness in summer legitimate; frosts in the autumn the same, and rains in spring not objectionable. He was not an exacting man. And I call to mind now that he always admired thunder. You remember, child, your father always admired thunder?"

"He adored it."

"No doubt it reminded him of battle," said Laura.

"Yes, I think perhaps it did."

THE ADVENTURES OF COLONEL SELLERS, 1873

Clad in their Sunday best, a very proper Atlanta couple sets out from home in the vehicle called a tea cart to pay a call. Although the solemnity of

the Victorian Sabbath gradually eased, a prim visit after midday dinner or a trip to a museum was about as far as many decent folk dared go.

Their good manners hammered into them since their infancy, 18 scrubbed, dressed-up boys and girls cheerfully wait for the adult signal

before diving into an imposing array of cakes spread out before them at a birthday party in a prosperous New York City home.

"It is curious to see how emphatically fond of picnics Americans are," wrote Mrs. M. E. W. Sherwood, author of a book of advice on family amusements. "A universal national hunger seems to seize the tired cit as the first warm day of May beams upon us." To satisfy this hunger, American city dwellers packed off to go picnicking in the lavish style shown by the ladies at right and by San Francisco's freewheeling Bohemian Club *(above)*. In the same extravagant way, they went hunting, fishing, canoeing (railways advertised canoe racks on freight cars) and camping. More and more women began to share in these outdoor pastimes—and a good thing, too, noted Mrs. Sherwood, who observed primly that a lady camper "acts as a temporary restraint on the too volatile spirits of the party."

Roughing it in their Old Ladies Home (note sign) beneath a giant sequoia, California ladies listen as their group leader reads aloud.

Sober lives demanded sober endings, with properly protracted periods of mourning for the departed. Members of this Richmond, Virginia, famil

go on wearing funereal black as they gather ceremoniously on their estate to plant a tree three months after the death of a grandmother.

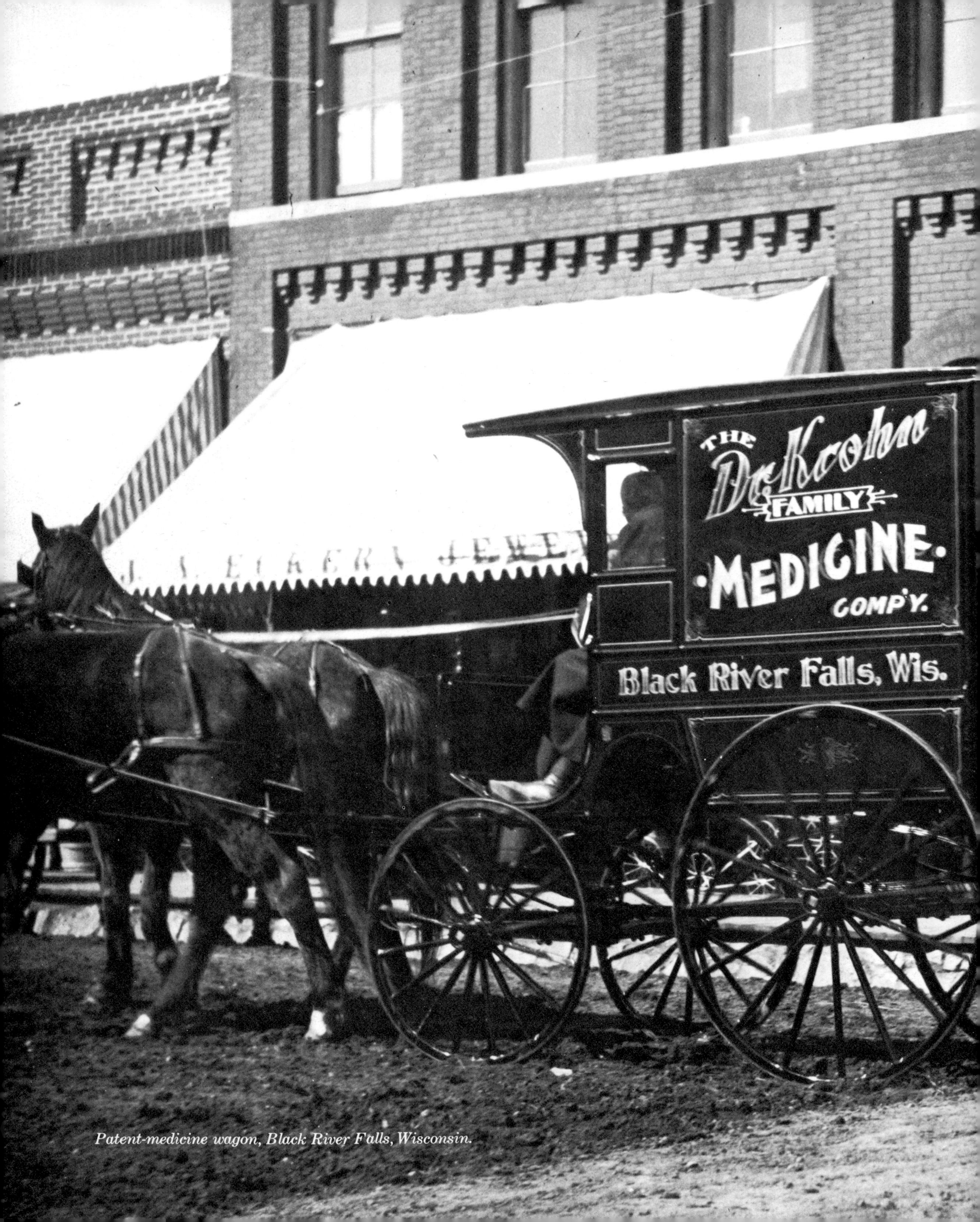

Patent-medicine wagon, Black River Falls, Wisconsin.

Nostrums

Cure-Alls with a Kick

To draw the line nicely, and fix definitely where the medicine may end and the alcoholic beverage begin, is a task which has often perplexed and still greatly perplexes revenue officers.

COMMISSIONER OF INTERNAL REVENUE, 1883

When Johnny came marching home from the Civil War, he was likely at some time to have suffered from one of the so-called camp diseases—dysentery, malaria or typhoid. In those primitive medical times, he was also likely to have treated himself with a patent medicine such as Radway's Ready Relief, with which a noncom of the 8th Maine dosed some troops afflicted by typhoid and dysentery and claimed to have cured them. Johnny carried the home-remedy habit into civilian life, thus giving a great boost to the patent-medicine industry.

In the period 1870 to 1900, virtually every ailment had its own ready cure: indigestion (Hostetter's Celebrated Stomach Bitters), chronic fatigue (Ayer's Sarsaparilla), aching muscles (Barker's Liniment—"Joy to the World, Relief Has Come"). There were elixirs for those who felt they lacked sex appeal. Egyptian Regulator Tea would bring "graceful plumpness" to flat-chested girls. Rengo medicine would "turn fat into muscle" for flabby men.

Most nostrum promoters presented their products as derivatives of America's popular folk-cure tradition: home-brewed remedies concocted by simple people whose earthy wisdom about the body and its ills gave them no need of fancy doctoring. And the public fell for it. When a fiftyish Massachusetts housewife marketed her cure for "female weakness," the public responded so warmly that Lydia E. Pinkham's Vegetable Compound grossed $300,000 in 1883—just 10 years after Mrs. Pinkham sold her first six bottles for $5.00. Many patents were billed as Indian cures (Who had more instinctive wisdom than the red man?). One fast seller was the buffalo salve (for scabby scalps) ballyhooed by the braves in the touring Kickapoo Indian Medicine Company. But the most aggressive patent-medicine pushers used the new art of newspaper advertising *(pages 212-213)* to expand their markets.

There were, of course, two fundamental facts about the whole patent-medicine business. It was a fraud, and a particularly dangerous fraud when it advertised nostrums for incurable diseases such as "consumption" (tuberculosis). Second, virtually all the most popular patents were loaded with hard drugs or alcohol. Dr. King's New Discovery for Consumption contained chloroform and opium, which quieted the consumptive's cough and raised his spirits for a short time, but left the tubercle bacillus to flourish. And the amount of plain alcohol in other common cures ranged from a ladylike 18 per cent in Mrs. Pinkham's Compound to a robust 44 per cent in Hostetter's Bitters.

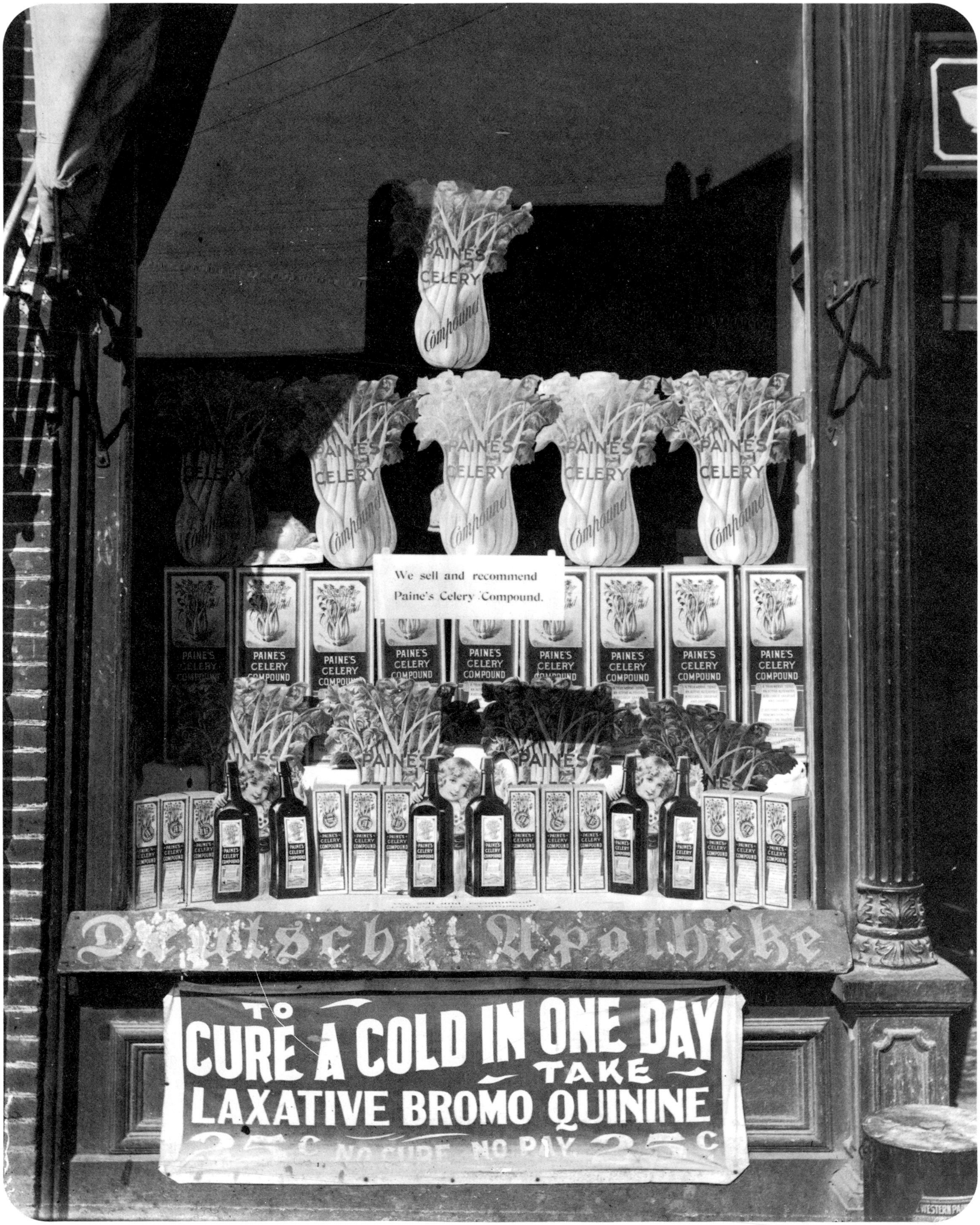

In 1898 a Junction City, Kansas, store sold a tonic whose 21 per cent alcoholic content kept it—and the consumer—from freezing in winter.

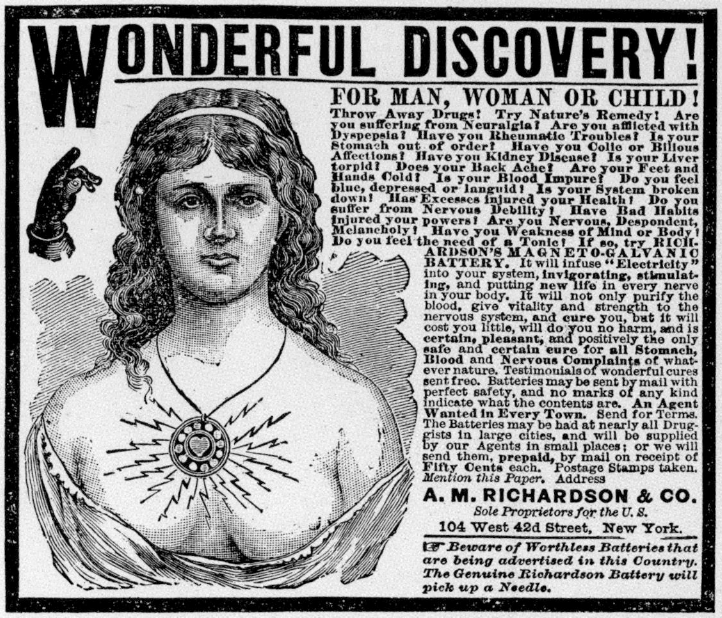

WONDERFUL DISCOVERY!
FOR MAN, WOMAN OR CHILD!
Throw Away Drugs! Try Nature's Remedy! Are you suffering from Neuralgia? Are you afflicted with Dyspepsia? Have you Rheumatic Troubles? Is your Stomach out of order? Have you Colic or Billous Affections? Have you Kidney Disease? Is your Liver torpid? Does your Back Ache? Are your Feet and Hands Cold? Is your Blood Impure? Do you feel blue, depressed or languid? Is your System broken down? Has Excesses injured your Health? Do you suffer from Nervous Debility? Have Bad Habits injured your powers? Are you Nervous, Despondent, Melancholy? Have you Weakness of Mind or Body? Do you feel the need of a Tonic? If so, try RICHARDSON'S MAGNETO-GALVANIC BATTERY. It will infuse "Electricity" into your system, invigorating, stimulating, and putting new life in every nerve in your body. It will not only purify the blood, give vitality and strength to the nervous system, and cure you, but it will cost you little, will do you no harm, and is certain, pleasant, and positively the only safe and certain cure for all Stomach, Blood and Nervous Complaints of whatever nature. Testimonials of wonderful cures sent free. Batteries may be sent by mail with perfect safety, and no marks of any kind indicate what the contents are. An Agent Wanted in Every Town. Send for Terms. The Batteries may be had at nearly all Druggists in large cities, and will be supplied by our Agents in small places; or we will send them, prepaid, by mail on receipt of Fifty Cents each. Postage Stamps taken. Mention this Paper. Address
A. M. RICHARDSON & CO.
Sole Proprietors for the U. S.
104 West 42d Street, New York.
Beware of Worthless Batteries that are being advertised in this Country. The Genuine Richardson Battery will pick up a Needle.

THE IDEAL SIGHT RESTORER
IDEAL SIGHT RESTORER
THE INESTIMABLE BLESSING OF SIGHT.
AVOID SPECTACLES & EYEGLASSES. HEADACHE & SURGICAL OPERATION. ILLUSTRATED PAMPHLET ON THE EYE. MAILED FREE.
THE IDEAL COMPANY, 239 BROADWAY, NEW YORK.

DR. SCOTT'S ELECTRIC TOOTH BRUSH.
A Remarkable Invention!!
Great Annoyance has been caused to all people using Tooth Brushes by the bristles coming out in the mouth. The Pall Mall Electric Association of London now take pleasure in introducing to the American public a Tooth Brush which they guarantee free from this troublesome defect, common to all other Tooth Brushes. The bristles are inserted in the handle by a patented process, which renders it simply impossible for them to come out in use. They are
WARRANTED THE MOST DURABLE IN THE WORLD.
In addition to this, the handle of the Brush is made of a newly invented material permanently charged with an electro-magnetic current, which acts, without any shock, immediately upon the nerves and tissues of the teeth and gums. The act of brushing causes this current to flow into the nerve cells and roots of the teeth, and, like water poured upon a plant, it invigorates and vitalizes every part, arresting decay, building up and restoring the natural whiteness of the enamel, and quickly imparting pearly teeth and healthful, rosy gums to all using it.
The handle is strong, beautifully polished, not affected by acids, impervious to moisture, and forever free from that unpleasant, musty odor exuding from wet, bone handles.
Read the following:
The "DENTAL REVIEW" says:
"The Electric Tooth Brush answers a long felt want, and we are convinced that it will prevent decay, and in a rational and healthy manner quickly restore the white Natural Color of the teeth unless decay is too far advanced. We congratulate the proprietors and the public upon its introduction, and believe its sale will be almost unlimited. We understand that it has already made its way into the toilets of leading London society, and we wish it all success, as it deserves."
THE ROYAL DENTAL SOCIETY of England
Testify in the strongest terms as to the quick benefits following the use of this Brush, and many experts in dentistry declare it to be the greatest invention in dental appliances since the manufacture of false teeth.
J. C. VARLEY, Esq., the Eminent Electrician, writes:
"GENTLEMEN: Your Electric Tooth Brush must prove a boon to humanity. In all of my connection with electricity and its effects, I have never known it likely to do direct good to so many people as in its application to your Tooth Brush. You have my full encouragement and indorsement, and henceforth no other Tooth Brush shall be used in my family."
DR. SCOTT'S "ELECTRIC" LONDON
Ask for Dr. SCOTT'S. For sale by all Druggists and Dentists, or we will mail it on receipt of 55 cents, post-paid.
50 CENTS EACH. POST-PAID.
It is time that a long-suffering public should know that the ordinary tooth brushes sold at 20c., 25c., and 30c., each, are all defective ones or "seconds," as they are called in the trade. Every maker carefully sorts out these defective brushes and sells them at a low price, while his first quality retail at from 35c. to 60c. each.
You may rely upon this being the invariable rule, as any honest druggist will tell you if you ask him.
A BEAUTIFUL BRUSH We will send it on trial, post-paid, on receipt of 55 cents, which will be returned if not as represented.
Seven Brushes will be mailed for the price of six, or request your nearest druggist, dentist, or fancy store to obtain one for you, and be sure Dr. Scott's name is on the Brush. MONEY RETURNED if not as REPRESENTED.
As soon as you receive the Brush, if not well satisfied with your bargain, write us, and we will return the money. What can be fairer!
Remittances should be made payable to GEO. A. SCOTT, 842 Broadway, New-York. They can be made in Checks, Drafts, Post-Office Orders, Currency, or Stamps. Agents wanted in every town. MENTION CENTURY.

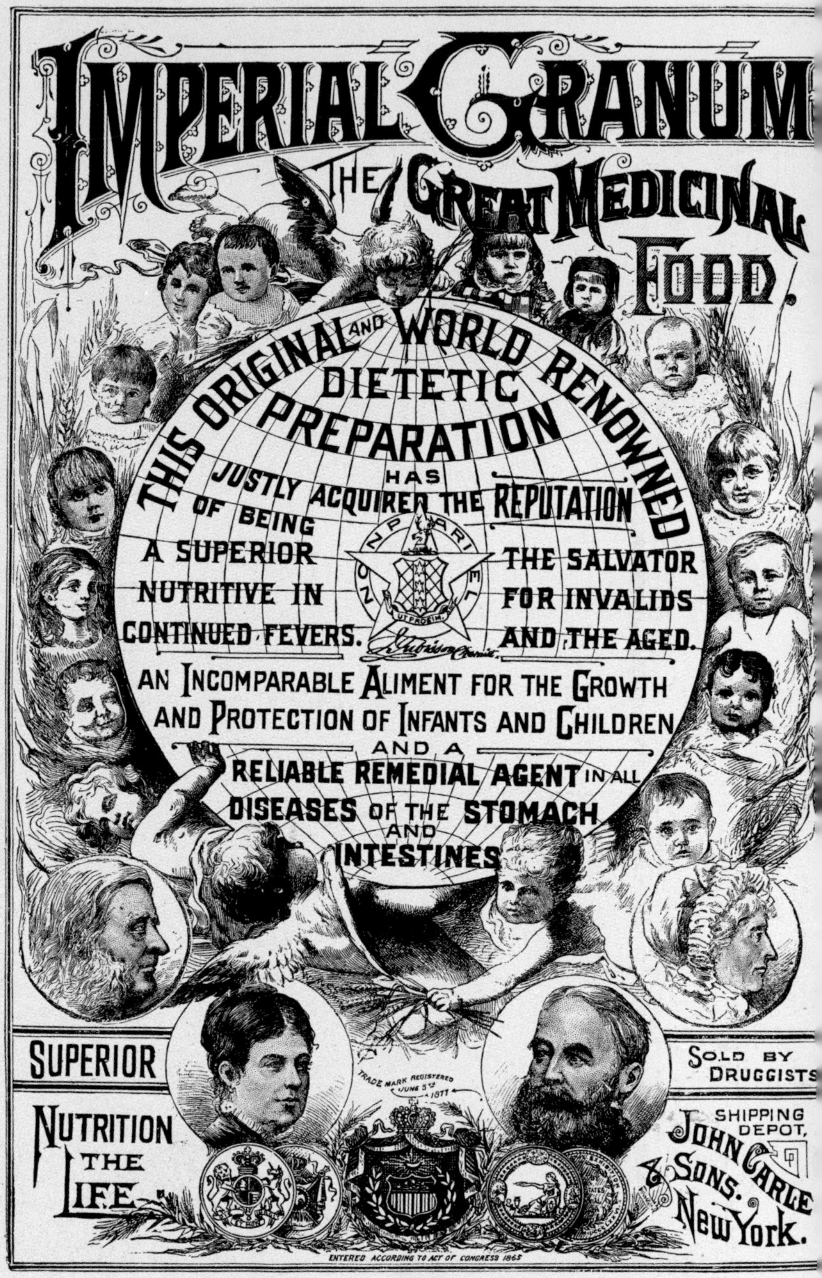

IMPERIAL GRANUM
THE GREAT MEDICINAL FOOD.
THIS ORIGINAL AND WORLD RENOWNED DIETETIC PREPARATION HAS JUSTLY ACQUIRED THE REPUTATION OF BEING
A SUPERIOR NUTRITIVE IN CONTINUED FEVERS.
THE SALVATOR FOR INVALIDS AND THE AGED.
AN INCOMPARABLE ALIMENT FOR THE GROWTH AND PROTECTION OF INFANTS AND CHILDREN
AND A
RELIABLE REMEDIAL AGENT IN ALL DISEASES OF THE STOMACH AND INTESTINES
SUPERIOR NUTRITION THE LIFE
SOLD BY DRUGGISTS
SHIPPING DEPOT, JOHN CARLE & SONS. New York.
ENTERED ACCORDING TO ACT OF CONGRESS 1865

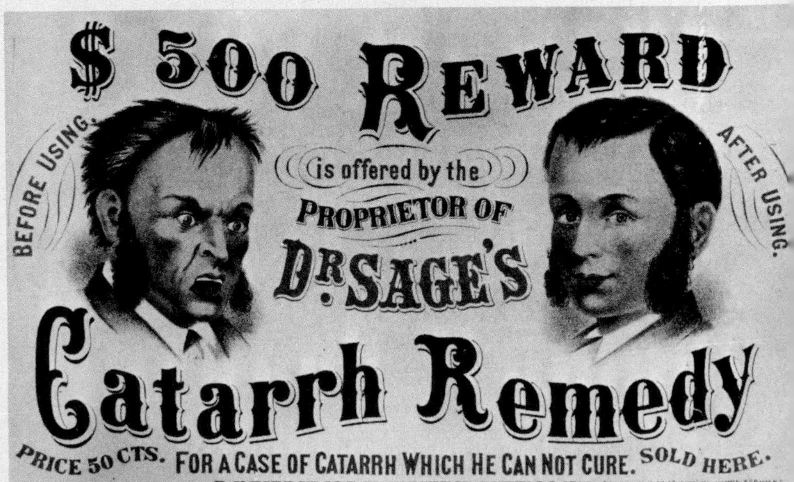

$ 500 REWARD
BEFORE USING.
AFTER USING.
is offered by the
PROPRIETOR OF
DR SAGE'S
Catarrh Remedy
PRICE 50 CTS.
FOR A CASE OF CATARRH WHICH HE CAN NOT CURE.
SOLD HERE.
R.V.PIERCE, M.D. PROPRIETOR, BUFFALO, N.Y.

Home-remedy makers were the most prolific advertisers in the U.S. during the 1880s. Nostrum peddling proved the best possible training for

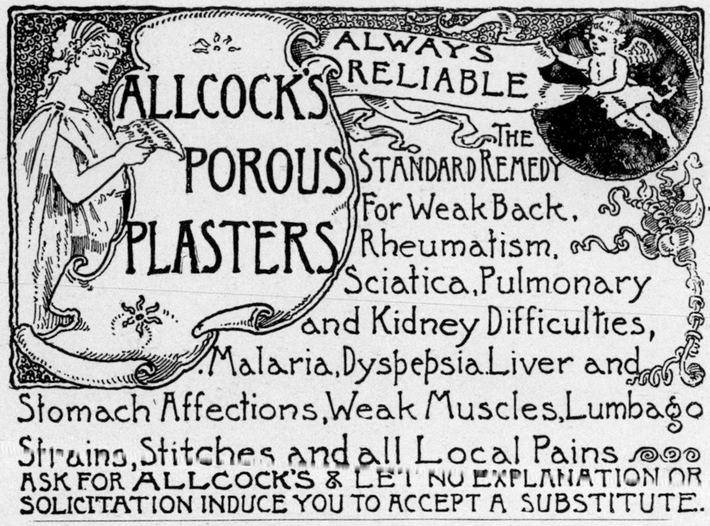

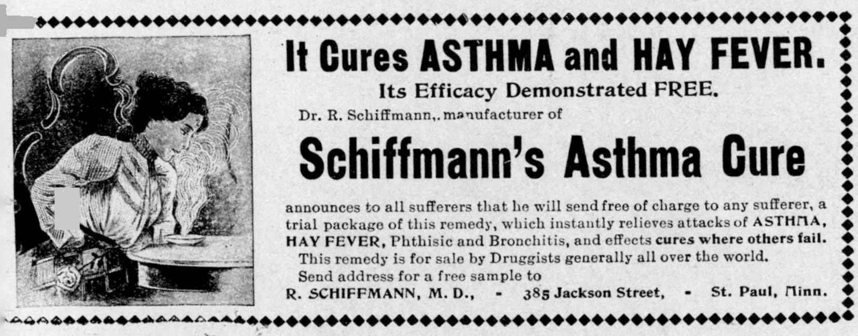

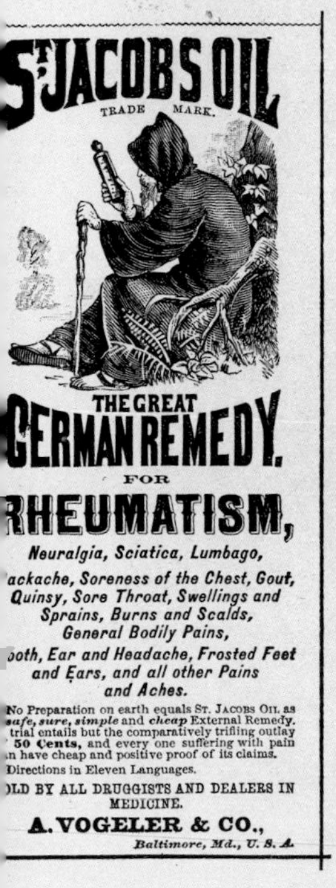

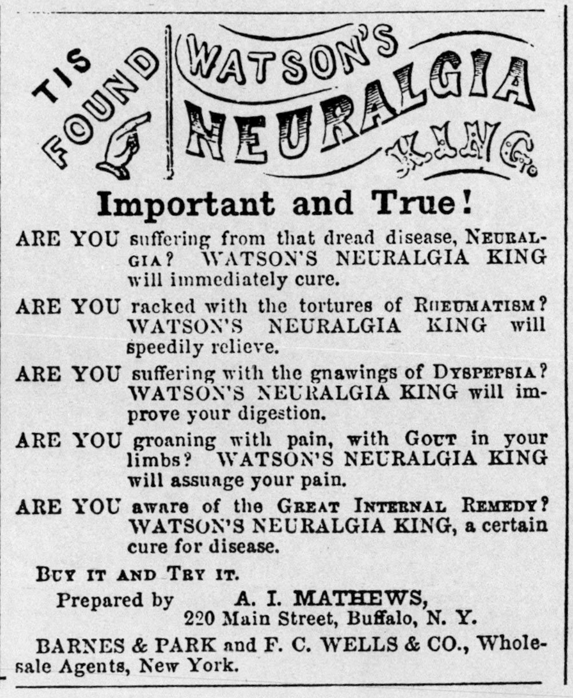

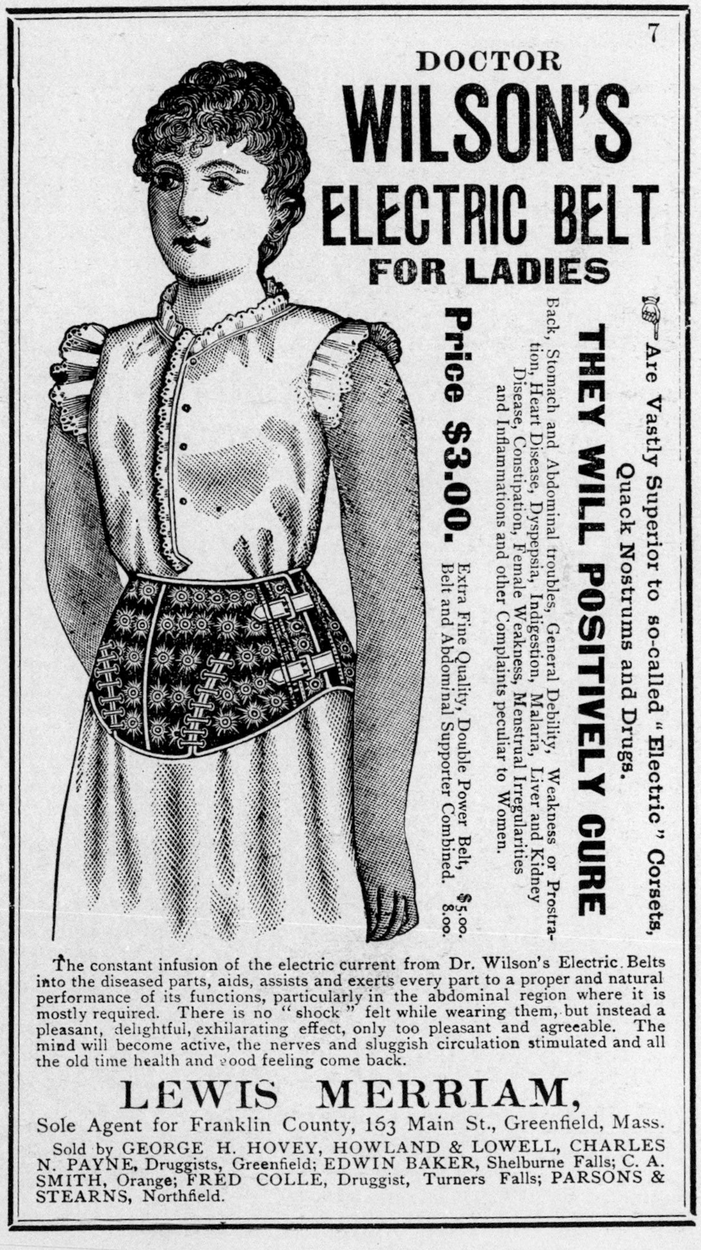

copywriters in the nation's pioneer ad agencies; the products were basically so useless it took a good man to make them seem worth buying.

Patent-medicine companies sent drugstores bushels of trade cards like these, to use as free handouts. Card-swapping became such a big fad

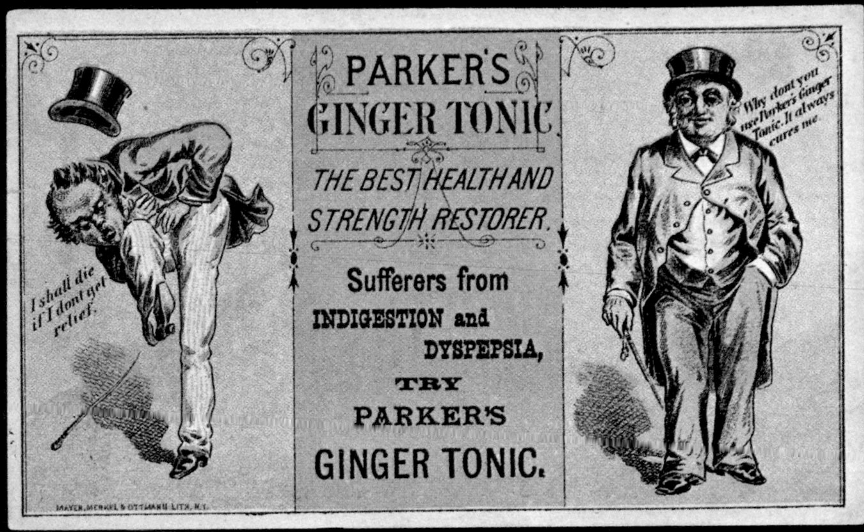

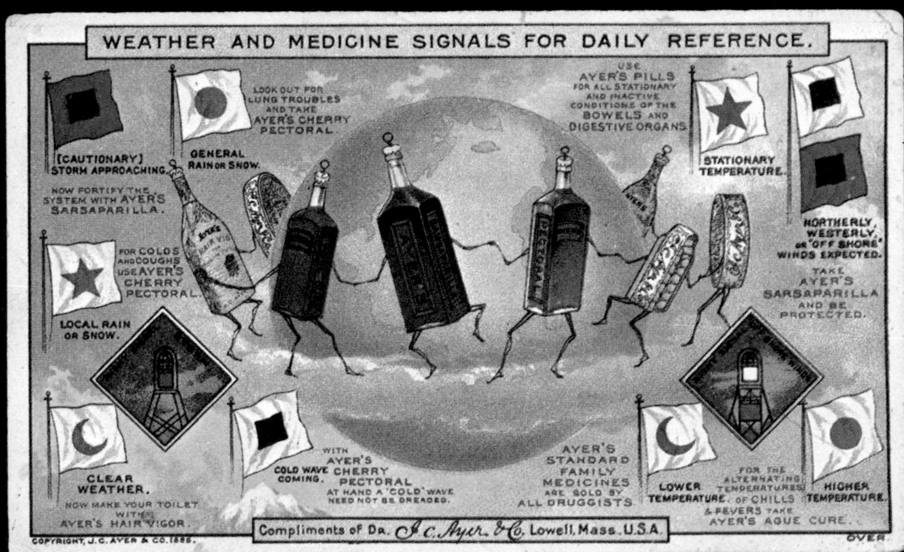

among kids, who bedeviled druggists for the latest printings, that a popular song was written with the refrain, "Mister, got a pikcha card?"

As early as the 1840s, nostrum makers began giving away almanacs loaded down with patent-medicine advertising. By the 1890s some 30 million patent almanacs were being distributed annually to a population that numbered in the 60 millions. For rural families, these free almanacs were often the only new book of the year; and one company boasted that its almanac was "second only to the Bible in circulation." The almanacs were splattered with praise of the company's product, couched in the most elaborate prose—"The facts relating to [the product] we do not wish to embellish by hyperbole, or lessen the force by exaggeration"—but in with all the huckstering was a potpourri of astrology, long-range weather forecasts and jokes *(below)* that entertained U.S. farm families throughout the year.

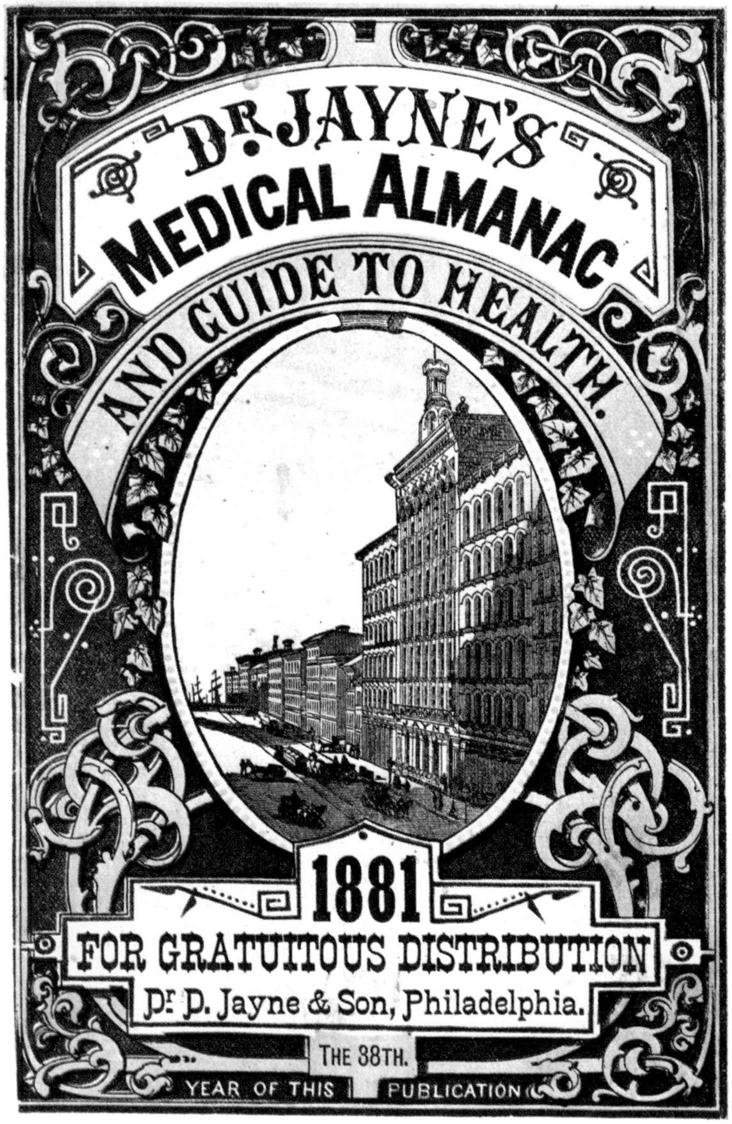

A lady once went to Dublin Castle in such very full dress that more bust than fabric was visible. "Did you ever see anything so unblushing?" said someone to the archbishop. "Never, since I was weaned," replied the wit.

A snob is a being on a ladder, who is quite as ready to kiss the feet of him who is above him as to kick the hand of him who is below.

When the girl who has encouraged a young man for several years tells him she can never be more than a sister to him, he can for the first time see the freckles on her nose.

You require in marriage precisely the same quality that you would in eating sausage—absolute confidence.

The politician of the insect world is the flea. He is ever itching for place, creates no end of disturbance, and you never know where to find him.

Any man who looks on the dark side of life will find it.

A widow weeping over the new-made grave of her husband finally dried her eyes and said, "There is one comfort in it anyhow; I shall know where he is at night."

The art of conversation is the art of hearing as well as being heard.

HOSTETTER'S ILLUSTRATED UNITED STATES ALMANAC

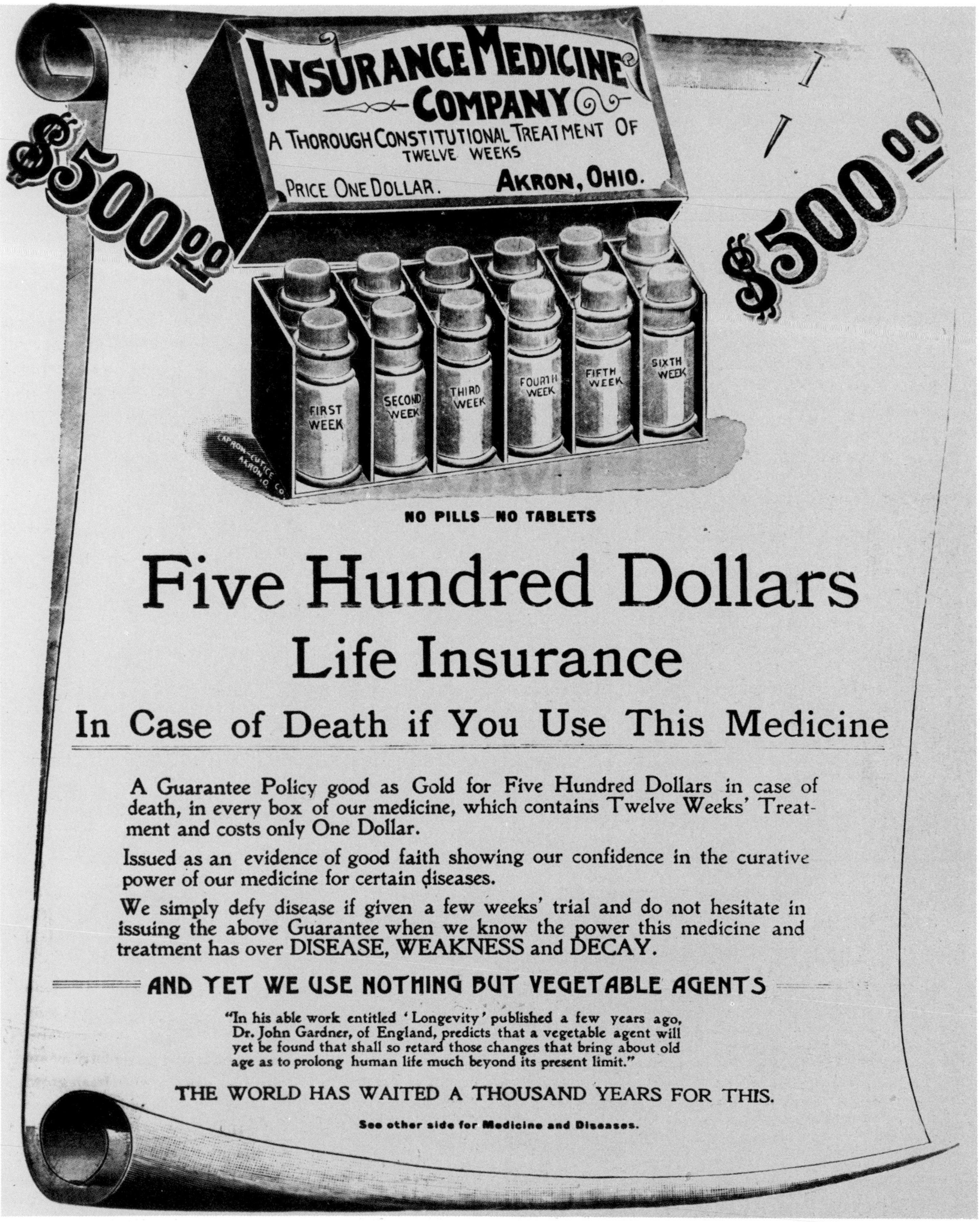
INSURANCE MEDICINE COMPANY
A THOROUGH CONSTITUTIONAL TREATMENT OF TWELVE WEEKS
PRICE ONE DOLLAR.
AKRON, OHIO.
$500.00
$500.00
FIRST WEEK
SECOND WEEK
THIRD WEEK
FOURTH WEEK
FIFTH WEEK
SIXTH WEEK
NO PILLS—NO TABLETS
Five Hundred Dollars
Life Insurance
In Case of Death if You Use This Medicine
A Guarantee Policy good as Gold for Five Hundred Dollars in case of death, in every box of our medicine, which contains Twelve Weeks' Treatment and costs only One Dollar.
Issued as an evidence of good faith showing our confidence in the curative power of our medicine for certain diseases.
We simply defy disease if given a few weeks' trial and do not hesitate in issuing the above Guarantee when we know the power this medicine and treatment has over DISEASE, WEAKNESS and DECAY.
AND YET WE USE NOTHING BUT VEGETABLE AGENTS
"In his able work entitled 'Longevity' published a few years ago, Dr. John Gardner, of England, predicts that a vegetable agent will yet be found that shall so retard those changes that bring about old age as to prolong human life much beyond its present limit."
THE WORLD HAS WAITED A THOUSAND YEARS FOR THIS.
See other side for Medicine and Diseases.

Any nostrum user or his family could take final comfort from the generous, good-as-gold offer of this modest patent-medicine maker.

ROCKWOOD'S PORTRAITS

The City

Laying cable-car track, New York, 1891.

The Magic Metropolis

The thoroughfares are crowded, busy and bustling; and abounding signs of life and energy in the people are everywhere apparent.

BRITISH AUTHOR SIR JOHN LENG, *AMERICA IN 1876*

"We cannot all live in cities, yet nearly all seem determined to do so," journalist Horace Greeley commented in the late 1860s. Despite such warnings, in the next three decades the United States became a nation dominated by its urban centers. Between 1870 and 1900 the population of Detroit leaped from 79,500 to 285,700; Los Angeles from 5,700 to 102,400; Atlanta from 21,700 to 89,800; Philadelphia from 674,000 to 1,293,000.

Most of the new urban dwellers had come from the farm. Some had been pushed off the land by mechanized farm equipment that enabled one man to do the work of six. Others, particularly the young, were ambitious dreamers hankering to exchange what Wisconsin-born author Hamlin Garland described as the "filthy drudgery of the farm yard" for the promise of a "care-free companionable existence" in town. In the city, they were joined by millions of immigrants, lured by the hope of finding America's streets paved with gold; five million entered the U.S. in the 1880s alone, and nearly all settled in cities.

Once there, many of the new arrivals faced a harsh awakening. Some immigrants found themselves stuffed into six-story tinderbox tenements; others were housed in dismal wooden row houses, thrown up right next to factories that smirched them with soot and smoke. Typhoid and cholera swept through such slums and in 1880 the Chicago *Times* reported in disgust: "The river stinks. The air stinks. People's clothing, permeated by the foul atmosphere, stinks. No other word expresses it so well as stink."

Yet rising above smoke and filth, the American city of 1870 to 1900 also presented a façade as filled with magic as had been the dreams of the immigrants. Skyscrapers soared up to 20 stories high, with electric elevators running miraculously up and down inside. Giant bridges reached across rivers over 1,000 feet wide. Horseless trolleys crisscrossed cities at the incredible speed of 20 mph. Towns sparkled at night with the marvel of electric street lighting; Cleveland inaugurated the first municipal arc light system in 1879, and the Bijou Theatre in Boston followed by electrically illuminating a theatrical performance for the first time, with a dazzling array of 650 bulbs.

At the turn of the century, the largest, wealthiest and most populous of these bursting urban centers was New York. And the description of that metropolis, offered in a phrase by a British visitor, was an eloquent summation of the U.S. city of the era: "a lady in ball costume, with diamonds in her ears, and her toes out at her boots."

Decked out in afternoon finery, a party of San Franciscans leaves the California Theater on Bush Street after a matinee in 1877.

In an effort to combat the ill effects of sedentary city life, clerks at the National Cash Register Co. in Dayton, Ohio, break for calisthenics.

There are certain injurious influences which are peculiar to cities, and affect the well-to-do as well as the poor. Walking on an even surface, the only variety of physical exercise which most business and professional men get in town, is well known to be a poor substitute for arm-exertion. A man may walk, in an hour, four miles on a city side-walk, and reach his desk tired, exhausted of force, and better only for the open air and a slight increase of the circulation. Had he spent half that time in a well ordered gymnasium, using chest and rowing-weights, and after a sponge-bath, if he had gone by rapid transit to his office, he would have found his work of a very different color, easier to do and taking less time to perform it. The remedy for this state of things is to cause every man and woman to realize the importance of arm exercise.

WALTER B. PLATT, M.D., BALTIMORE, 1887

Supported by 16-inch steel cables, the Brooklyn Bridge carries trains, trolleys and pedestrians across the East River to New York.

A Giant Stride for Builders

Steel arches of the Eads Bridge reach out across the Mississippi.

"With the waters of the Atlantic, the Pacific, the Gulf and the Lakes commingled, emblematic of the Union effected by these mighty spans, I christen this structure the Illinois and St. Louis bridge, and invoke the blessings of the Almighty on it." So spoke Mrs. Julius S. Walsh, wife of a St. Louis railroad magnate on July 4, 1874, as she stood in a black, grosgrain silk dress by the new 1,500-foot Eads Bridge spanning the Mississippi. Then she stepped forward and solemnly sprinkled the massive structure with the four waters from solid silver pitchers. In this genteel manner, America's first major steel structure *(above)* was officially opened.

With its inauguration came a new era in city building. Until then architects and engineers had been limited in the size of their structures by the brittle quality and weight of iron and masonry. But by the 1870s these materials had become inadequate as cities were pressing to expand outward across major rivers and upward into taller buildings. Only a superstrong, flexible building material could make such goals attainable, and it was found in the form of steel, just beginning to be mass produced.

The pioneer who took the first giant step with steel was Captain James Buchanan Eads, who masterminded the St. Louis bridge. Although Eads had never before attempted a bridge (he had built ironclad salvage vessels during the Civil War), he boldly drew up plans for a multispan structure of three cantilevered steel arches. Although one engineer protested, "I cannot consent to imperil my reputation by appearing to encourage the design's adoption; I deem it entirely unsafe," Eads convinced others who counted, and his plan was accepted. Throughout the seven-odd years of construction, Eads battled with manufacturers to obtain the quality of steel he needed, driving one supplier, Andrew Carnegie, to remonstrate, "Nothing that would and does please engineers is good enough for this work." But in the end Eads's perfectionism paid off. On July 2, 1874, his bridge passed a spectacular test of strength as 14 locomotives weighing a total of 700 tons paraded across the sturdy 520-foot center span. From then on, steel was the heart and spine of city building. In New York, engineer John Augustus Roebling designed the first suspension span to be supported by steel cables, the 1,600-foot Brooklyn Bridge *(left)*. Every bit as confident as Eads, Roebling had grandly predicted, "The contemplated work, when constructed in accordance with my design, will be the greatest engineering work of this Continent, and of the age." It was, enabling New York and outlying Brooklyn to unite in 1883 into one metropolis with a population that reached 3.4 million by 1900.

Elsewhere engineers and architects began to utilize steel to support buildings so tall they were called skyscrapers. William Le Baron Jenney tried it first in 1884 when he designed Chicago's towering, 10-story Home Insurance Building, which was to be supported by a metal skeleton. Like Eads and Roebling, Jenney endured the criticism of nervous doubters (at the last minute one building commissioner insisted that the Home Insurance skeleton be reinforced with massive brick walls). Nevertheless, within the decade bigger and better skyscrapers were rising over Chicago, St. Louis, New York and Buffalo *(following pages)*, topped in 1892 by Chicago's soaring 22-story Masonic Temple, in its day the tallest building in the world.

He who is ready to admit that exigency of site gives some excuse for "elevator architecture" will find a good deal to interest him in its practice at Chicago. In many cases their architects have succeeded admirably in steering a middle course between the ornate style of the palace on the one hand and the packing case with windows on the other; and the observer might unreservedly admire the general effect were it not for the crick in his neck.

JAMES FULLARTON MUIRHEAD, *THE LAND OF CONTRASTS*, 1898

MASONIC TEMPLE, CHICAGO, 1892

UNION TRUST BUILDING, ST. LOUIS, 1893

ST. PAUL BUILDING, NEW YORK, 1899

GUARANTY BUILDING, BUFFALO, 1895

By the 1890s, skyscrapers like these were providing compact office space for as many as 4,000 workers in the heart of America's cities.

William Penn waits to be raised atop Philadelphia's City Hall.

While a generation of brilliant pragmatists were solving the city's major construction problems, some others with a compulsion for elegance concentrated on beautifying the urban milieu with heroic statues and triumphal arches. In Philadelphia, for example, a gigantic bronze image of the city's founder, William Penn, was hoisted in 14 sections to its permanent home atop City Hall's 548-foot tower. Weighing 53,348 pounds, the superstatue boasted a hat nine feet in diameter; its waistline measured 24 feet; and its legs, 10 feet from ankle to knee.

Even more grandiose was the arch erected in New York in 1899 *(right)* to greet Admiral Dewey on his victorious return from Manila. Inspired by the Arch of Titus in Rome, it was adorned with the work of 30 artists. One sculptor, John Quincy Adams Ward, created the crowning touch, a four-horse chariot entitled "Naval Victory." A perfectionist, Ward had once remarked of his sculptures, "I am always afraid to ride or to drive near one of my statues. I don't believe I have stopped in front of one of them since it was put up." But this time Ward did not have to spend much time cringing in the face of his own imperfections. Within a year the great confection, made of plaster and wood for the occasion, had come crumbling down.

A more lasting contribution was that of the park builders, led by landscape architect Frederick Law Olmsted, whose avowed aim was to bring into the city, for all to share, "the beauty of the fields, the meadow, the prairie, of the green pastures and the still waters." Despite such Elysian phrases, Olmsted was in fact a hard-driving realist influenced by the ideals of Utopian Socialism. By the 1870s, his Greensward plan had transformed 800 acres of rocky wilderness in the middle of Manhattan into a vast and varied playground called Central Park. There were carriage roads, bridle paths, a zoo, a lake for boating and skating, and afternoon concerts where 40,000 people could listen from benches or sprawled on the grass. One visitor described the scene as "a veritable nation of working folk at rest." Inspired by Olmsted, other cities developed similar facilities and by 1880 there were 20 new city park systems being constructed at a cost of nearly $50 million.

On New York's Fifth Avenue, a colonnade leads to the 100-foot arch built to honor Spanish-American War hero Admiral George Dewey.

Chicago's park system is truly her diadem. They are found to be literally for the use of the people who own them. I have a fancy that a people who are so largely American would not suffer them to be otherwise. There are no signs warning the public off the grass, or announcing that they "may look, but mustn't touch." The people even picnic on the sward and find, ready at hand, baskets in which to hide the litter which follows.

JULIAN RALPH, *OUR GREAT WEST*, 1893

Bostonians take a 10-cent spin in a swan boat, an attraction of the Public Garden, one of America's popular city parks.

Owned by the Henry Ford Museum

Parkgoers skate in New York (below) and gawk at bears in the Chicago zoo.

Diversity in the Marketplace

Marshall Field's is draped in flags for the Columbian Exposition.

By the '70s American cities were teeming with people eager to buy the new factory-made goods—ranging from machine-produced shoes to canned meats—that were being turned out cheaply and in large quantities by the nation's manufactories. As a result, retail sales methods began to change radically, and so did the look of America's big urban marketplaces. Farmers' markets like the one in Detroit *(overleaf)* surrounded the produce area with stalls that sold a miscellany of hardware and dry goods. But the most striking innovations were the department store, the chain store and the shopping center, all launched by city merchants. Perhaps the most far-sighted of these was Chicago's Marshall Field, who built an ordinary dry-goods firm into one of America's first department stores *(above)* with annual sales that reached $35 million by 1890. As a young sales clerk earning $400 a year, Field had shown a positive genius at bringing in women customers and holding them at the counter with his earnest, attentive manner. He soon decided to cash in on this gift by forming his own firm, where the guiding maxim was "Give the lady what she wants." Field and company allowed lady shoppers to take out goods on approval, thereby giving a woman what she indeed most wanted—the option to change her mind. And Field also began to advertise directly to women in the *Chicago Magazine of Fashion, Music and Home Reading,* where he offered Jessie Oakley's Rose Geranium Toilet Soap, Bohemian blown glass or a $250 sage-green silk street dress. In 1885, responding to another basic female trait—nickle-nursing—Field opened a bargain basement discreetly called a branch department, and advertised goods that were "Less Expensive but Reliable." And in 1890, as a final come-on, he opened a restaurant offering chicken salad and various other delicacies, served up with a complimentary rose.

Another smart dry-goods clerk who could find his way into a lady shopper's heart was Frank W. Woolworth. One morning in 1874 he took a tray of random items and marked them down to five and ten cents. By the end of the day almost all were sold. Thereupon Woolworth quit his job and opened a five-and-ten cent store in Lancaster, Pennsylvania. On the first day sales amounted to a mere $127.65. But only six years later he had a chain of 25 stores with annual sales of over one million dollars.

At the same time that shopping facilities were expanding, shopping itself became a more elegant pastime. An English lady recorded these impressions of New York's 14th Street: "It is a perfect bazaar. Not only is there a brilliant display in the windows of everything from Paris-imported bonnets to pink-satin boots, but the sidewalk is fringed with open-air stalls, heaped high with pretty things, many of them absurdly cheap." Even New York, however, was put in the shade in 1890 when Cleveland opened a huge arcade *(right)* that housed 112 of the finest jewelers, stationers and leather goods shops, thus creating the nation's first true shopping center where ladies and gentlemen could choose among the merchandise or enjoy a Sunday stroll, to the accompaniment of band music.

Four tiers of stores and offices line the 390-foot esplanade of a glittering arcade that was opened in downtown Cleveland in 1890.

Farmers line up their wagons at Detroit's Central Market. When it opened in 1880, only meats and vegetables were sold, but within a decade fish,

dry goods, shoes, dishes and even books were added. Monthly sales conducted from the wagons totaled over $3,000; from stalls, nearly $7,000.

At a gala opening, the first cable car on Downey Avenue in Los Angeles glides by to the cheers of primly starched, flag-waving flower girls.

Getting Around

By 1870 about a dozen American cities had populations of more than 100,000. Carriages and horse trams were choking the streets, and new ways had to be found to transport the growing mobs of urban commuters. One group of New York financiers proposed digging a tunnel eight feet in diameter the length of Manhattan from the Battery to the Harlem River. Through it they promised to move 20,000 people an hour in cars propelled by a gigantic wind-making machine. This ingenious notion died in merciful obscurity. A better idea was the cable car, introduced in San Francisco in 1873. At a secret trial at 5 a.m. on August 1, the motorman chosen to pilot the first car froze at the controls, fearing the cable would break, whereupon inventor Andrew Hallidie jumped in to take his place and triumphantly ran the car down Clay Street. The new machine became an instant popular success, and lines soon opened in Los Angeles *(left)*, Denver, Seattle, Omaha and other cities. Though some nervous passengers continued to share the original motorman's qualms, most cable-car riders agreed with visitor Rudyard Kipling, "If it pleases Providence to make a car run up and down a slit in the ground for many miles, why shall I seek the reasons for this miracle?"

Even more miraculous was the electric trolley car, perfected by an ingenious engineer named Frank Sprague in Richmond, Virginia. Sprague also held a secret run. But the secret was poorly kept, and a sizable cluster of fascinated citizens was on hand to see the test trolley break down on a hill, from which it was ignominiously rescued by four mules. By February 2, 1888, however, a smooth-running system was ready for business and within two years 200 other cities had installed electric trolleys. By 1900 there were 30,000 cars with 15,000 miles of track, and the trolley had become an integral part of American life, inspiring ballads such as the "Song of the Trolley" in honor of the new marvel: "I am coming, I am coming, hark you hear my motor humming/ For the trolley's come to conquer, so you cannot keep it back/ And Zip! the sparks are flashing, as the car goes onward dashing/ While the wheels are whirring smoothly along a perfect track."

In 1872 new rows of four-story town houses rise along Boston's Commonwealth Avenue in the freshly land-filled Back Bay Area.

A New Life Style

The Navarro apartment house borders New York's Central Park.

"Gentlemen will never consent to live on mere shelves under a common roof," a conservative New Yorker huffed as he contemplated an odd new phenomenon of city living—the apartment house. He was typical of the prosperous American city dweller, who had always lived in a town house; to him, apartments were tenements fit only for the great unwashed. But by the early 1870s, in spite of a hustle of residential building *(left)*, new private homes could not keep pace with the rise of city populations. Besides, town houses were becoming too expensive—even a modest one rented for $1,800 a year. Furthermore, the servants needed to maintain such an establishment were demanding salaries as high as $15 or $20 a month.

By 1870 it was apparent that a more compact and economical city dwelling unit was needed. It was provided, paradoxically, by a young New Yorker of impeccable family background, Rutherford Stuyvesant, who boldly opened New York's first apartment house, a five-story walk-up on East 18th Street. He patterned it after Parisian buildings, right down to the watchful concierge. And he described the apartments—six rooms and a bath that rented for $1,000 to $1,500 a year—with the fashionable-sounding name French Flats. Nicknamed Stuyvesant's Folly by skeptics, the building was nonetheless fully rented before it had even been finished. Within the next two decades a variety of taller and more elaborate apartment houses sprang up, including the eight-story Navarro Flats *(above)* and the nine-story Dakota, the latter built at a cost of two million dollars. The Dakota boasted 15-foot ceilings, mahogany paneling, marble floors and nine hydraulic elevators—a necessity for the new mode of vertical living, but a horror to some of its passengers, as an article of the day reported *(below)*. By 1890, with one and a half million needing homes in Manhattan, apartment living was so well accepted that complaints about shortages began to be heard. "We often hear of specially desirable small apartments," wrote one periodical, "but when we attempt to find them they are like the will 'o the wisp."

The elevator in modern buildings has only one drawback—the sickness it causes when the car is suddenly stopped. To people of a delicate constitution this sickness is often such a serious matter that to them the elevator is a dangerous blessing. Elevator sickness is caused by the same law that throws a person to the ground when he gets off a moving car in the wrong way. The stoppage of the elevator car brings a dizziness to the head and sometimes a nausea at the stomach. The internal organs seem to want to rise into the throat. The feet being next to the car floor stop with the car, while other portions of the body continue moving. If the body as a whole can be arrested at the same time with the feet, there will be no sickness. This can be done by placing the head and shoulders against the car frame. Then there will be no sickness, and, according to the "Scientific Press," it is a sure preventive.

SCIENTIFIC AMERICAN, JULY 12, 1890

Tenement buildings line an alley in San Francisco's Chinatown.

Italians gather outside their homes in an old Colonial section of Philadelphia. By 1890 one fourth of the city's population was foreign-born.

In the aftermath of the Blizzard of '88, tiny Brooklynites explore among great mounds of snow. On some streets, drifts reached 30 feet.

Nature against the City

"The wind howled, whistled, banged, roared and moaned as it rushed along," reported the New York *Sun*. It was March 12, 1888, and the most famous blizzard in American history had begun to reveal to New York what havoc the elements could bring to a metropolis. In 1871 Chicago, with a fire department of only 17 horse-drawn engines, had been helpless against a devastating fire *(overleaf)*. Now New York, dependent entirely on volunteer wagon and shovel brigades, was equally defenseless against a raging snowstorm. Within 24 hours, all horsecars, cable cars and El trains were at a halt, street signs were obliterated, the mails stopped. The city was paralyzed.

Most New Yorkers huddled at home—the rich beside potbellied stoves under the glow of gas lamps, the poor in unlighted, unheated tenements. But some brave souls were seized by a spirit of adventure. Donning oilskins and toboggan caps and covering their shoes with socks or burlap bags, they set out into the driving gale. One gentleman gave the New York *Sun* an account, excerpted below, of his trek downtown from his home on the upper West Side.

I had to get downtown, and I went to a livery stable to get a conveyance. There was one cutter, one horse and one driver left. I hired all three for $15. We started down Third avenue, and the wind tore by us at such a rate that the horse staggered about like a drunken man. The surface cars were deserted and most were off the track. The sidewalks were deserted as well. As we kept moving southward, the sleet striking my face made me feel as if it was raining carpet tacks. We tilted nearly over several times and twice we ran into pillars of the elevated road, for we couldn't see where we were going half the time. I arrived at THE SUN *office at 12:31 o'clock having made the trip in a little more than two hours, and I don't believe anybody beat it. I am not going home to-night. I have telegraphed to expect me in May.*

Construction crews begin to rebuild Chicago after the Great Fire of 1871, a holocaust that destroyed 17,450 buildings and left 100,000 homeless. A

week after the disaster, 6,000 temporary structures were up, and within 20 years a new Chicago had become the nation's second largest city.

Posters on a New York billboard, circa 1896.

Entertainment

Standing Room Only

Mistress: Maggie, have you put fresh water in the goldfish bowl?
Maid: No, they ain't drunk up what I gave 'em yesterday.

VAUDEVILLE SKIT, 1890s

As the Civil War ended, Americans looked around and discovered that they were beginning to have both the time and the money to have some fun. Between 1870 and 1900, as the population rose from 39 to 76 million, annual income per capita went up from $779 to $1,164. Meanwhile, the work day for most citizens had decreased from 12 hours to 10 hours, and for many, Saturday was becoming a half holiday. With this combination of cold cash and leisure at their disposal, they began buying entertainment—going to shows, circuses and sports events—with such exuberance that one shocked European visitor accused them of "gross sensuality" and said they were displaying a positive "mania for heaping up the elements of pleasure in excessive quantities."

When this mass quest for fun first got under way, the country had nothing that could be called commercial entertainment on a nationwide basis. Circuses still traveled by horse-drawn wagon and thus were restricted to regional or local tours. In the theater the producers promoted their shows in the old-fashioned manner, plugging thousands of forgettable dramas and providing headlines barely bigger than the copyright notice for the actors who could really draw the crowds *(right)*. Sport was still afflicted by the ancient, upper-class stricture that the best athletes were gentlemen amateurs who would never play for pay. Thus the best-known teams were ostentatiously amateur and patently second rate; they played just for sport and exercise, before small, informal crowds, according to rules that varied from town to town.

But as smart promoters began profiting from all the new money and leisure time, these barriers to big-time entertainment were quickly brushed aside. Baseball led the way in 1869, when the Cincinnati Red Stockings fielded the first admittedly professional team, whose mercenaries earned up to $1,400 a season while proving that any good pro could beat the fancy pants off a gentleman and put on a better show doing it. On a 12,000-mile cross-country tour, playing against amateur clubs, they won 64 games without a loss and drew crowds of 3,000 and more. Other clubs rushed to join the play-for-pay movement, and by 1876 the leading teams had joined to form the National League of Professional Baseball Clubs, which set up strict rules and standards for its members. Sharp rivalries now grew up between different cities. Heroes such as Providence's Charlie (Old Hoss) Radbourne helped to draw as many as 20,000 fans at 50 cents a head for games with Philadel-

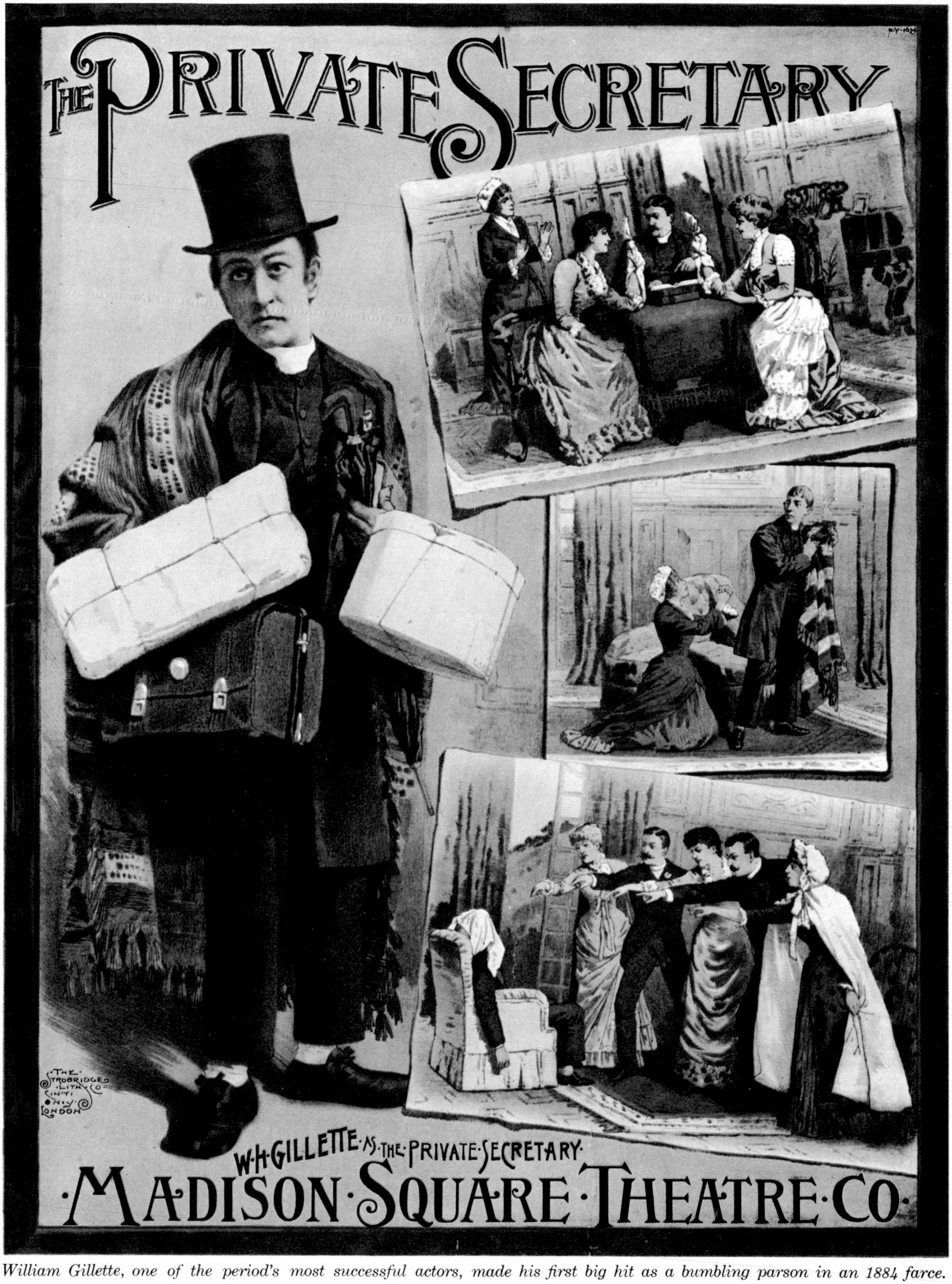

William Gillette, one of the period's most successful actors, made his first big hit as a bumbling parson in an 1884 farce.

phia, Cleveland and Buffalo. In 1886 *Harper's Weekly* announced, "The fascination of the game has seized upon the American people, irrespective of age, sex or other condition." Indeed, it even reached the White House. In 1889, when the Chicago White Stockings wound up a triumphant, round-the-world tour, they were invited to meet President Grover Cleveland in Washington. Afterwards Mike (King) Kelly, the lordly catcher of the Chicago club, had a scornful comment on the encounter. "The President's hand was fat and soft," he declared. "I squeezed it so hard that he winced."

During the 1880s, the theater also became big-league entertainment. A few top performers of the legitimate stage, such as Ada Rehan *(page 261)* and John Drew, achieved star billing and enjoyed long-run successes. In 1894, William Gillette's *Too Much Johnson* stayed on Broadway for 216 performances. And as Gillette's farce proved, the great ticket-buying masses preferred light, noisy, fast-moving entertainment, and they got it in a torrent of outdoor extravaganzas, lurid melodramas and lively variety shows.

Most popular of them all was the variety show, a catch-all entertainment that encompassed three basically similar productions. When a hodge-podge of songs, dances, comedy skits and specialty acts was performed in blackface, it was called a minstrel show. If it was peppered with blue humor and decorated with buxom ladies in revealing tights, it was burlesque. And if it was cleaned up for family consumption, it was vaudeville. Producers and performers switched freely from one type of variety to another, and sometimes the choice between burlesque and vaudeville for a night's entertainment was made when a stage manager peeked out at the audience and spied a cop.

Besides a wide range of standard acts (dialect comedians, magicians, song-and-dance teams, ventriloquists), a typical variety bill would include a couple of sensational novelties. One such was a man named Blatz who, billed as The Human Fish, submerged himself in a glass tank of water where he nonchalantly ate a banana, played a bubbling trombone and apparently fell asleep while reading a newspaper. The versatile Hernandez, a contortionist and guitar player, displayed both of his talents simultaneously without missing a chord or a backward somersault. And the great Kar-Mi *(page 265)* swallowed all but the muzzle of a revolver, which promptly fired, knocking a target from the hand of an assistant.

Such heroics, while they might pack the house, brought little beyond applause to the variety performer. His pay in the 1880s was $20 a week in the big cities and $15 a week on the road—a little more than the $12 a week earned by a first-rate plumber. To earn his pay a trouper might have to visit seven towns in a week and perform five times a night; indeed, shows in the West sometimes went on until daybreak or as long as the customers at the bar, which often faced the stage, were still buying drinks.

Yet through shrewd promotion these troupers could be worth a fortune to the showman who booked them. A Manhattan impresario named Tony Pastor, who had been the first to take the step of laundering the lines of his burlesque acts, wound up with a devoted family audience that eventually supported a chain of 47 theaters. A competitor, Harry Miner, did so well with burlesque and amateur nights that he could even afford to run for Congress. One of the most spectacular successes was that of two well-matched partners, B. F. Keith and E. F. Albee. In 1885 these veterans of the dime-show business *(opposite)* combined two theaters in Boston, the Gaiety and the Bijou, and transformed them into the first modern big-time vaudeville palace, featuring continuous performances throughout the afternoon and evening. From Boston their activities spread to Providence, Philadelphia, New York and beyond. Eventually the partnership controlled more than 400 theaters from coast to coast, and they were able to exercise something close to monopolistic powers in booking talent and setting salaries.

The circus, too, had its share of empire-builders whose genius at expansion and promotion extended into outright rascality. One notorious grifter, John V. (Pogey) O'Brien, worked with gamblers and thieves to defraud his partners and employees in some 23 circuses. Another promoter, Adam Forepaugh *(page 257)*, came honestly to the own-

Cheap circuses called dime shows worked the routes that were too remote for big-tent operators. Standard dime shows featured freaks, acrobats and variety numbers. But in deference to puritanical country people who considered entertainment sinful, posters stressed the shows' dubious educational value.

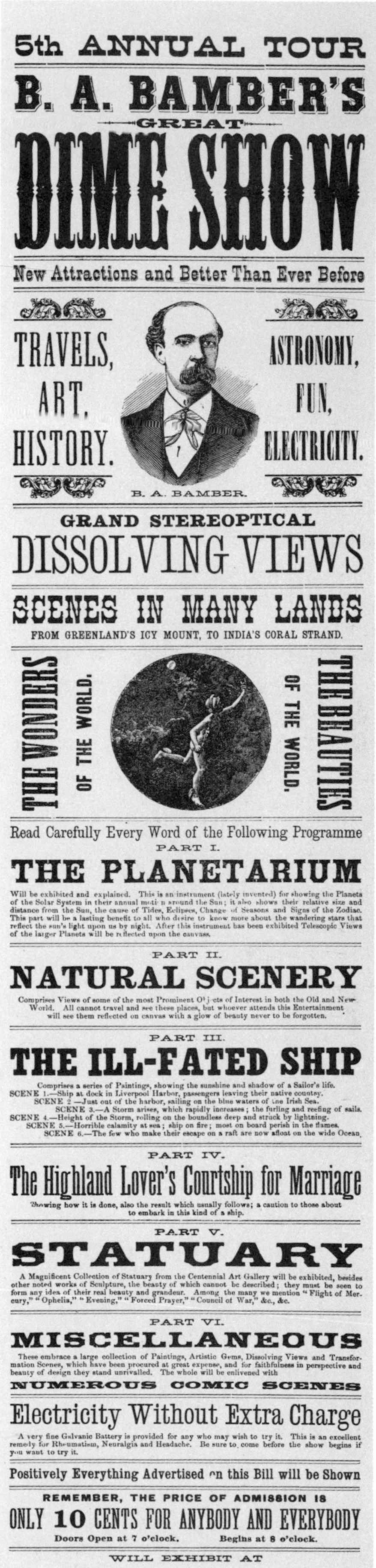

ership of his circus but then stopped at nothing to pull crowds into his big tent. In 1884, when he learned that P. T. Barnum's circus had imported a $75,000 white elephant, Forepaugh promptly created another with a bucket of whitewash; then he shamelessly printed up scurrilous handbills—aptly called rat sheets in circus jargon—describing Barnum's beast as a "rank fraud."

Such slander aroused little sympathy for Phineas Taylor Barnum, whom everyone knew to be the brassiest faker of them all. At one time Barnum exhibited an elderly Negro woman as George Washington's nurse (she would have had to have been at least 120 years old). During another season Barnum sewed together the top half of a dead monkey and the bottom half of an embalmed fish and displayed the result as a Fiji Island mermaid. He even went so far as to make a fake of a fake, exhibiting a plaster replica of the so-called Cardiff Giant, itself a carved stone phony being shown in upstate New York as the petrified remains of a primitive man.

However, as Barnum himself often and arrogantly declared, "There's a sucker born every minute"; and all of them, it seemed, were clamoring to pay their money to be deliciously fooled by old P. T. His circus grossed $400,000 in its first season, 1871. Three years later, after his greatly enlarged show had become the first circus to travel nationwide by railroad car, Barnum's gate receipts—50 cents each from about 20,000 customers a day—roughly doubled his enormous operating costs of $5,000 a day.

As the '90s rolled on, shows of all kinds got bigger and gaudier, and so did the crowds. Burlesque barkers and minstrel-show posters bragged of larger casts than their rivals ("Fifty—count 'em—fifty performers!"), and the biggest shows usually outdrew smaller ones. This compulsion to bigness reached a climax of sorts in Boston, where theatrical manager John Stetson found himself dissatisfied with the staging of a scene depicting the Last Supper. Considering the problem for a moment, Stetson quickly solved it to his own satisfaction: with only 12 apostles the stage was too bare. Turning to an assistant, the maestro roared: "I know what I want! Gimmee twenty-four!"

In the entertainment boom that followed the Civil War, trotting races and baseball became the favorite spectator sports. Countless new trotting tracks were built all over the country, and one of them, the Chicago Driving Park (right) promptly drew a record crowd of 35,000. In baseball, many a club could hardly cope with its soaring attendance. A new team called the New Yorks, soon to be rechristened the Giants, began playing in a 6,000-seat polo stadium in 1883 and was inundated by crowds of 12,000 and more. The overflow had to sit in carriages or stand in the outfield (below). A second and larger Polo Grounds was built in time for the 1891 season. Here, only three years later, the Giants set a year's attendance record for the National League of 400,000.

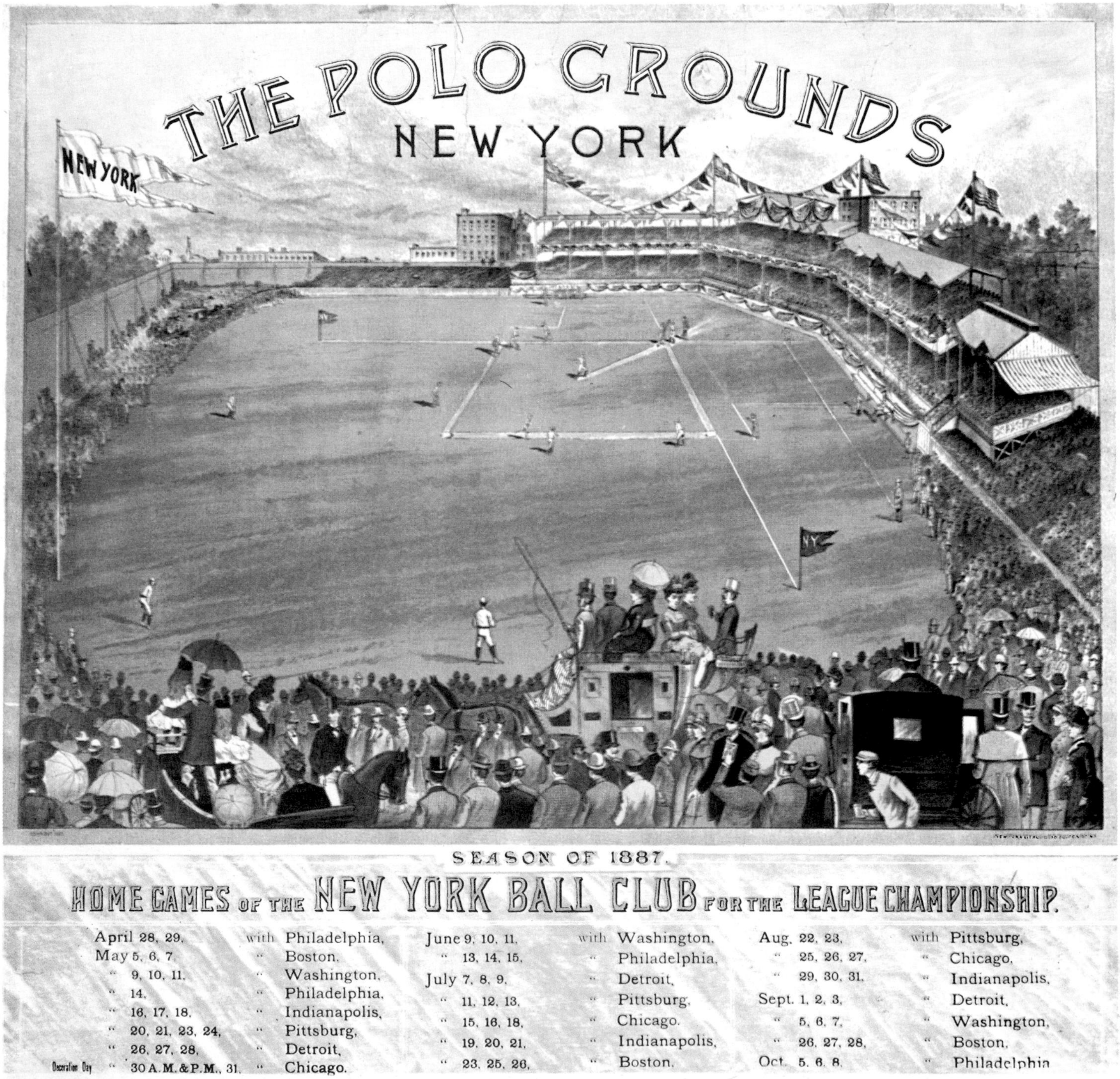

THE POLO GROUNDS
NEW YORK
NEW YORK
N.Y.
SEASON OF 1887.
HOME GAMES OF THE NEW YORK BALL CLUB FOR THE LEAGUE CHAMPIONSHIP.
April 28, 29. with Philadelphia,
May 5, 6, 7. " Boston,
" 9, 10, 11. " Washington,
" 14. " Philadelphia,
" 16, 17, 18. " Indianapolis,
" 20, 21, 23, 24. " Pittsburg,
" 26, 27, 28. " Detroit,
Decoration Day " 30 A.M. & P.M., 31. " Chicago.
June 9, 10, 11. with Washington,
" 13, 14, 15. " Philadelphia,
July 7, 8, 9. " Detroit,
" 11, 12, 13. " Pittsburg,
" 15, 16, 18. " Chicago.
" 19, 20, 21. " Indianapolis,
" 23, 25, 26. " Boston,
Aug. 22, 23. with Pittsburg,
" 25, 26, 27. " Chicago,
" 29, 30, 31. " Indianapolis,
Sept. 1, 2, 3. " Detroit,
" 5, 6, 7. " Washington,
" 26, 27, 28. " Boston,
Oct. 5, 6, 8. " Philadelphia

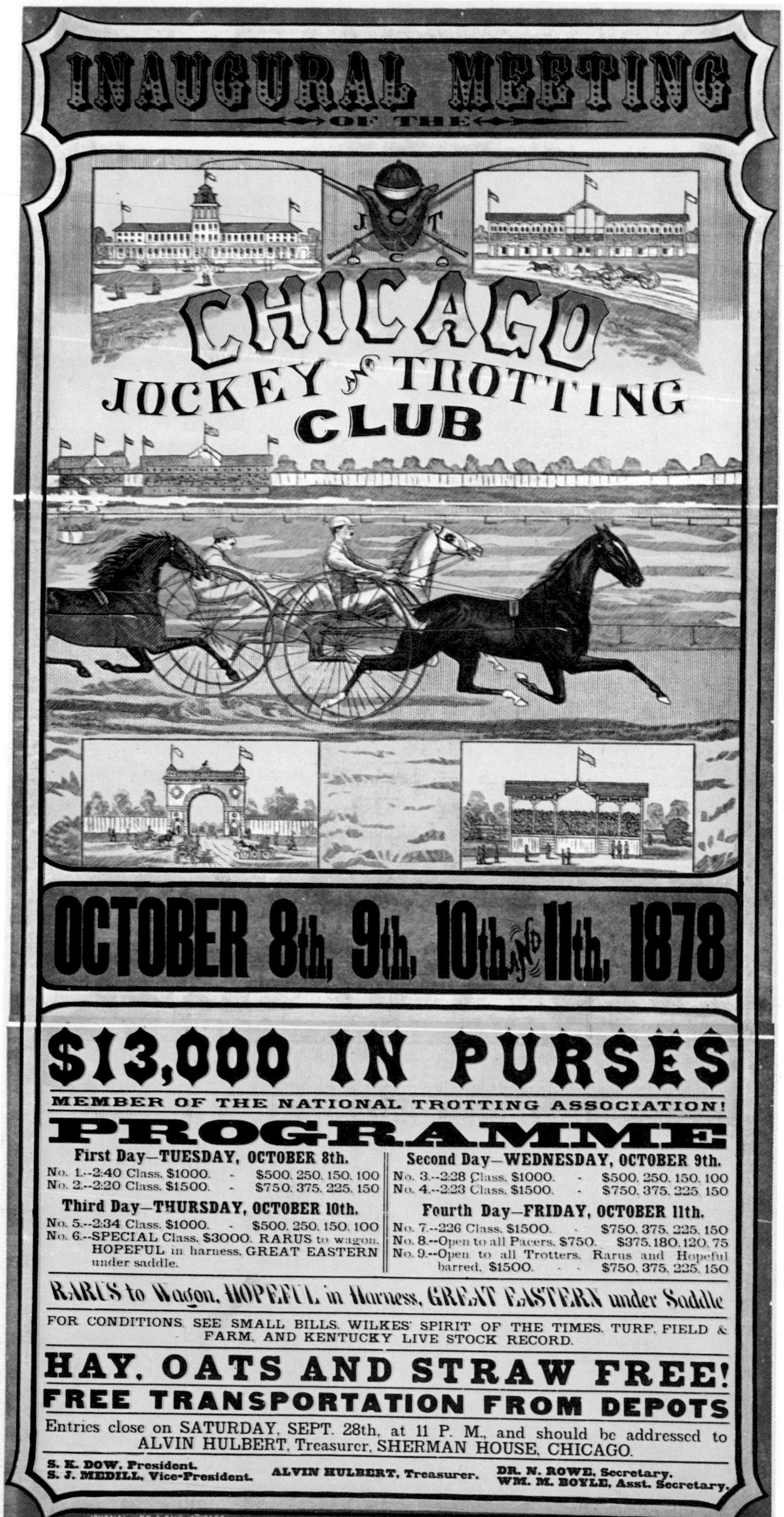

INAUGURAL MEETING
OF THE
CHICAGO
JOCKEY AND TROTTING
CLUB
OCTOBER 8th, 9th, 10th AND 11th, 1878
$13,000 IN PURSES
MEMBER OF THE NATIONAL TROTTING ASSOCIATION!
PROGRAMME
First Day—TUESDAY, OCTOBER 8th.
No. 1.--2:40 Class. $1000. - $500. 250. 150. 100
No. 2.--2:20 Class. $1500. - $750. 375. 225. 150
Second Day—WEDNESDAY, OCTOBER 9th.
No. 3.--2:28 Class. $1000. - $500. 250. 150. 100
No. 4.--2:23 Class. $1500. - $750. 375. 225. 150
Third Day—THURSDAY, OCTOBER 10th.
No. 5.--2:34 Class. $1000. - $500. 250. 150. 100
No. 6.--SPECIAL Class. $3000. RARUS to wagon. HOPEFUL in harness. GREAT EASTERN under saddle.
Fourth Day—FRIDAY, OCTOBER 11th.
No. 7.--226 Class. $1500. - $750. 375. 225. 150
No. 8.--Open to all Pacers. $750. $375. 180. 120. 75
No. 9.--Open to all Trotters. Rarus and Hopeful barred. $1500. - - $750. 375. 225. 150
RARUS to Wagon, HOPEFUL in Harness, GREAT EASTERN under Saddle
FOR CONDITIONS SEE SMALL BILLS. WILKES' SPIRIT OF THE TIMES. TURF. FIELD & FARM, AND KENTUCKY LIVE STOCK RECORD.
HAY, OATS AND STRAW FREE!
FREE TRANSPORTATION FROM DEPOTS
Entries close on SATURDAY, SEPT. 28th, at 11 P. M., and should be addressed to ALVIN HULBERT, Treasurer, SHERMAN HOUSE, CHICAGO.
S. K. DOW, President.
S. J. MEDILL, Vice-President.
ALVIN HULBERT, Treasurer.
DR. N. ROWE, Secretary.
WM. M. BOYLE, Asst. Secretary.
JOURNAL - PR & ENG. CHICAGO.

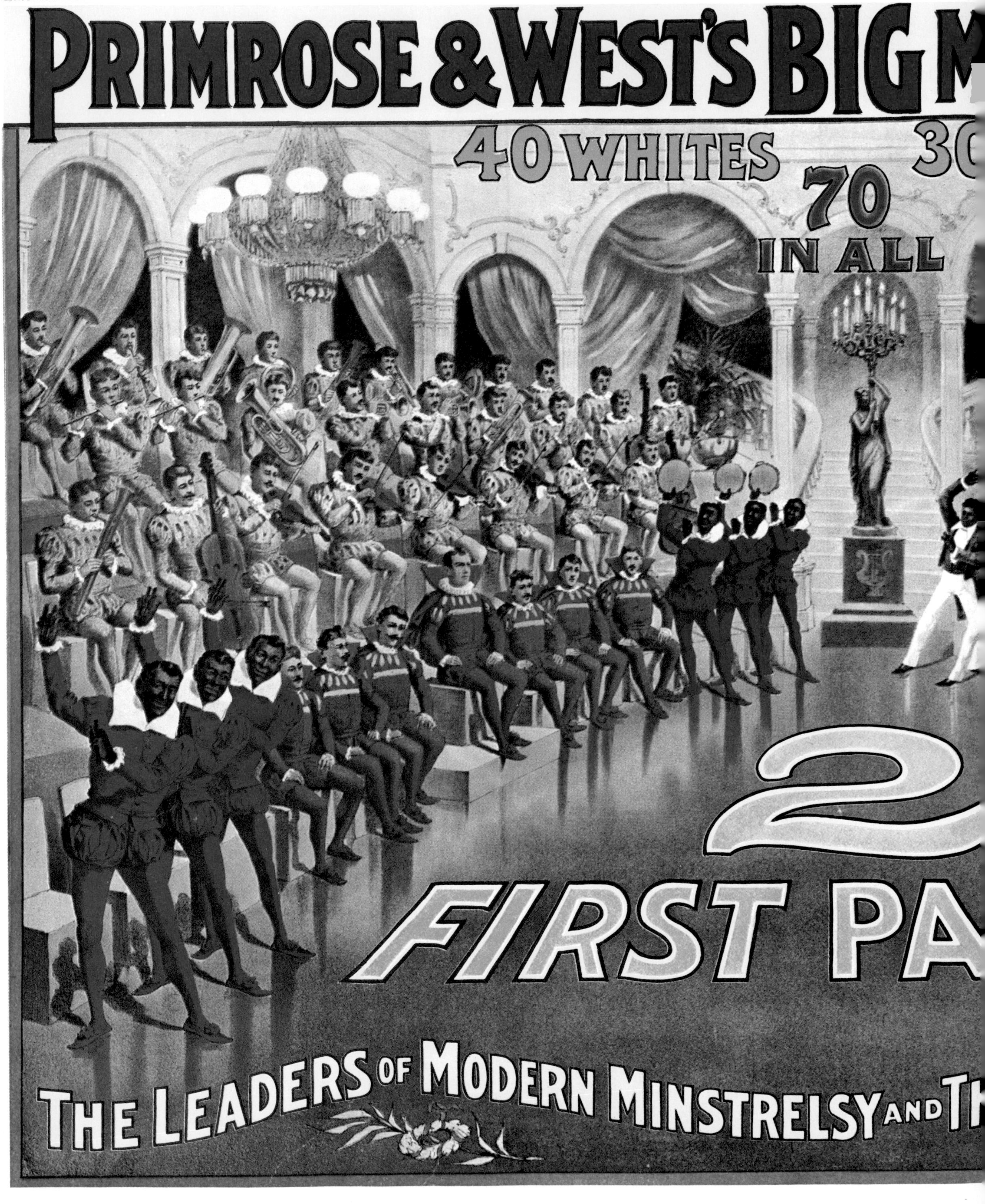
PRIMROSE & WEST'S BIG M
40 WHITES
30
70
IN ALL
2
FIRST PA
THE LEADERS OF MODERN MINSTRELSY AND TH

During the 1880s the homely minstrel show suddenly blossomed into extravagant entertainment. Up until then, hardy little troupes of white men done up in black face or occasional groups of Negroes traveled the countryside doing a blend of sweet ballads, shuffling dances and deep-dish humor. In the '70s a few veterans of the burnt-cork circuit decided to go big time. Two old troupers, George Primrose and William West, helped lead the trend by beefing up their shows with full-sized orchestras and dozens of song-and-dance men decked out in elegant costumes. By 1894 the Primrose and West show was one of the most successful large-scale productions. It was also one of the boldest, presenting white and black performers on the same stage with equal billing.

The circus became a nationwide business in 1872, when showman P. T. Barnum took his huge troupe out of its horse-drawn wagons and began moving it cross-country on 65 railroad cars. Nine other large outfits followed suit, including the Forepaugh and Wallace shows; and business became so good that the total number of circuses swelled to 50 by 1885. Meanwhile, the entrepreneurs engaged in a wild scramble for profit and advantage. Big shows like the Sells Brothers swallowed up lesser ones. Not even Barnum's "Greatest Show on Earth" was safe; in 1888 he lost control to his partner James Bailey, and eventually the Ringling Brothers moved in to absorb Barnum's old show.

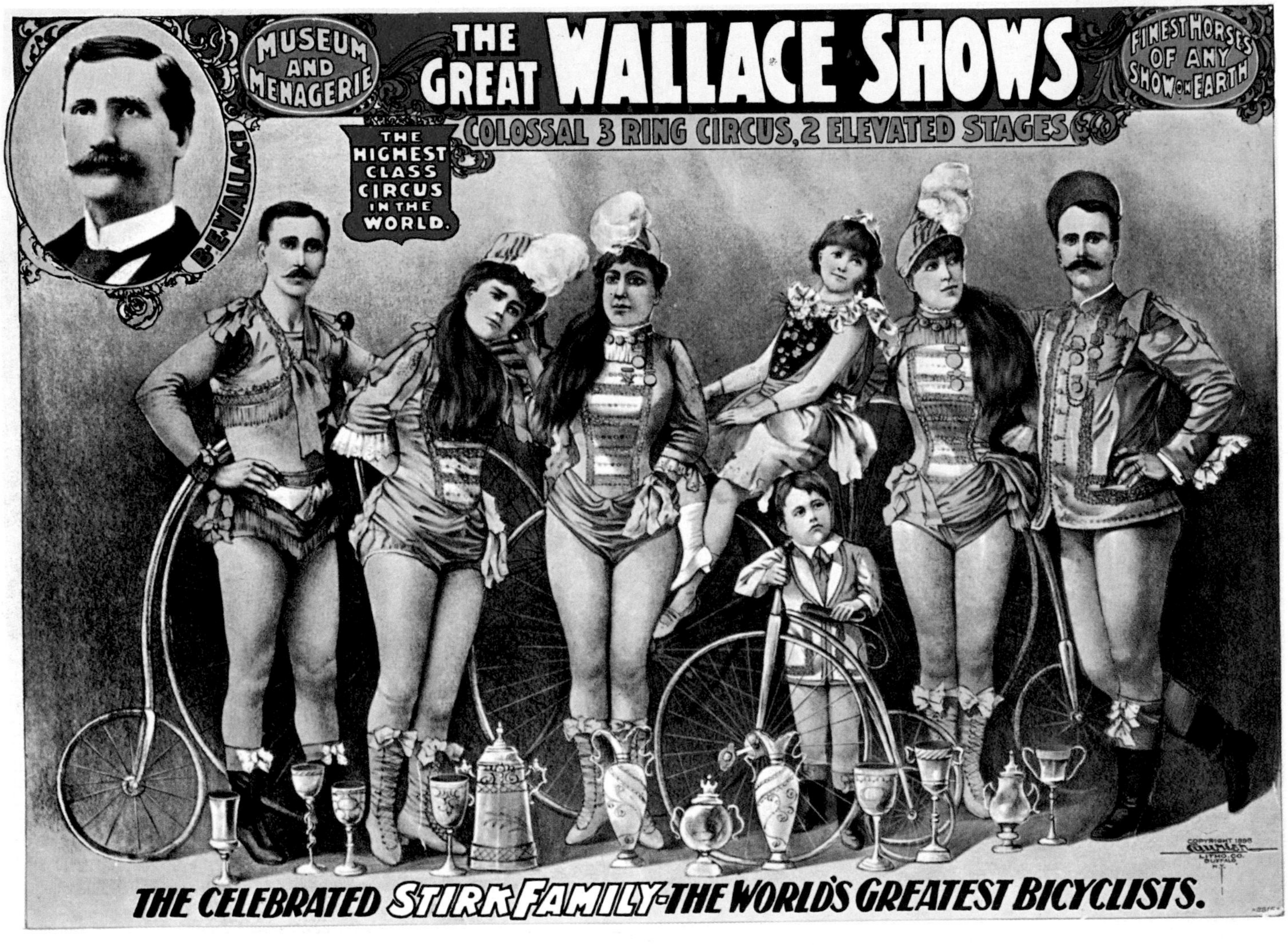

THE ADAM FOREPAUGH AND SELLS BROTHERS
AMERICA'S GREATEST SHOWS CONSOLIDATED
THE LARUE-WALTONS.
A SEXTETTE OF MATCHLESS ACROBATS. SIX SPLENDID ATHLETES UNEQUALLED IN THEIR WONDERFUL PERFORMANCES - ALL ARE FULL SIZED MEN, NO BOYS OR CHILDREN APPEARING IN THEIR ACT.

THE ADAM FOREPAUGH AND SELLS BROTHERS
AMERICA'S GREATEST SHOWS CONSOLIDATED
MADAME YUCCA.
THE FEMALE HERCULES, THE STRONGEST WOMAN ON EARTH - HANDSOME, MODEST AND GENTEEL, IN THE COSTUME OF THE PARLOR SHE PERFORMS FEATS OF STRENGTH NEVER ATTEMPTED BY ANY OTHER MAN OR WOMAN ON EARTH. EVERY FEAT ON THIS ILLUSTRATION IS ACTUALLY PERFORMED AT EACH EXHIBITION

THE ADAM FOREPAUGH AND SELLS BROTHERS
AMERICA'S GREATEST SHOWS CONSOLIDATED
THE GREAT LIVINGSTONE, DAVENE & DE MORA TROUPE
OF CHAMPION ACROBATS, POSTURERS & HAND BALANCERS. THE WONDERFUL EUROPEAN SENSATIONAL MALE & FEMALE ARTISTS IN A PERFORMANCE ABSOLUTELY NEW TO AMERICA

The taste of some playgoers still ran to moralizing melodramas, which needed no star to ensure their long life. The Prisoner of Zenda, for example, ran for 112 performances in New York in 1895 and then moved to new triumphs in the sticks, where troupes of obscure actors sometimes played 14 towns in as many days.

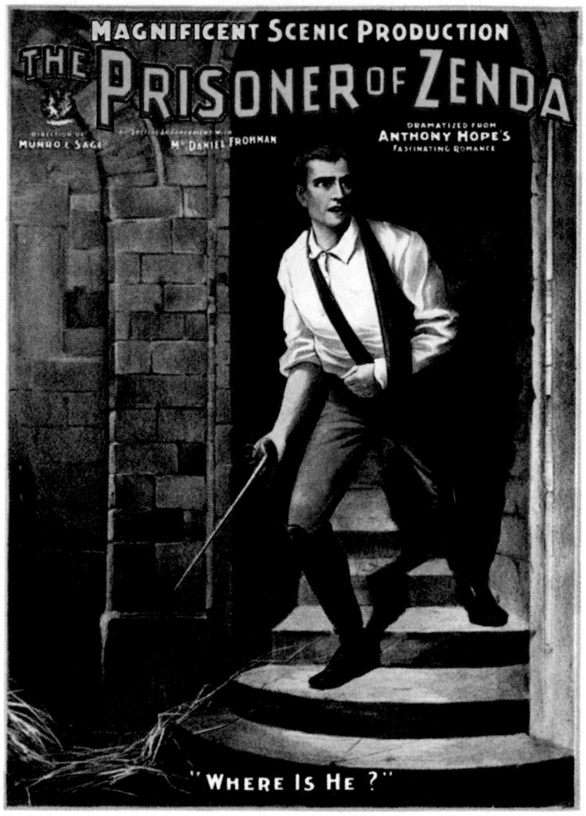

THE COMPANION PLAY TO THE FATAL WEDDING
FOR HER CHILDREN'S SAKE
BY THEO. KREMER
MANAGEMENT SULLIVAN, HARRIS & WOODS
"IF YOU STRIKE MY MOTHER, I'LL SHOOT!"

Capitalizing on her eye-boggling figure (note inset), Sylvia Starr became a popular performer in the burlesque circuit.

First lady of the legitimate stage, Ada Rehan played 200 roles, her greatest being in Taming of the Shrew in 1887.

THE LONG ISLAND RAILROAD.
PAIN'S
GREAT WAR SPECTACLE
GILMORE'S BAND.

For sheer spectacle, none of the period's outdoor extravaganzas could surpass Henry J. Pain's show, which began in 1879 and became a summertime institution for New Yorkers. Amid bursting rockets, a cast of 500 enacted such epic events as the London fire or the siege of Vera Cruz. The Long Island Railroad promoted the spectacular to lure passengers onto their seashore line; as a result the 20,000-seat amphitheater at Manhattan Beach was filled for almost every performance.

A SENSATION! AN INNOVATION!

ALL LADIES! ALL LADIES!!

GRAND INAUGURAL TOUR OF AMERICA!

Of the Famed European Sensational Attraction,

LILLY CLAY'S

Lilly Clay
Marion Singer
Mertie Houck
Palma Schroder
Beatrice Vaughn
Alice Burnard
Victoria North
Louise Lellie
Elsie Hall
Topsy Robina
Fannie Stockton
Angie Pelham
Lillie Ashford
Clara Wilton
Lizzie Badger.

Alice Townsend
Nellie Brooks
Clara Coleman
Gertrude Keith
Lida Morse
Etta Warren
Louise Lester
Kate Harcourt
Ella Grant
Sadie Torrey
Edith Raymond
Laura Lawrence
Nellie Miles
Jennie Witherell
Alice Benden.

COMPANY OF LADIES ONLY

MISS LILLY CLAY .... SOLE DIRECTRESS AND MANAGERESS
Miss Etta Warren .... Stage Manageress
Miss Louise Lester .... Leader of Orchestra
Miss Kate Harcourt .... Ticket Agent
Miss Ella Grant .... Doorkeeper
Miss Laura Lawrence .... Treasurer
Miss Sadie Torrey .... Band Mistress
Miss Lottie Beaumond .... Chief of Ushers
Miss Edith Raymond .... Press Agent

THE ONLY REAL NOVELTY.

That you will witness this Season. Nothing like it ever before seen. The Theatre transformed for this occasion into a veritable

GARDEN OF EDEN

30 | A COTERIE OF CHARMING AND CULTURED ENGLISH AND AMERICAN LADY ARTISTS | 30

Appearing in the Great London and Paris Success, and now presented for the first time in America, aptly entitled

AN

ADAMLESS EDEN

PRODUCED WITH REGAL SPLENDOR AND MAGNIFICENCE

Lady Comedians, Lady Vocalists, Lady Specialists, Lady Instrumental Soloists | Lady Musical Directors, Lady Ticket Sellers, Lady Doorkeepers, Lady Ushers

This startlingly original and entirely novel entertainment is divided into

Three Separate and Distinot Features

The Magnificence of the BRILLIANT MUSICAL RECEPTION SCENE, very appropriately entitled

SOMETHING NEW

Has rarely been equalled and certainly never surpassed, and is participated in by the entire

COTERIE OF LOVELY LADY LYRIC STARS

In a Grand Selection of Operatic Gems, Popular Home Ballads, Solos, Duets, Trios, Quartettes, Sextettes, Majestic March Songs and Choruses. Fusilades of Chaste Bon Mots and Witty Repartee, by the Corps of Original and Funny Lady Comediens.
Also introducing a complete

15 GRAND ORCHESTRA OF LADIES 15

Under the conductorship of the Eminent Lady Directress, Miss LILLY CLAY.

Lady Violinists, Lady Cornettists, Lady Flutists, Lady Clarionettists, Lady Trombone Players, Lady Pianists, Lady Harpists, Lady Bass Players, | Lady Oboe Players, Lady French Horn Players, Lady Bombardon Players, Lady Tympani Players, Lady Drummers

Violin, Cornet, Clarionet, Harp, Piano, Trombone, Bombardon, Xylophone, and Concertina Solos by the Lady Soloists, finishing the scene with a Grand Selection by the

LADIES UNIFORMED MILITARY BAND

MISS SADIE TORREY, BAND MISTRESS.

Clad in the gorgeous Scarlet and Gold Uniforms of the French Imperial Guard, and rendering in a masterly manner the most difficult martial music. This feature is followed by the introduction of the

PHALANX OF AMERICAN AND EUROPEAN LADY SPECIALTY ARTISTS!

In Series of Sensational Vaudeville Surprises.

This really new and original entertainment concluding with the OPERA DI CAMERA,

AN ADAMLESS EDEN!

For the last two successive years the rage of London and Paris, and now offered to our patrons, as reconstructed and localized by that well-known Author and Playwright, Leonard Grover, Esq., and presented with a completeness of detail, seldom seen outside of the Great Metropolitan cities, with

Rich and Appropriate Costumes, by .... Groshau, of Paris
Grand Ballet D'Action, by the .... Maitre De Ballet, Novissimo

And all the charming and original music as arranged by ROBERT RECKER, Esq., and

A PHENOMENAL CAST OF CHARACTERS

REGULAR PRICES OF ADMISSION PREVAIL

NOTWITHSTANDING THE NOVELTY OF THE ATTRACTION.

Secure Choice Reserved Seats three days in advance at the usual places, without extra charge, and at the Box Office of the Theatre, of the Lady Ticket Agents and Treasurees on the day of performance, for which purpose the Box Office will be open all day.

Metropolitan Job Print, 38 Vesey Street, New York.

In all the fast-changing world of entertainment, the shows that drew the largest total audience were the variety shows. Virtually every town had a hall where a traveling troupe could strut its stuff. Some of the stuff, like the Adamless Eden shows, was pretty lusty: in the western town of Tombstone, the brassy artists took time out between their bawdy burlesque routines to dance with the cowboys at 50 cents a whirl. In the 1880s, however, many troupes began offering cleaned-up shows that drew big family audiences under the fancy French name of vaudeville. An impresario like Harry Miner, whose Bowery Theatre was a stronghold of burlesque, added variety to his spice in the '90s by instituting regular amateur nights. Other companies took advantage of the circus' off-season by hiring acrobats, sharpshooters and sword swallowers (below).

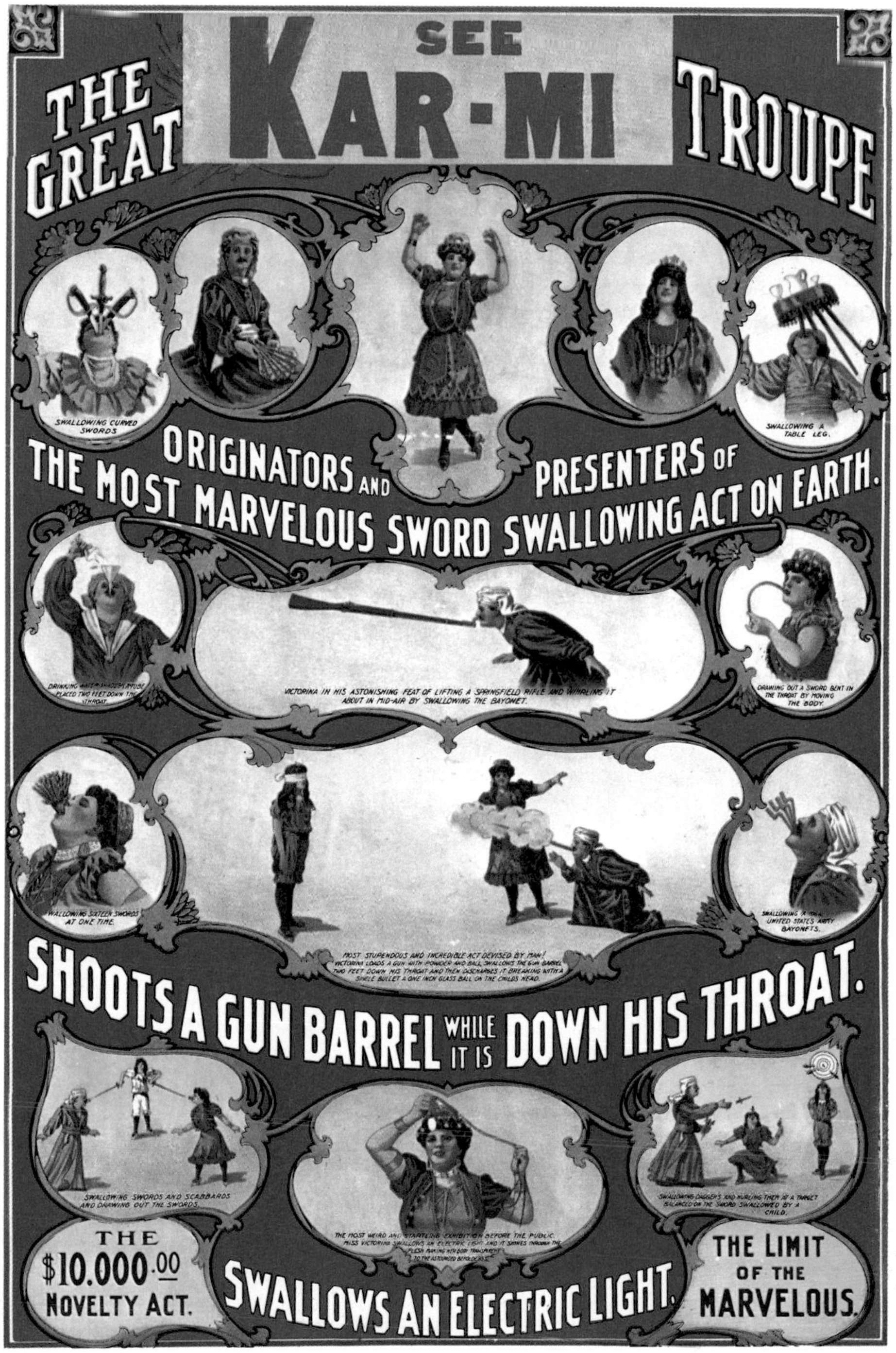

The Greatest Showman on Earth

In 1883 the remote cow town of Omaha, Nebraska, was treated to the grand opening of a show that would reign as America's favorite for two decades. It was Buffalo Bill Cody's Wild West, and the locals gladly paid the 50 cents admission to see its famous star. Virtually every American knew of Buffalo Bill: how he earned his nickname hunting buffalo for railroad-building crews, how he had ridden on the Pony Express, fought the Indians, scouted for the U.S. Cavalry and performed for 11 seasons as a professional actor—all this and more by the age of 37.

Cody gave the Nebraskans their money's worth with a cast of trail-hardened cowboys putting on a dazzling display of stunt riding, fancy roping and deadeye marksmanship. Bill himself topped them all with rifle and shotgun, hitting dozens of small glass balls while running or riding at full tilt.

The crowd loved it, and so did the press as Bill took his show on tour. Reporters began hailing The Wild West as "the best open-air show ever seen" and praising Bill as the showman who "out-Barnumed Barnum." On the crest of such raves, the show set attendance records across America and throughout Europe. Eighty-three thousand people bought tickets in one day in London; and during a full, five-month season more than a million people turned up to watch Buffalo Bill do his stuff.

Bill also doubled as front man and producer, hobnobbing confidently with other celebrities who came to see the show. Once he took the Prince of Wales and four kings for a ride in the show's stagecoach, and he delighted the poker-playing prince by describing his passengers as "a royal flush." As producer, Bill steadily improved the quality of his big troupe. In 1885, he took on as sharpshooter a very comely young woman, Mrs. Phoebe Ann Butler, and gave her star billing as Annie Oakley, "Little Sure Shot." Later he used his foreign tours to recruit the best horsemen in Europe for the sensational acts entitled "Rough Riders of the World" *(gatefold, opposite).*

Bill's most exotic talent catch was Sitting Bull, the Sioux chieftain whose braves had slaughtered the troops of General George Custer at Little Bighorn in 1876. The warrior chief signed on in 1885 for a $125 bonus and $50 a week, much of which he gave away to the poor urchins who hung around the show. When, at tour's end, Sitting Bull went back to his people, Bill gave his friend a rare prize: a performing horse that went into its act when a gun was fired.

To Cody's sorrow, he had not seen the last of that gift horse. In 1890, when Sitting Bull's Sioux were growing warlike on their Dakota reservation, a troop of Indians, recruited by the government, went to arrest the great chief. Sitting Bull refused to leave his people, and in the ensuing skirmish he was shot dead. Meanwhile the trick horse, at the cue of gunfire, kept rearing and pawing the air, convincing the Indians that the fallen chief's spirit had entered its body. Masterless but unharmed, the beast was returned to Bill to perform again in The Wild West show.

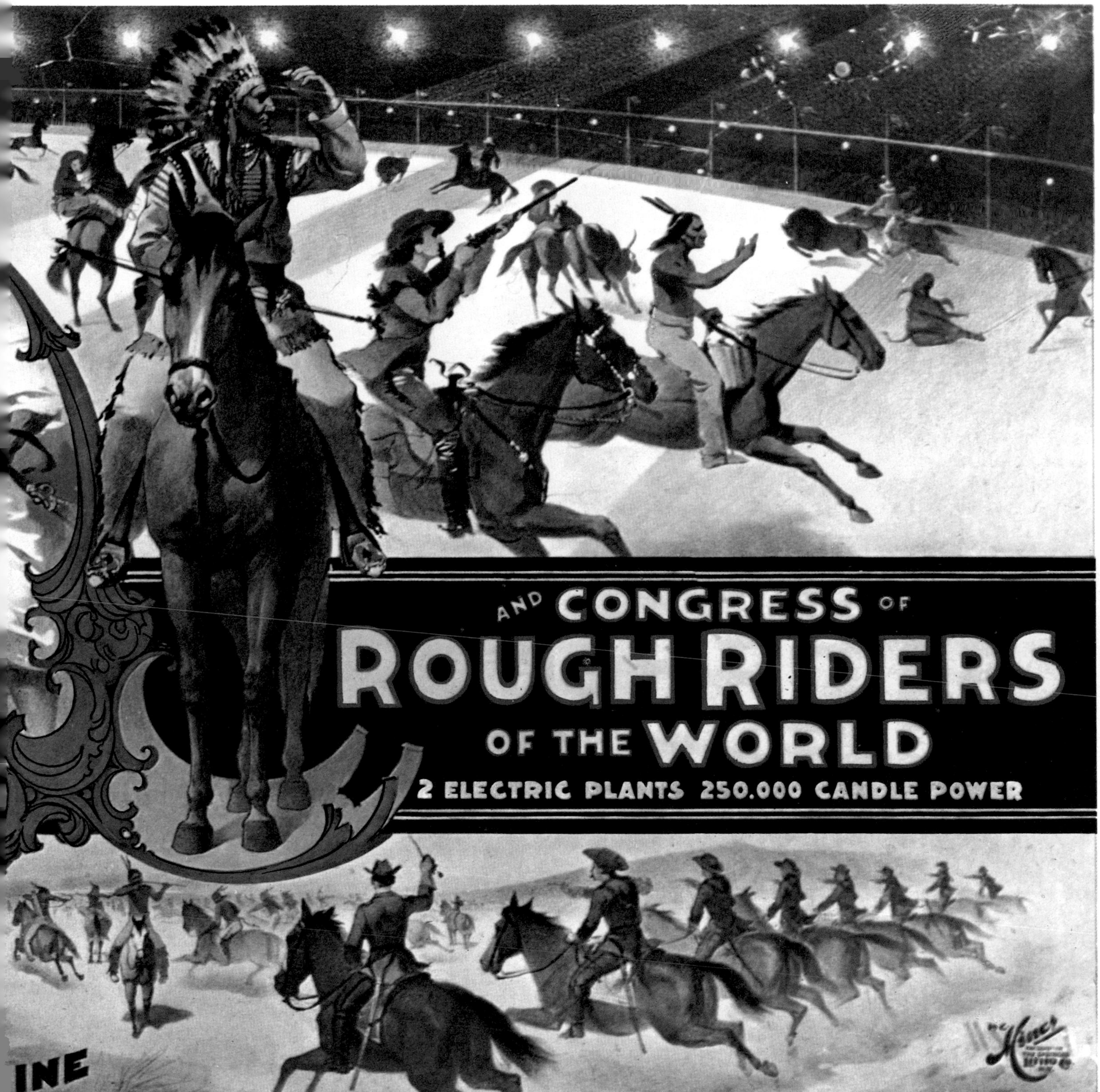

Buffalo Bill's Western spectacular was the 19th Century's most popular show: 41,448 saw a single performance in Chicago in 1884.

Family Portrait

The Brooks family at its annual reunion, New Hampshire, 1895.

God Bless Our Home

In Hannibal, Missouri, when I was a boy, everybody was poor, but didn't know it; and everybody was comfortable, and did know it. MARK TWAIN, *AUTOBIOGRAPHY*

Mark Twain's world was typical of that in most U.S. families at a time when over 45 million people still lived on farms or in scattered villages with populations of less than 5,000. Despite the lure of city life and the call of the open frontier, family ties were close; and children in school recited with reverence these lines from McGuffey's *Reader:* "We are all here! Father, Mother, Sister, Brother, All Who hold each other dear."

This sentimentalizing on the sacred quality of family life showed through every layer of American society. Men with hard hands and moist eyes sang such ballads as "Home Sweet Home" ("Be it ever so humble, there's no place like home") as they bellied up to the bar. And the gayest times of the year were the anniversaries, when the wanderers came home if they could and the family celebrated the simple fact of being together—and feeling close to one another. Author Hamlin Garland recalled one such gathering of a clan in Onalaska, Wisconsin: "It was Sunday and all my aunts and uncles were in holiday dress and a merry, hearty group they were. One roguish young fellow snatched me from the wagon and carried me under his arm to the threshold where a short, gray-haired smiling woman was standing. 'Mother, here's another grandson for you,' he said as he put me at her feet."

At the heart of this family-oriented life was, of course, the old homestead itself. And when itinerant photographers began to tour the countryside with their horse-drawn darkrooms, the whole clan would turn out to pose before the house, bringing such treasures as a new bicycle, a drum, a sewing machine, an accordion, the best chinaware and the family pets *(right).* It was the photographer's job to compose the picture, and one periodical had this advice to give to those about to sit: "Do not interfere with the arrangement of the pose. It is true that not one photographer in ten is an artist as well; but an intelligent sitter will soon discern whether he is in the hands of an artist or a muff."

Artistic or not, photographs like the ones on the following pages had deep meaning for the people in them. Some were framed and hung with pride in living rooms; others were carefully preserved in the family album or sent to relatives back in the old country. They caught the full essence of an age in which the young Henry Ford said of his home in Dearborn, Michigan, "It was Mother's idea. More than once I've heard Mother say, if we couldn't be happy here in this house, we'd never be happy anywhere else."

The Fields, outside their home in Natchez, Mississippi, 1895.

The King family, Dallas, Texas, 1890.

The Walters, Lubert County, Georgia, 1896.

Scandinavian family, Madison, Wisconsin, circa 1877.

The Lugo family, Bell, California, circa 1888.

The E. B. Leightlys, Massillon, Ohio, circa 1890.

Three generations of a Norwegian family, DeForest, Wisconsin, circa 1875.

Nebraska farmer and his brood, East Custer County, 1888.

A golden wedding anniversary in the Dow family, Manchester, New Hampshire, 1895.

Credits

The sources for the illustrations in this book appear below. Credits for pictures from left to right are separated by semicolons, from top to bottom by dashes.

Fabric design by Charles Mikolaycak.
6,7–Courtesy of the Bancroft Library, University of California, Berkeley. 8,9 –Florida State University Library. 10,11–Missouri Historical Society. 12,13 –Collection of Mrs. Edith LaFrancis. 14,15–San Francisco Maritime Museum. 16,17–The Huntington Library, San Marino, California. 18,19–David R. Phillips, Chicago. 20,21–Haynes Foundation, Bozeman, Montana. 22,23–Minnesota Historical Society. 24–The Society of California Pioneers. 27–Historical Collections, Security Pacific National Bank (3)–No Credit; Woody Gelman. 29–Sy Seidman. 31 –Courtesy of the Bancroft Library, University of California, Berkeley. 32,33–The Bettmann Archive. 35–Minnesota Historical Society. 36,37–Wells Fargo Bank History Room, San Francisco; Helen Greenway courtesy Library of Congress. 38,39 –Wells Fargo Bank History Room, San Francisco. 40,41–Brown Brothers. 42,43 –Minnesota Historical Society. 45–Pinkerton's, Inc. 46,47–Helen Greenway courtesy Pinkerton's, Inc.; Pinkerton's, Inc. 48–The Valentine Museum, Richmond, Virginia. 50,51–Quotations and photos reprinted from *Professional Criminals of America, 1886* by Thomas Byrnes. Copyright © 1969 Chelsea House Publishers. Reprinted by permission. 52,53–University of Washington Library, Special Collections; Minnesota Historical Society. 54,55–Frances Benjamin Johnston courtesy Library of Congress. 57–Sy Seidman. 58–State Historical Society of Wisconsin; Courtesy Mrs. Earl Moore, Weston, Connecticut–Courtesy of The New-York Historical Society, New York City. Quotations courtesy Sy Seidman. 59–Courtesy of The New-York Historical Society, New York City, except bottom left Paulus Leeser courtesy The Bettmann Archive. Quotations courtesy Sy Seidman. 60–Paulus Leeser courtesy John Noble, New York–Paulus Leeser courtesy Sy Seidman; Evanston Historical Society, Evanston, Illinois; Joe Clark courtesy Detroit Historical Museum–Travis County Collection, Austin Public Library, Texas; Jacksonville Museum, Oregon. 61–Courtesy John Noble, New York; Courtesy Sy Seidman. Both Paulus Leeser. 62–Paulus Leeser courtesy Charles Mikolaycak. 63–Paulus Leeser courtesy Sy Seidman. 64–Paulus Leeser courtesy John Noble, New York–Joe Clark courtesy Detroit Historical Museum. 65–Courtesy John Noble, New York except center Sy Seidman and upper right Museum of the City of New York. All Paulus Leeser. 66,67–Paulus Leeser courtesy Sy Seidman–Evanston Historical Society, Evanston, Illinois; State Historical Society of Wisconsin. 68–Paulus Leeser courtesy Sy Seidman. Quotations courtesy *The Dallas Morning News.* 69 –Paulus Leeser courtesy Sy Seidman; Paulus Leeser courtesy Museum of the City of New York–Chicago Historical Society. Quotations courtesy Historical Society of Pennsylvania. 70–Paulus Leeser courtesy Sy Seidman. 71–Paulus Leeser courtesy John Noble, New York–Paulus Leeser courtesy Culver Pictures–Frances Benjamin Johnston courtesy Museum of Modern Art. Quotations courtesy Presbyterian Historical Society, Philadelphia, Pennsylvania. 72–Joe Clark courtesy Detroit Historical Museum; Paulus Leeser courtesy Sy Seidman–Paulus Leeser courtesy The Bettman Archive. 73–Top and left Joe Clark courtesy Detroit Historical Museum. Upper right and bottom Paulus Leeser courtesy Sy Seidman. Center right Evanston Historical Society, Evanston, Illinois. 74–Paulus Leeser courtesy John Noble, New York; Society for the Preservation of New England Antiquities–Joe Clark courtesy Detroit Historical Museum except pink ornament State Historical Society of Wisconsin. 75–Paulus Leeser courtesy Museum of the City of New York. 76,77–W. D. Johnson photo from U.S. Geological Survey. 79 –Denver Public Library Western Collection. 82,83–Montana Historical Society, Helena. 84–U.S. Geological Survey Records Photo No. 57-HS-566 in the National Archives. 85–U.S. Geological Survey Records Photo No. 57-HS-997 in the National Archives. 86,87–Library of Congress. 88,89–Minnesota Historical Society; University of Washington Library, Special Collections. 90,91–Library of Congress. 92 –The Kansas State Historical Society, Topeka. 93–Haynes Foundation, Bozeman, Montana. 94,95–Division of Manuscripts, University of Oklahoma Library. 96,97 –Minnesota Historical Society; Montana Historical Society, Helena. 98,99–Montana Historical Society, Helena. 100,101–Haynes Foundation, Bozeman, Montana. 102,103–Haynes Foundation, Bozeman, Montana. 104,105–Joe Clark owned by the Henry Ford Museum. 106,107–A. Y. Owen courtesy Division of Manuscripts, University of Oklahoma Library; University of Washington Library, Special Collections. 108,109–Division of Manuscripts, University of Oklahoma Library. 110,111 –Florida State University Library. 113–The Byron Collection, Museum of the City of New York. 114,115–Brown Brothers. 116,117–Buffalo and Erie County Historical Society, Buffalo, New York; Courtesy of The New-York Historical Society, New York City. 118–Courtesy National Woman's Christian Temperance Union. 121 –Culver Pictures. 122,123–The Massillon Museum, Massillon, Ohio. 125–Culver Pictures. 126,127–Courtesy Peabody Museum of Salem; Oregon Historical Society. 128–From *The Life and Adventures of Nat Love* published by Arno Press and The New York Times (1968); Courtesy of the Bancroft Library, University of California, Berkeley. 129–The Huffman Pictures, Miles City, Montana; Florida State University Library. 130–Collection of Mrs. Edith LaFrancis. 131–The Manchester Historic Association, New Hampshire. 132,133–The Huntington Library, San Marino, California; Collection of Mrs. Edith LaFrancis. 134,135–New York State Historical Association, Cooperstown. 136,137–Collection of Mrs. Edith LaFrancis except upper left Louisiana Collection, Tulane University Library and bottom left Clarke Historical Library, Central Michigan University, Mt. Pleasant, Michigan. 138,139–Collection of Mrs. Edith LaFrancis. 140,141–Kansas State Historical Society, Topeka. 143–The Bettmann Archive. 144–From *Pennsylvania Reversible Writing Book* (1880) courtesy Sy Seidman. Background from *Payson, Dunton and Scribner's National System of Penmanship* (1870) courtesy Sy Seidman. 145 –Teaching Machine charts reprinted by permission from *Lithopinion* #11, the graphic arts and public affairs journal of Local One, Amalgamated Lithographers of America, New York, except left center and bottom from *Theory of Spencerian Penmanship for Schools and Private Learners* (1874). 146,147–From *McGuffey's New Eclectic Spelling Book* (1865) courtesy Sy Seidman; from *McGuffey's Third Eclectic Reader* (1879) courtesy Sy Seidman; From *A Complete Course in Geography* by William Swinton (1879) courtesy The New York Public Library–From *The Franklin Sixth Reader and Speaker* (1875) courtesy Sy Seidman. 148–From *American History for Schools* by G. P. Quakenbos (1877)–From *The Normal Music Course* (1888) courtesy Silver Burdett Company. 149–Courtesy Bert Landsman Morein, New York City. 150,151–Minnesota Historical Society. 152 through 163 –Ken Kay courtesy Collection of Regional History and Archives, Cornell University. 164,165–The Bettmann Archive. 167–Microfilm by 3M IM/Press from the research collections of The New York Public Library. 169–Brown Brothers. 170,171,172–Microfilm by 3M IM/Press from the research collections of The New York Public Library. 174,175–Courtesy of Micro Photo Division, Bell & Howell Company. 176–Microfilm by 3M IM/Press from the research collections of The New York Public Library. 177–Courtesy of Micro Photo Division, Bell & Howell Company. 178,179–Courtesy of the Bancroft Library, University of California, Berkeley. 181–Robert W. Kelley courtesy Oregon Historical Society. 182,183–Minnesota Historical Society; Courtesy of the Bancroft Library, University of California, Berkeley–The Staten Island Historical Society. 184,185–*The Ladies' Home Journal* (June 1893); Montana Historical Society, Helena. 186,187–Courtesy of the Bancroft Library, University of California, Berkeley. 188–Norman Collection courtesy Thomas H. Gandy except bottom Brown Brothers. 189–Norman Collection courtesy Thomas H. Gandy. 190–Culver Pictures except bottom left and bottom center New York State Historical Association, Cooperstown. 191–Historical Collection, Title Insurance & Trust Company, San Diego. 192–New York State Historical Association, Cooperstown. 193–Culver Pictures except bottom left New York State Historical Association, Cooperstown. 194,195–Norman Collection courtesy Thomas H. Gandy; Minnesota Historical Society; The Massillon Museum, Massillon, Ohio. 196,197–Courtesy of the Bancroft Library, University of California, Berkeley. 198–From the collections of the Michigan Historical Commission. 200,201–Atlanta Historical Society. 202,203–The Byron Collection, Museum of the City of New York. 204,205–Courtesy of the Bancroft Library, University of California, Berkeley. 206,207–The Valentine Museum, Richmond, Virginia. 208,209 –State Historical Society of Wisconsin. 211–J. J. Pennell Collection, Regional History Department, Kenneth Spencer Research Library, University of Kansas. 212–The Bettmann Archive; Culver Pictures–Sy Seidman–Culver Pictures; Courtesy of The New-York Historical Society, New York City. 213–Courtesy of The New-York Historical Society, New York City; The Bettmann Archive; Brown Brothers–Sy Seidman–Culver Pictures; Brown Brothers; The Bettmann Archive. 214–Top Sy Seidman (2). Center Brown Brothers. Bottom Culver Pictures (2). 215 –Brown Brothers; Culver Pictures–Culver Pictures; Sy Seidman–The Bettmann Archive. 216,217–The Bettmann Archive. 218,219–The J. Clarence Davies Collection, Museum of the City of New York. 221–Courtesy of the Bancroft Library, University of California, Berkeley. 222,223–Social Ethics Collection, Harvard University. 224–Photoworld, Inc. courtesy History of Photography Collection, Smithsonian Institution. 225–Missouri Historical Society. 226–Courtesy C. W. Condit; Missouri Historical Society. 227–Courtesy of The New-York Historical Society, New York City; Courtesy C. W. Condit. 228–Archives, Philadelphia City Hall. 229 –Courtesy of The New-York Historical Society, New York City. 230–The Staten Island Historical Society; Owned by the Henry Ford Museum–Photoworld, Inc. 232 –Courtesy Marshall Field & Company. 233–Cleveland Public Library. 234,235 –Burton Collection, Detroit Public Library. 236,237–The Huntington Library, San Marino, California. 238–Print Department, Boston Public Library. 239–Courtesy of The New-York Historical Society, New York City. 240,241–Courtesy of the Bancroft Library, University of California, Berkeley; Social Ethics Collection, Harvard University. 242,243–Way Collection, Brooklyn Public Library. 244,245–Chicago Historical Society. 246,247–The Bettmann Archive. 249–Lee Boltin courtesy Museum of the City of New York. 251–Woody Gelman. 252,253–Henry Beville courtesy Library of Congress. 254,255–Lee Boltin courtesy of The New-York His-

torical Society, New York City. 256,257–Henry Beville courtesy Library of Congress. 258–Lee Boltin courtesy of The New-York Historical Society, New York City; Culver Pictures–Henry Beville courtesy Library of Congress (2). 259–Henry Beville courtesy Library of Congress. 260–Henry Beville courtesy Library of Congress. 261–Lee Boltin courtesy Museum of the City of New York. 262,263–Henry Beville courtesy Library of Congress. 264–Lee Boltin courtesy Museum of the City of New York; Henry Beville courtesy Library of Congress. 265–Henry Beville courtesy Library of Congress. 266–Collection of Huntington Hartford. 267,268,269–Henry Beville courtesy Library of Congress. 270,271–The Manchester Historic Association, New Hampshire. 273–Norman Collection courtesy Thomas H. Gandy. 274,275–David R. Phillips, Chicago. 276–Courtesy of the Bancroft Library, University of California, Berkeley. 277–State Historical Society of Wisconsin. 278,279–Courtesy History Division, Los Angeles County Museum of Natural History. 280–The Massillon Museum, Massillon, Ohio. 281–State Historical Society of Wisconsin. 282,283–Solomon D. Butcher Collection, Nebraska State Historical Society. 284,285–The Manchester Historic Association, New Hampshire.

Bibliography

Bartlett, Richard A., *Great Surveys of the American West.* University of Oklahoma Press, 1962.
Beer, Thomas, *The Mauve Decade.* Alfred A. Knopf, 1926.
Bishop, Morris, *A History of Cornell.* Cornell University Press, 1962.
Brown, Dee, *The Year of the Century: 1876.* Charles Scribner's Sons, 1966.
Carson, Gerald, *One for a Man, Two for a Horse.* Doubleday & Co. Inc., 1961.
Carson, Gerald, *The Polite Americans.* William Morrow & Co., 1966.
Dorf, Philip, *The Builder: A Biography of Ezra Cornell.* The Macmillan Co., 1952.
Cubberley, Ellwood P., *Public Education in the United States.* Houghton Mifflin Co., 1947.
Dillon, Richard, *Wells Fargo Detective: The Biography of James B. Hume.* Coward-McCann, Inc., 1969.
Dulles, Foster Rhea, *America Learns to Play.* Appleton-Century Company, Inc., 1940.
Fox, Charles P., and Tom Parkinson, *The Circus in America.* Country Beautiful, 1969.
Glaab, Charles N., and A. Theodore Brown, *A History of Urban America.* The Macmillan Co., 1967.
Holbrook, Stewart H., *The Golden Age of Quackery.* The Macmillan Co., 1959.
Horan, James D., and Paul Sann, *Pictorial History of the Wild West.* Crown Publishers, Inc., 1954.
Horan, James D., *Desperate Men: Revelations from the Sealed Pinkerton Files.* G. P. Putnam's Sons, 1949.
Kouwenhoven, John A., *The Columbia Historical Portrait of New York.* Doubleday & Co., Inc., 1953.
Leonard, Irving A., *When Bikehood was in Flower.* Bearcamp Press, 1969.
Lewis, Oscar, *San Francisco: Mission to Metropolis.* Howell-North Books, 1966.
Loomis, Noel M., *Wells Fargo: An Illustrated History.* Clarkson N. Potter Inc., 1968.
Mayer, Grace M., *Once Upon a City.* The Macmillan Co., 1958.
Mayer, Harold M., and Richard C. Wade, *Chicago: Growth of a Metropolis.* University of Chicago Press, 1969.
Morris, Lloyd, *Incredible New York.* Random House, 1951.
Nevins, Allan, *The Emergence of Modern America.* The Macmillan Co., 1927.
Palmer, Arthur Judson, *Riding High: The Story of the Bicycle.* E. P. Dutton & Co., Inc., 1956.
Pierce, Bessie Louise, ed., *As Others See Chicago.* The University of Chicago Press, 1933.
Randel, William P., *Centennial.* Chilton Book Co., 1969.
Ridge, Martin, and Ray A. Billington, eds., *America's Frontier Story.* Holt, Rinehart & Winston, 1969.
Ross, Marjorie Drake, *The Book of Boston–The Victorian Period 1837-1901.* Hastings House Publishers, 1964.
Russell, Don, *The Lives and Legends of Buffalo Bill.* University of Oklahoma Press, 1960.
Schlesinger, Arthur M., *The Rise of the City 1878-1898.* The Macmillan Co., 1933.
Silverberg, Robert, *Bridges.* MacRae Smith Co., 1966.
Still, Bayrd, *Mirror for Gotham.* New York University Press, 1956.
Sullivan, Mark, *Our Times: The United States 1900-1925, Vol. II.* Charles Scribner's Sons, 1939.
Swanberg, W. A., *Pulitzer, Vol. VIII.* Charles Scribner's Sons, 1967.
Tilden, Freeman, *Following the Frontier.* Alfred A. Knopf, 1964.
Wilson, Mitchell A., *American Science and Invention.* Barnes & Noble, 1960.
Young, James H., *The Toadstool Millionaires.* Princeton University Press, 1961.

Acknowledgments

The editors of this book wish to thank the following persons and institutions for their assistance:

Frank Aydelotte and Jane Riss, University of Kansas; Frances Barger, *The Dallas Morning News;* Lawrence Belles and Mikel Darling, Evanston Historical Society, Evanston, Illinois; Amelia D. Bielaski, Curator, Smith-Telfer Collection, New York State Historical Association, Cooperstown; Larry Booth, Director, Historical Collection, Title Insurance & Trust Company, San Diego; Nellie C. Carico, U.S. Geological Survey; Dr. Edwin H. Carpenter, Western Americana Bibliographer, Henry E. Huntington Library and Art Gallery, San Marino, California; Harry Collins, Brown Brothers, New York; John Cumming, Director, Clarke Historical Library, Central Michigan University, Mt. Pleasant; Virginia Daiker and Mrs. Elena Millie, Prints and Photographs Division, Library of Congress; Mrs. Alice Dalligan, Curator of Manuscripts, Burton Historical Collection, Detroit Public Library; Eugene Decker and Robert Richmond, Kansas State Historical Society, Topeka; Mrs. Evelyn Draper, Archivist, Rollins College, Winter Park, Florida; Wilson Duprey, Curator of Prints, and James Gregory, Librarian, The New-York Historical Society, New York; Barbara Friedman, Photographs and Maps Librarian, Oregon Historical Society, Portland; Dr. Thomas H. Gandy, Natchez, Mississippi; Woodrow Gelman, Nostalgia Press, Malverne, New York; Dorothy Gimmestad, Assistant Head, Audio-Visual Library, Minnesota Historical Society, St. Paul; Mrs. Jennifer Goldsborough, Society for the Preservation of New England Antiquities, Boston; Sinclair Hitchings and Mrs. Nancy Davidson, Print Department, Boston Public Library; Lowell Hocking, Director, Jacksonville Museum, Jacksonville, Oregon; Daniel W. Jones, Special Projects, NBC, New York City; Alison Kallman, New York City; Mrs. Jessie Kincheloe, Historical Picture Collection, Title Insurance & Trust Co., Los Angeles; Charlotte LaRue, John Noble and James Strobridge, Museum of the City of New York; Ellen Leiman, Little Meadow, Pennsylvania; Louisiana State Museum, New Orleans; John M. Cahoon, History Division, Los Angeles County Museum of Natural History; Mrs. Elsa B. Meier, Acquisitions Archivist, Louisiana State University Library, Baton Rouge; Harriett C. Meloy, Acting Librarian, Montana Historical Society, Helena; Allen Morris, Florida State Pictorial Archivist, Chief Clerk of the House, Tallahassee; Mrs. Irene Simpson Neasham, Director, Wells Fargo Bank History Room, San Francisco; Sol Novin, Culver Pictures, New York; George O'Neil, Director of Public Relations, Pinkerton's Inc., New York City; Bob Parkinson, Circus World Museum, Baraboo, Wisconsin; Margot Pearsall, Detroit Historical Museum; Philip Pines, Curator, Hall of Fame of the Trotter, Goshen, New York; Robert C. Pettit, Curator of Collections, Dee Hermonie, Opal Jacobsen, Louise Small, Nebraska Historical Society, Lincoln; Mrs. Virginia Plisko and Mrs. Elizabeth Lessard, The Manchester Historic Association, Manchester, New Hampshire; Victor R. Plukas, Bank Historian, Security Pacific National Bank, Los Angeles; Davis Pratt, Curator of Still Photography, Harvard University; Mrs. Elizabeth Rademacher, Michigan Historical Commission Archives, Lansing; Jack Redding, Baseball Hall of Fame, Cooperstown, New York; Martha and Ray Samuel, New Orleans; Sy Seidman, New York City; Barbara Shepherd, Collection of Regional History and University Archives, Cornell University, Ithaca; Dr. John Barr Tompkins, Head of Public Services, Bancroft Library, University of California, Berkeley; Paul Vanderbilt, Curator, Elise Hall and Joan Severa, Iconographic Collection, State Historical Society of Wisconsin; Robert A. Weinstein, Los Angeles; Philip J. Welchman, Executive Director, and Dr. Elliot Evans, Curator, The Society of California Pioneers, San Francisco.

Index

Numerals in italics indicate an illustration of the subject mentioned.

Printed in U.S.A.